THE MYTH OF THE IMPERIAL PRESIDENCY

THE MYTH OF THE IMPERIAL PRESIDENCY

How Public Opinion Checks
the Unilateral Executive

DINO P. CHRISTENSON
DOUGLAS L. KRINER

THE UNIVERSITY OF CHICAGO PRESS

CHICAGO AND LONDON

The University of Chicago Press, Chicago 60637
The University of Chicago Press, Ltd., London
Published 2020

29 28 27 26 25 24 23 22 21 20   1 2 3 4 5

ISBN-13: 978-0-226-70422-7 (cloth)
ISBN-13: 978-0-226-70436-4 (paper)
ISBN-13: 978-0-226-70453-1 (e-book)
DOI: https://doi.org/10.7208/chicago/9780226704531.001.0001

Library of Congress Cataloging-in-Publication Data

Names: Christenson, Dino, author. | Kriner, Douglas L., author.
Title: The myth of the imperial presidency : how public opinion checks the
    unilateral executive / Dino P. Christenson, Douglas L. Kriner.
Description: Chicago ; London : The University of Chicago Press, 2020. | Includes
    bibliographical references and index.
Identifiers: LCCN 2019054894 | ISBN 9780226704227 (cloth) | ISBN 9780226704364
    (paperback) | ISBN 9780226704531 (ebook)
Subjects: LCSH: Obama, Barack. | Trump, Donald, 1946– | Executive power—
    United States. | Separation of powers—United States. | Public opinion—Political
    aspects—United States. | United States—Politics and government. | United
    States—Politics and government—2009-2017. | United States—Politics and
    government—2017–
Classification: LCC JK516 .C48 2020 | DDC 352.23/50973—dc23

LC record available at https://lccn.loc.gov/2019054894

TO OUR INSPIRING MOMS,

VINCENZA AND DEBBIE

CONTENTS

ACKNOWLEDGMENTS

This book is the culmination of a broader project that began about seven years ago. As a result, we are indebted to a large number of colleagues, friends, and family members who have helped us along the way.

For constructive feedback and suggestions received over the course of the project, we would like to thank Adam Berinsky, Anthony Bertelli, Jan Box-Steffensmeier, Fang-Yi Chiou, Jeffrey Cohen, Chris Dawes, Jamie Druckman, David Glick, Jeff Jenkins, Will Howell, Sam Kernell, George Krause, Dave Lewis, Molly Roberts, Larry Rothenberg, Andrew Rudalevige, Gina Sapiro, Sharece Thrower, Adam Warber, Herb Weisberg, Graham Wilson, and our anonymous reviewers. We are particularly grateful for the continued dialogue with our friends and colleagues Andrew Reeves and Jon Rogowski; engaging their work has strengthened our own. Various chapters benefited greatly from seminar participants at Clemson; Cornell; Emory; New York University; Penn State; Rochester; University of California, San Diego; University of South Carolina; University of Southern California; Washington University in St. Louis; the American Political Science Association; and the Midwest Political Science Association.

We thank Boston University and Cornell University for generous financial support of our work, and Ishaan Bakhle and Lucas Wesselius for excellent research assistance. Christenson would like to thank Matthew Blackwell for related conversations and support while a visiting scholar at Harvard University's Institute for Quantitative Social Science (IQSS), as well as Gary King for making his time there possible. He would also like to thank Azer Bestavros and the Hariri Institute. Kriner would like to thank Vincent Della Sala for helpful conversations and support while a visiting scholar at the Jean Monnet European Centre, University of Trento.

We would be remiss if we did not thank the outstanding team at the University of Chicago Press who helped bring this project to fruition. We would specifically like to thank our editor Chuck Myers, for his guidance and insight throughout the project, as well as Sandy Hazel, Susan Karani, Melinda Kennedy, Adriana Smith, and Alicia Sparrow. We also thank Tobiah Waldron for indexing assistance.

Finally, we would like to take a moment to acknowledge our great debt to our families, specifically Erin, Peter, Thomas, and Vincenza Christenson, as well as Jillian Goldfarb and Gary and Debbie Kriner. These poor folks have listened to countless versions of each chapter and virtually every idea in rambling audio format. They have tolerated sudden departures from the topic at hand to those in the book over our meals and holidays together, not to mention picked up the slack around our homes so we could concentrate on this work. Despite all that and more, they have continued to encourage us. This book would not be possible without their love, support, and, frankly, their patience and tolerance.

CHAPTER ONE

An Imperial Presidency?

While the dramatic expansion of the federal government following the New Deal and World War II greatly increased the institutional resources of the executive branch, every postwar president has struggled mightily to translate this leverage into mastery over politics and policymaking. In 1960, the father of modern presidency scholarship, Richard Neustadt, argued that the president's constitutional powers are so meager and the executive's reliance on other actors so great that presidential power amounts to little more than the power of persuasion. Three decades later, despite the office's continued growth, Neustadt saw little reason to change his assessment. When thinking about presidential power, he argued, "weak *remains* the word with which to start."[1]

To overcome legislative inertia, presidents routinely rely on powers not specifically enumerated in Article II of the US Constitution. But they do more than simply endeavor to persuade other actors to behave as they would like. Instead, presidents can eschew persuasion altogether and employ a range of unilateral instruments to effect significant changes in policy without needing to secure congressional assent. To their supporters, such actions illustrate the energy and dispatch of the executive branch to meet the needs of the nation as extolled by Alexander Hamilton in *Federalist 70*. To their opponents, unilateral initiatives prompt plaintive cries of usurpation.

Has the rise of presidential unilateralism fundamentally upset the constitutional balance of power in American politics? Most civics classes present an abidingly clear vision of separation of powers. Congress creates the law. Presidents take care that it is faithfully executed. However, reality has never been so clear-cut. Presidents have long asserted and the courts have affirmed the chief executive's power to effect major changes in public policy with the stroke of a pen, absent any legislative sanction from Congress. By employing a range of tools including executive orders, memoranda, proclamations, and national security directives, presidents have materially influenced many of the most important domestic and foreign policy issues facing the country. Presidents have unilaterally taken us to war; dramatically expanded the territorial size of the nation; ended slavery in the South; interned tens of thousands of US citizens in concentration camps; desegregated the armed forces; reduced pollution in the air we breathe and the water we drink; authorized warrantless electronic surveillance on Americans' communications; and shielded millions of undocumented persons from deportation.

Unilateral executive action has always been a part of the fabric of American governance. However, it has perhaps never been as central to politics as it is today. Presidents have long faced an uphill battle in securing support for their policy agendas on Capitol Hill. Even "successful" presidents' scorecards feature as many failures as victories. Building coalitions and navigating the obstacle-ridden legislative process—always an arduous task—has become virtually Sisyphean in our contemporary polity. Congress is more polarized than it has been in a century.[2] Obstructionism in its myriad forms is rampant.[3] Blocked by gridlock on Capitol Hill, it is little wonder that presidents from both parties have repeatedly turned to unilateral action to pursue key elements of their policy agendas. Indeed, unilateralism has become so pivotal that presidency scholars Terry Moe and William Howell argue that "it virtually defines what is distinctively modern about the modern American presidency."[4]

Even presidents who pledge to reverse the trend ultimately find unilateralism indispensable. While campaigning for the presidency in 2008, Illinois senator Barack Obama ran under the banner of "change we can believe in." To be sure, Obama promised (and would eventually deliver) a serious break from many of the policies, both foreign and domestic, of the incumbent George W. Bush administration. But Obama also promised to roll back what he viewed as the dangerous and excessive unilateralism of the Bush team. At a campaign stop in Pennsylvania, the former president of the *Harvard Law Review* chastised Bush for too often going it alone: "I take the Constitution very seriously. The biggest problems that we're facing right now have to do with George Bush trying to bring more and more power into the executive branch and not go through Congress at all. And that is what I intend to reverse when I become president of the United States."[5] But once in office, Obama, like his predecessors, succumbed to the siren song of unilateralism. On the eve of his 2014 State of the Union address, President Obama warned Congress that should it intransigently refuse to consider his policy prescriptions for the nation's ills, he would act on his own. "We are not just going to be waiting for legislation in order to make sure that we're providing Americans the kind of help that they need," he declared. "I've got a pen, and I've got a phone. And I can use that pen to sign executive orders and take executive actions and administrative actions that move the ball forward."[6]

While running to succeed President Obama, Donald Trump routinely bashed the "illegal and overreaching" executive actions of his predecessor while simultaneously boasting of the sweeping changes he would unleash unilaterally.[7] In his very first days in office, Trump followed through on many of his promises. Most of his early executive actions focused on erasing the Obama legacy by dealing major blows to the implementation of the Affordable Care Act; strengthening immigration enforcement; greenlighting the stalled Keystone XL and Dakota Access oil pipelines; reducing protections for wildlife; shrinking national monuments and parks; pulling out of the Paris climate agreement; cutting scientific research on the environment; and slowing the processing of refugees. But Trump also struck out in new directions with orders easing environmental strictures on infrastructure permits; expanding offshore oil drilling; banning many transgender Americans from serving openly in the military; renegotiating the North American Free Trade Agreement (NAFTA); and, perhaps most stridently, declaring a national emergency to build his signature border wall with Mexico.

Confronted with these bold assertions of unilateral power, many politicians, pundits, and scholars have argued that *imperial* rather than *weak* best characterizes the contemporary presidency. Arthur Schlesinger Jr.'s 1973 classic is perhaps most remembered for its description of presidential wartime power grabs that rendered the American president "the most absolute monarch (with the possible exception of Mao Tse-Tung of China) among the great powers of the world." However, Schlesinger's diagnosis was considerably broader. Vietnam alone did not make Lyndon Johnson and Richard Nixon imperial. Rather, the greater danger lay in the inevitable spillover of claims of unilateral authority from the foreign to the domestic sphere: "If the President were conceded these life-and-death decisions abroad, how could he be restrained from gathering unto himself the less fateful powers of the national polity?"[8]

Recent scholarship has challenged Schlesinger's claims of presidential wartime supremacy.[9] Yet his broader warning about presidents' increasing willingness to bypass the legislative process, trample on constitutional

norms, and instead effect policy change with the stroke of a pen continues to reverberate loudly. Equally important, the quiescent Congress that
aided and abetted the rise of the imperial presidency all too often seems
equally feckless when confronting contemporary presidential power
grabs.[10] The Bush administration's aggressive use of the presidency's unilateral powers to respond to the terrorist attacks of 9/11 prompted a chorus
of critics to lament the rise of a "new" imperial presidency.[11] Even in the
Obama era, legal scholar Bruce Ackerman argued that presidential unilateralism is the proximate cause underlying the "decline and fall of the
American Republic."[12] During the Trump administration, it took fewer
than three weeks before some began to warn about the return of the imperial presidency in perhaps an even more pernicious form.[13]

More broadly, many observers see clear parallels between recent presidents' embrace of unilateralism and the actions of authoritarian leaders
that have triggered democratic backsliding across the globe. In their 2018
best seller *How Democracies Die*, comparative politics scholars Steven
Levitsky and Daniel Ziblatt argue that presidents' increasing willingness
to employ unilateral powers previously reserved for wartime emergencies
to pursue their domestic agendas has weakened "the guardrails of democracy" and driven the growing authoritarian tilt in American politics.[14]
Similarly, in "How to Lose a Constitutional Democracy," legal scholars
Aziz Huq and Tom Ginsburg warn that the Constitution's parchment barriers provide little check against democratic "retrogression" fueled by an
authoritarian executive.[15]

Such jeremiads tap into Americans' long, conflicted relationship with
executive power. Having freed themselves from the tyrannical regime of
George III, members of the Founding generation took great pains to avoid
recreating a monarchy in *terra nova*. Indeed, their initial solution to the
problem under the Articles of Confederation was simply to avoid having
an executive branch altogether! By 1787, there was a clear need for greater
energy and dispatch in government to meet the challenges threatening the
American experiment in self-government. Gradually, the delegates to the
Constitutional Convention devised an independent executive that would
both serve as a check on Congress and provide energy and efficiency in
administration. However, the design and powers of the nascent presidency
proved to be among the most controversial features of the new Constitution. Even the careful compromises reached in Philadelphia failed to sat-
isfy critics concerned about inevitable executive aggrandizement. One of
the most prescient critiques focused precisely on unilateral action—the

ability of presidents to both make and execute law, independent of Congress. In his fifth letter, the antifederalist writer Cato warned that without concrete and indisputable limits on presidential power, "you might as well deposit the important powers of legislation and execution in one or a few and permit them to govern according to their disposition and will."[16]

The Framers plainly anticipated presidential power grabs, so they created an intricate system of checks and balances to blunt and contain such impulses. However, this Newtonian system of counterpoised forces has all but collapsed in the face of an ascendant presidential juggernaut. Why have Congress and the courts failed to fight back? Here, existing scholarship offers a clear and cogent answer: while both branches possess the constitutional authority to check brazen assertions of unilateral power, both are institutionally ill equipped to exercise it in practice.[17] Consider House Speaker John Boehner's response to President Obama's overt threats to act unilaterally in 2014 if Congress refused to move on his priorities. In a letter to his fellow legislators, Boehner charged that Obama had willfully and repeatedly "circumvented the Congress through executive action, creating his own laws and excusing himself from executing statutes he is sworn to enforce—at times even boasting about his willingness to do it, as if daring the American people to stop him."[18] The country elected a president, Boehner inveighed, not a king! Yet such bombastic rhetoric was all that congressional opponents of the president could muster. Any legislative efforts to overturn executive actions would have to overcome multiple procedural hurdles, a Democratic filibuster in the Senate, and, ultimately, President Obama himself wielding a veto pen. In short, legislation to check the unilateral president was dead on arrival.

Historically, the federal courts have also proved reluctant to strike down assertions of unilateral presidential power. Such cases put the courts in a precarious situation, forcing them to rely on the very person they are contemplating ruling against to enforce their decisions. As a result, courts have developed a variety of instruments, such as the political questions doctrine, to avoid having to rule on many legal challenges to presidential unilateralism.[19] And when they do hear such challenges, they have sided with the president and upheld unilateral directives the overwhelming majority of the time.[20]

Yet the very weakness of these formal institutional constraints on the unilateral president suggests that most prior analysts of unilateral power are asking the wrong question—and looking for the answer in the wrong places. That presidents have enjoyed great success when acting unilaterally and that other actors have routinely seemed all but powerless to check the unilateral executive are unsurprising. Indeed, these situations are precisely what we would expect when analyzing the relative institutional strengths and weaknesses of the three branches. The true puzzle is the relative *paucity* of major unilateral actions, not their frequency. If Congress and the courts are all but powerless to undo that which the president has wrought unilaterally, what forces prevent presidents from acting unilaterally even more aggressively to bring government policies across the gamut of foreign and domestic issues into closer alignment with their preferences?

Our question in no way seeks to minimize what presidents have achieved unilaterally. But for every policy priority that they have pursued unilaterally, there are many more to which they have consciously eschewed a unilateral solution. By any metric, the number of significant unilateral actions—those of major political or policy importance—is modest. When presidents act unilaterally, they usually succeed in moving policy closer to their preferences. Yet in many other cases presidents could act unilaterally, but they ultimately choose not to do so. Why?

When contemplating unilateral action, presidents, we argue, anticipate more than the likelihood of Congress enacting legislation over their veto to undo an executive action or the probability of the federal courts striking it down. They also consider the longer-term consequences of acting unilaterally in one sphere for their other priorities. A key component of this calculation is domestic public opinion. Will voters rally around unilateral action? Or will they punish a president who pushes too aggressively on the bounds of his or her authority?

But why are presidents so carefully attuned to public opinion, when public opinion can do little to directly check their exercise of the office's vast unilateral authority? In short, the president's standing among the public is perhaps the most ubiquitous and salient measure of a president's political capital and thus ability to advance his or her agenda in Washington. It informs other political actors' assessments of the president's power, which in turn shapes how they react in a range of settings. Almost every president openly perceives public support as critically important to legislative success. For example, President Obama declared that educating the public and rallying opinion to his side were the most essential facets of his job, as only public pressure could break the partisan gridlock on Capitol Hill.[21] While skeptical of presidents' ability to lead public opinion effectively in most cases, George Edwards echoes Obama's assessment that broad public support is often essential to presidents successfully overcoming the hurdles that derail most legislative initiatives.[22] As a result, presidents have strong incentives to avoid taking unilateral action if it risks provoking a popular backlash that would threaten their broader standing among the public. A short-term victory won unilaterally would prove to be a Pyrrhic one if it jeopardized the rest of a president's legislative agenda.

While public support is always a form of political currency, at the ballot box the *vox populi* becomes the *vox dei*. Most directly, an erosion of public support threatens that which every first-term president desires above all else: a second term.[23] The electoral ramifications of public support for the president are considerably broader, however. Congressional elections have become increasingly "presidentialized" as attitudes toward the president have come to dominate how many Americans view the parties and candidates for downballot races.[24] Waning public support for the president could thus significantly shape the partisan balance of power in Congress, with major consequences for the president's short- and long-term political prospects. Finally, a president's legacy, both legislative and particularly unilateral, is most secure when defended by a copartisan successor. Even second-term presidents have incentives to court public opinion, as the outgoing president's approval rating remains one of the most important predictors of a fellow partisan taking his place behind the Resolute Desk.[25]

As a result, legacy-minded presidents should rationally defer taking executive action—even when they know that Congress and the courts are unlikely to overturn it—if they believe that the long-term political costs of pursuing an unpopular policy exceed the benefits of doing so. This calculation depends heavily on public opinion and, in particular, presidential approval. Critically, Congress and the courts remain relevant to understanding contemporary unilateral politics. But the primary way in which they influence presidential calculations is by combating the unilateral president in the arena of public opinion, not by exercising their formal constitutionally designed checks.[26] Even when they cannot block or overturn a unilateral action, other political actors remain relevant through their special capacity to mobilize the public and bring popular pressure to bear on the White House. Presidents therefore anticipate the political costs of unilateral action and the capacity of other political actors to increase those costs, and they adjust their willingness to use the office's unilateral power accordingly.

The imperial presidency is chimerical. When contemplating unilateral action, presidents are significantly more constrained than often supposed.

Importantly, however, the nature of this constraint is more political than constitutional. Public opinion—not formal checks by Congress and the courts—serves as the primary check on the unilateral executive.

THE PAUCITY OF MAJOR UNILATERAL ACTION

A superficial glance at the empirical evidence suggests that presidential unilateral action has been anything but rare in the modern era. Between 1945 and 2018, presidents issued more than four thousand executive orders. While executive orders are perhaps the most prominent weapon in the president's unilateral arsenal and have the advantage of having their legal status firmly codified and enshrined by the courts, they are far from the only unilateral instrument routinely used by presidents. Indeed, while the rate at which presidents have issued executive orders has decreased, on average, in raw terms over the past fifty years, they are increasingly employing alternate instruments, such as executive memoranda, to pick up the slack.[27] When we examine the sum total of unilateral executive directives, the raw numbers are overwhelming at first glance.

However, any analysis relying on simple counts comes with an important caveat: many and indeed most of these executive actions are of little if any policy-relevant importance. For example, president Barack Obama repeatedly reminded critics concerned about the expansion of presidential unilateral power that he issued far fewer executive orders than his predecessors. Moreover, many of the executive orders he issued were trivial in scope. For example, an April 2016 order authorized the Peace Corps to change its logo. Two August 2016 orders updated the chain of succession at the US Treasury and Veterans Affairs Departments. President George W. Bush is often remembered for being particularly aggressive in exercising the unilateral power of the presidency to its fullest. While Bush undoubtedly ordered a number of highly consequential actions, the ultimate impacts of most of his orders were decidedly mundane as well. For example, a December 2002 executive order set procedures for allowing most federal offices to close for Christmas Eve. Other orders were clearly more policy relevant, such as the 2002 order to create the President's Commission on the Postal Service and a 2004 order to create a Committee on Ocean Policy. But the ultimate policy implications of such orders were limited, and all but imperceptible to most Americans.

To answer whether the rising tide of presidential unilateralism truly threatens our separation of powers framework, we must try to separate the proverbial wheat from the chaff and home in on the subset of politically important unilateral initiatives. Measuring significance is intrinsically difficult and somewhat subjective. However, one method developed by previous scholars relies on media coverage to determine significance. Executive orders that receive even a modicum of media coverage are likely to be more important, on average, than those that receive no such attention. To this end, we build on the work of prior scholars and identify every executive order mentioned in coverage by the *New York Times* from 1953 through 2018.[28] If an order received even a single mention, we coded it as a significant executive order. This represents a low threshold, particularly compared to the criteria developed by political scientists to identify significant pieces of legislation enacted by Congress.[29] Nonetheless, using such a highly inclusive metric paints a decidedly different picture concerning the prevalence of significant unilateral action.

The top panel of figure 1.1 presents the total number of executive orders issued each year. The frequency with which presidents have issued these orders has declined from the heady days of the immediate aftermath of World War II. Still, the graph makes clear that all presidents, Democrats and Republicans alike, have routinely issued dozens of executive orders each year. However, the bottom panel of figure 1.1 shows that most of these orders did not merit even a single mention anywhere in the *New York Times*, perhaps the most important newspaper of national record; this suggests that most executive orders are not substantively significant.[30] From the beginning of Ronald Reagan's presidency through 2018, presidents have issued, on average, just ten executive orders per year that were mentioned in the *Times*. Moreover, while some of these orders did indeed have significant policy consequences, many of those receiving media coverage were nonetheless quite limited in scope and importance. For example, executive orders creating the Armed Forces Service Medal, establishing the Microgravity Research Board, updating the order of succession at the US Department of Housing and Urban Development, and instructing federal agencies to take steps to promote physical fitness all received coverage in the *Times*.

An important limitation of the data presented in figure 1.1 is that they focus exclusively on executive orders. Restricting the analysis to executive orders affords several advantages. Perhaps most important, since 1935 all executive orders are required by statute to be published in the *Federal Register*. Executive memoranda, by contrast, are published at the discretion of the president. Similarly, many national security directives are classified, which complicates efforts to compile a comprehensive list.[31] Moreover, the legal status of executive orders, in contrast to some other types of unilat-

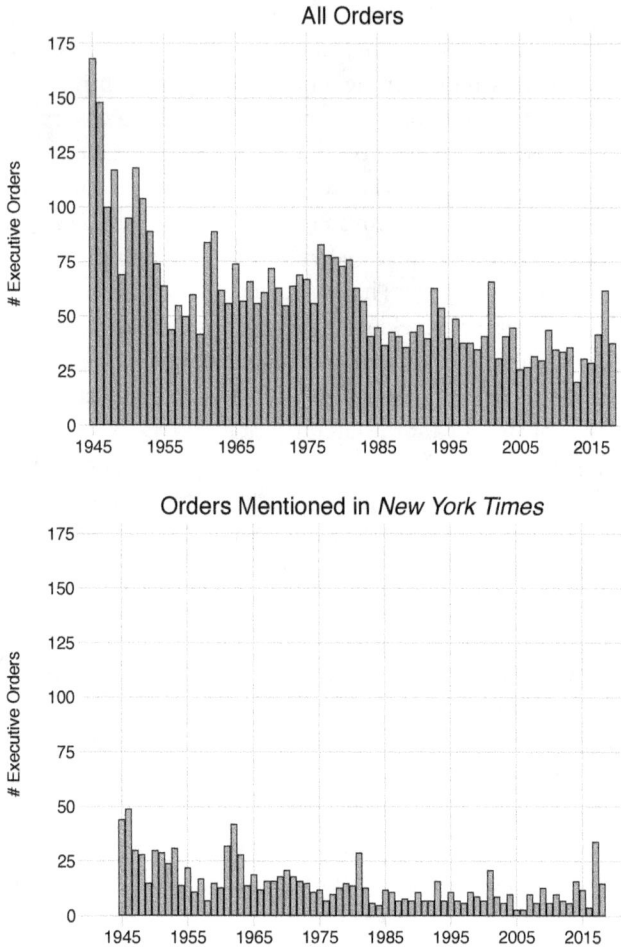

Figure 1.1. The scarcity of significant executive orders, 1945–2018

eral instruments, is long established and firmly codified by the courts. Yet many of the most important unilateral actions of recent years—from President Bush's decision to create a system of military tribunals to try terror suspects and to authorize the National Security Agency to conduct warrantless wiretaps on Americans' electronic communications, to President Obama's initiatives to shield millions of undocumented immigrants from deportation—were promulgated through other instruments, not executive orders. This raises the possibility that examining only executive orders could cause us to significantly underestimate the extent of presidential unilateralism.

To alleviate concerns that the data in figure 1.1 may miss a number of important unilateral actions, we conducted a broader search to identify every unilateral action (e.g., memoranda, proclamations, executive agreements) mentioned even once in the *New York Times* from 2001 through 2018.[32] The top panel of figure 1.2 shows that even when we expand the search parameters to include other high-profile unilateral actions in addition to executive orders, presidential unilateralism is still far from rampant.[33] Presidents Bush and Obama averaged just under fifteen unilateral directives reported in the *Times* per year. Some of these, including President Bush's creation of military tribunals to try suspected terrorists and

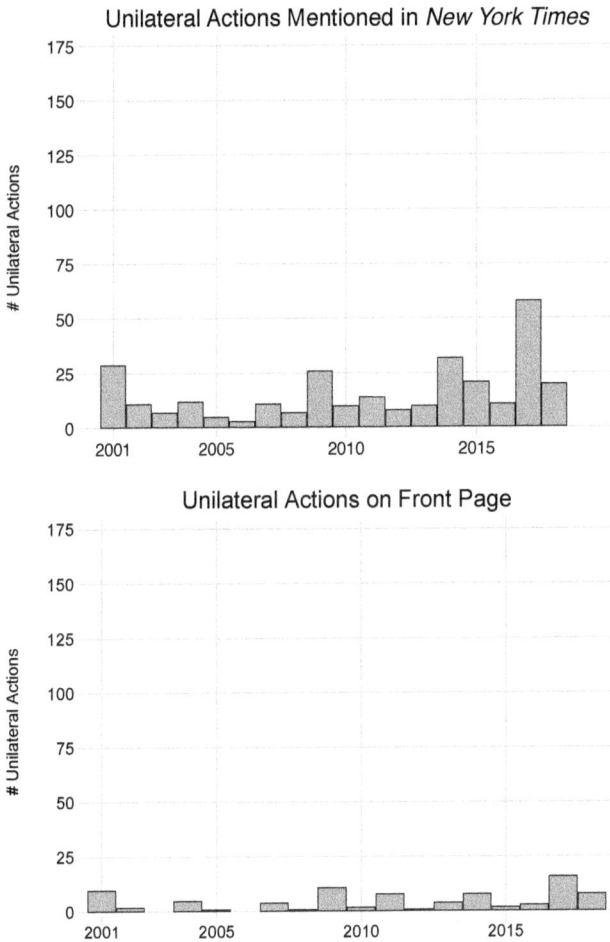

Figure 1.2. Significant unilateral actions, 2001–2018

President Obama's nuclear deal with Iran, clearly had significant policy consequences. However, many of these executive actions—such as President Obama's executive orders to create an advisory council on antibiotic resistance and to tighten antifraud protections on federally issued credit cards—while substantively meaningful, were of limited impact. The clear outlier here is president Donald Trump, who in 2017 issued as many executive actions covered in the *Times* as President Obama did in his entire first term in office. But President Trump's pace slackened considerably in 2018, and questions remain as to how aggressively he will rely on unilateral powers for the remainder of his presidency. Throughout this book, we explore the extent to which the politics of unilateral action differ under Trump. In particular, we explore whether the businessman-turned-politician is less responsive than his predecessors to political checks on this power.

A final way to home in on the most important unilateral actions—those constituting bold action with significant consequences for politics and policy—is to focus on executive actions that received at least one mention in a *front-page* story in the *Times*. The resulting list captures most of the high-profile executive actions in recent years, including President Bush's actions restricting federal stem cell research, denying Geneva Convention rights to terror suspects, and creating the Offices of Homeland Security and Faith-Based and Community Initiatives, as well as President Obama's orders to close the US military prison at Guantanamo Bay, Cuba, and to shield hundreds of thousands of undocumented immigrants from deportation. Even among this narrower set, however, not all the executive actions were of earth-shattering significance. For example, the resulting list includes President Bush's 2007 executive actions to ease Thanksgiving holiday air travel. Nevertheless, this final procedure helps us focus more squarely on the subset of executive actions most likely to have major policy consequences.

The bottom panel of figure 1.2 shows the number of executive actions meriting mention on the front page of the *New York Times* from 2001 through 2018. As the figure makes clear, such unilateral actions are surprisingly rare. President Trump's first year in office again produced the highest tally, with sixteen orders. Yet five years during this period produced either zero or only one unilateral action important enough to merit mention in even a single front-page article. On average, presidents issued roughly five such unilateral actions per year over the last three administrations.

Most Americans are familiar with some of the most brazen assertions of unilateral power by recent presidents—including Obama's creation of the Deferred Action for Childhood Arrivals (DACA) immigration program and Trump's declaration of a national emergency to build the US-Mexico border wall, cases in which they both acted unilaterally to effect policy changes explicitly rejected by Congress. But a broader assessment of the data on unilateral activity as a whole places these exceptional cases within a more general context. To be sure, presidents can and do issue bold unilateral directives that effect significant changes in public policy absent any congressional action. Such instances are historically rare, however, even in the contemporary era, when unilateralism has allegedly reached its zenith. Perhaps the most surprising fact about recent trends in major unilateral action is its relative scarcity.[34]

THE PIVOTAL POLITICS PARADIGM

Debates over the propriety, scope, and extent of presidential unilateral power are almost as old as the republic itself. In 1793, desperate to keep the fledgling nation out of European entanglements, president George Washington famously issued his Proclamation of Neutrality. By declaring that the United States would remain neutral in the conflagration between England and France, Washington claimed for the executive the right to define the nation's foreign policy posture until Congress exercised its power to declare war. His decision was highly controversial and pitted two erstwhile allies, Alexander Hamilton and James Madison, against each other. The former, unsurprisingly, championed the president's prerogative to act. The latter lambasted the move as an usurpation of congressional authority.

President Thomas Jefferson negotiated and agreed to the Louisiana Purchase without any prior congressional approval. President Abraham Lincoln took steps to put the Union on a war footing in 1861 while Congress was not in session, including an attempted resupply of Fort Sumter, the institution of a naval blockade against Confederate ports, and the suspension of the writ of habeas corpus. In 1863, Lincoln issued perhaps the most sweeping unilateral directive of all time, the Emancipation Proclamation. At the turn of the twentieth century, president Theodore Roosevelt went perhaps further still in declaring a broad, undefined residuum of presidential power to act unilaterally in the national interest, whether in the domestic sphere by protecting millions of acres of pristine wilderness from development or in the international realm by pursuing gunboat and dollar diplomacy absent congressional sanction.

Courts have grappled with questions of the constitutionality of unilateral presidential actions almost since the Founding. In the 1804 case *Little v. Barreme*, the Supreme Court struck down an order by president John Adams issued during the quasi war with France that authorized US naval vessels to seize ships sailing to and from French ports. Chief justice John Marshall argued that had Adams acted alone, the order would have been constitutional. However, because Congress had explicitly authorized the seizure only of ships sailing *to* French ports (and the *Barreme* was sailing *from* a French port), the order was unconstitutional. Additional nineteenth-century cases involved challenges to specific presidential unilateral actions, such as *Ex Parte Merryman* and Lincoln's unilateral suspension of the writ of habeas corpus. But in the 1930s, the Supreme Court issued a series of rulings putting presidential unilateral powers on a firmer legal footing. Two cases, *United States v. Curtiss-Wright* and *United States v. Pink*, established the president's power to enter the United States into international agreements and held that these agreements have the same legal status as treaties. A third case, *United States v. Belmont*, recognized the president's power to issue executive orders and held that those orders have the force of federal law, including preeminence over state law.[35]

Ironically given their prominence, presidency scholars had long paid relatively little attention to unilateral powers.[36] Perhaps the most important reason for this oversight is that the most influential book on the presidency of the last fifty years, Richard Neustadt's *Presidential Power*, explicitly downplayed the importance of unilateral power.[37] Presidents can rarely rely on their power to "command," Neustadt argued. Even superficially successful instances of command often came at a long-term political cost that exceeded the immediate policy benefit.

Arthur Schlesinger Jr.'s *The Imperial Presidency* reawakened scholarly interest in presidential unilateral power. While Watergate and president Richard Nixon's downfall ushered in an era of congressional resurgence, by the 1980s and 1990s presidential unilateralism again seemed to be on the march. This prompted a new wave of scholarly interest in the president's unilateral tool kit and its increasing prominence on the national political stage. Analysts presented illustrative case studies of presidents effecting major policy changes unilaterally in domains as diverse as civil rights and foreign policy. Moreover, empirical assessments showed that the use of such unilateral tools has increased in recent decades.[38]

The dominant theoretical paradigm for understanding unilateral politics emerged from a new model of the lawmaking process developed by political scientist Keith Krehbiel. For decades, scholars had used a simple median voter model as a heuristic to help make sense of legislative behavior.[39] But Krehbiel's model noted that this framework does not accurately describe the US legislative system, which has multiple supermajoritarian requirements. Specifically, in the Senate a minority can filibuster a bill supported by the majority and prevent it from receiving a final up or down vote. As a result, sixty votes are required to secure passage of most major legislative initiatives in the Senate. Furthermore, once passed by both chambers of Congress, a bill still must be signed by the president to become law. If a bill moves policy away from the president's preferences, he will veto it. In this case, a two-thirds majority is needed to override the presidential veto. Hence, the crucial players in the American context are what Krehbiel terms the filibuster pivot and the veto pivot—the legislators who are key in determining whether a bill can secure sixty votes to stop a filibuster or a two-thirds vote to override a presidential veto.[40] Perhaps the most important result of Krehbiel's model is that many policies are "gridlocked"—that is, no bill that would change the status quo can be passed and signed by the president. The ideological space between the filibuster and the veto pivots is christened the "gridlock interval." Status quo policies within this ideological space cannot be changed by normal legislative procedures. This theory of lawmaking offers keen insight into our contemporary institutional malaise. Partisan polarization widens the gridlock interval by moving the pivotal players further to the ideological extremes. This in turn makes legislative action all but impossible for a growing number of issue areas.

William Howell embraced the basic framework of the pivotal politics model, but with an important modification. Presidents can do more than veto legislation. They can also be first movers in the US system by acting unilaterally. Once this adjustment is made, even the basic model yields a surprising result: the very same institutional setup that makes it so difficult for presidents to achieve their policy priorities legislatively gives them tremendous advantages when acting unilaterally.[41] Indeed, the model suggests that presidents can move any status quo policy lodged within the gridlock interval closer to their preferences, provided that the new policy remains within that interval, secure in the knowledge that Congress will not be able to undo legislatively what the president has changed unilaterally.[42]

As a result, the dominant unilateral politics model predicts that presidents should be able to act unilaterally with little risk of being overturned by Congress on a wide range of issues. Moreover, since all they need is enough support in Congress to sustain their veto, presidents are even more empowered in an era of intense partisan polarization.[43] In a polarized era, it is hard to imagine a presidential move for which the president could not recruit the necessary one-third plus one members of either the House of Representatives or the Senate to sustain a veto. As Neal Katyal describes it, the veto has become a tool that can "entrench presidential decrees," all but completely undermining legislative checks on presidential assertions of unilateral power.[44] Presidents have always enjoyed significant institutional advantages when acting unilaterally. But polarization has expanded the gridlock interval, rendering Congress increasingly powerless to enact legislation reversing executive action.

Of course, formal models are simplifications of reality. Are the congressional checks on the unilateral president stronger than such models propose? Howell argues no.[45] In fact, Congress may be even weaker than the unilateral politics model predicts. The formal model assumes that Congress will vote to override a presidential veto on any bill amending policy changed by an executive order that is closer to the veto pivot's preferences than the unilaterally created policy. But the task for legislators is not so simple. Congress as an institution is plagued by a collective action dilemma when it tries to defend its institutional prerogatives. Besides, even when acting to constrain the president is in enough members' personal political as well as collective institutional interests, it is exceedingly difficult to build and maintain large coalitions throughout a legislative process riddled with transaction costs.[46] As a result, the modern congressional constraint on presidential unilateral action may be even weaker than suggested by the pivotal politics model. These institutional weaknesses of Congress may render it unable to challenge unilateral actions successfully, even when a supermajority of members would prefer legislation to overturn a presidential order and restore the status quo.[47] In summarizing the institutional barriers to effective legislative redress, Terry Moe and William Howell conclude, "The bottom line, then, is that the Constitution's incomplete contract sets up a governing structure that virtually invites presidential imperialism."[48]

Consistent with Moe and Howell's insight, many of the most prominent unilateral actions of recent years clearly illustrate how presidents can secure policy victories unilaterally when they are blocked legislatively. For example, on October 26, 2001, Congress granted the George W. Bush administration sweeping power to identify and prosecute suspected terrorists. However, less than three weeks later President Bush also signed an order creating a system of military tribunals to try terror suspects outside the reach of civilian courts. The new, unilaterally created tribunal system fundamentally undermined a central compromise at the heart of the Patriot Act: suspected terrorists must be charged with a crime within seven days of their detention and also have access to the federal judicial system.[49] The order's release prompted bipartisan outcry on Capitol Hill, with such disparate voices as Rep. Bob Barr (R-GA) of Clinton impeachment fame and stalwart liberal Rep. Dennis Kucinich (D-OH) railing against the president's action.[50] This strong opposition on Capitol Hill may well have derailed any presidential effort to create the tribunals legislatively. However, congressional opponents of the president's action could not muster the requisite two-thirds majorities in both chambers to overturn that which Bush had wrought unilaterally. As a result, the order stood.[51]

Similarly, when President Bush's secret order authorizing the National Security Agency to electronically eavesdrop on the international communications of US citizens was revealed by the *New York Times* in 2005, it provoked a firestorm of criticism.[52] The reaction on Capitol Hill strongly suggests that Bush would have faced an uphill battle had he chosen to seek legislative changes to the Foreign Intelligence Surveillance Act to permit the new program. It was far easier to create the program unilaterally and then beat back congressional efforts to rein in the program post ex facto.

By contrast, president Barack Obama aggressively lobbied Congress to pass immigration reform by advancing both comprehensive immigration reform and a narrower set of less controversial reforms colloquially known as the Development, Relief, and Education for Alien Minors (DREAM) Act. With the reforms hopelessly stalled in Congress, in June 2012 Obama instituted many of the DREAM Act's provisions unilaterally through the Deferred Action for Childhood Arrivals (DACA) program. In short, the president succeeded in effecting change unilaterally that he simply could not extract from Congress legislatively.

While most analysts focus primarily on Congress and its ability—or inability—to constrain the unilateral executive, the unilateral politics model also recognizes a role for courts. While the courts have long held that unilateral actions, such as executive orders, if properly issued have the full force of law, the courts retain the capacity to strike down an executive action if they determine it exceeds discretionary authority delegated by statute or the president's inherent constitutional authority. Yet, as Alexander Hamilton noted in *Federalist 78*, the judiciary, having "no influence over either the purse or the sword," is often the weakest branch of the US government. This is particularly true in the context of unilateral action. To strike down an executive action, the court must rely on the very actor it is reproaching to enforce its ruling. The result is that judicial challenges to unilateral action historically have been exceedingly rare, and successful ones rarer still.[53]

The unilateral politics model thus offers a very clear expectation about the frequency and volume of unilateral action. Presidents should routinely use unilateral action to pursue their goals across a wide range of policies, secure in the knowledge that neither Congress nor the courts are likely to reverse them.

This dominant paradigm also casts in a very different light the most controversial action of the Donald Trump presidency so far—his February 2019 decision to declare a national emergency to build the Mexican border wall. In the winter of 2018, President Trump fought desperately to secure congressional funding for the wall. However, appropriators refused to budge. The government shut down. And eventually, Trump caved and signed legislation reopening the government without wall funding. Undeterred, he quickly decided to achieve unilaterally what he could not legislatively. In many narratives, Trump's gambit is portrayed as a brazen usurpation of power rivaling Harry Truman's nationalization of the steel mills by executive order during the Korean War.

The reaction thus far to Trump's declaration perfectly fits the predicted script. Congressional Democrats unanimously denounced the president's usurpation of Congress's power of the purse (outlined in Article I of the Constitution). Even in the contemporary era of intense partisan polarization, they were joined by a substantial number of Republicans. Indeed, twelve Republican senators ultimately broke with Trump and voted for legislation to rescind his national emergency declaration. But Trump promptly vetoed the joint resolution, effectively killing any effort at legislative redress. Of course, Trump may yet lose in court. The outcome is anything but certain, however, and the potential policy gains should he prevail are enormous.

We argue that the better question is not what explains Trump's audacity but rather what explains the reticence of other presidents to similarly use (or abuse?) their unilateral power—emergency or otherwise—to effect similarly dramatic shifts in policy when blocked by a gridlocked legislature. Many Republicans sought to dissuade Trump by warning him that such a move could open a Pandora's box for future Democratic presidents to exploit emergency powers in order to pursue policies that would be anathema to the party and Trump's conservative base. What would stop a future Democratic president from declaring gun violence—which in 2017 was responsible for 20% of deaths among Americans between the ages of fifteen and twenty-four—a national emergency requiring unilateral presidential action?[54] Or, as senator Lamar Alexander (R-TN) warned, what would prevent the next president from declaring "a climate change emergency to close coal plants and build wind turbines, or a health care emergency and force into Medicare the 180 million Americans with health insurance on the job?"[55]

Given the frailty of the institutional checks on unilateralism, presidents clearly have great opportunities to act alone. And yet both the more systematic assessment of unilateral action in the preceding section and the case studies of forgone unilateral action in chapter 6 suggest that presidents have exercised considerable self-restraint. Why have they not pushed the bounds of their unilateral power even further? Why does Trump look more like an outlier than the norm? We argue that public opinion and informal political checks largely have succeeded in reining in presidents when formal institutional checks are unable to do so.

THE POLITICAL COSTS OF UNILATERAL ACTION

While 9/11 and its aftermath fueled scholarly assessments of the scope of unilateral power, over the last decade several strands of scholarship have instead explored some forces that may limit its exercise. For example, research by Fang-Yi Chiou and Larry Rothenberg as well as by Josh Chafetz acknowledges that Congress rarely overturns unilateral actions, but contends that it nevertheless enjoys a broader range of legislative tools including budgetary, appointment-making, and agenda-setting powers through which it influences the exercise of unilateral power.[56] Relatedly, Michelle Belco and Brandon Rottinghaus empirically show that much unilateral action, rather than representing a presidential end run around Congress, is actually collaborative with congressional majorities.[57] Hearkening back to Neustadt, another strand of literature led by Andrew Rudalevige and Josh Kennedy emphasizes the importance of the bureaucracy as a potential check on the president's unilateral impulses.[58] As Rudalevige has shown, many orders originate in the bureaucracy rather than in the White House or the Executive Office of the President, and thus presidents may need to bargain with bureaucrats over policy formulation. And of course, presidents may also be forced to bargain with the bureaucracy over program implementation after an order is signed, or even risk noncompliance.

The attention to other forms of institutional resistance to unilateralism offers an important corrective to the conventional wisdom asserting almost unbridled presidential unilateral power. We argue, however, that

such an approach focusing primarily on institutional responses to unilateralism misses a more fundamental omission in the dominant unilateral
politics model: its failure to understand the factors shaping the political
costs of unilateral action and how those costs, both real and anticipated,
inform presidents' strategic calculus.

When deciding whether to act unilaterally, presidents consider more
than simply the likelihood of Congress enacting legislation to overturn
their order or of the courts striking it down as unconstitutional. Rather,
presidents also consider the political costs of going it alone, and they
weigh these costs against the expected policy benefits of doing so.[59] Past
scholarship has occasionally acknowledged the existence of these more informal political costs, even if it has given them little sustained emphasis
or empirical testing. For example, Kenneth Mayer argues that presidents
will sometimes forgo acting unilaterally to avoid an anticipated "backlash."[60] Similarly, Moe and Howell note, "Should [presidents] go too far
or too fast, or move into the wrong areas at the wrong time, they would
find that there are heavy political costs to be paid—perhaps in being reversed on the specific issue by Congress or the courts, but more generally
by creating opposition that could threaten other aspects of the presidential policy agenda or even its broader success."[61] And of course, Richard
Neustadt's three "cases of command" were designed to argue that even
unilateral victories often come at a significant cost.[62]

While speculating that such political costs may exist, past scholarship tells us little about what form these costs might ultimately take and
which factors raise or lower the costs presidents risk incurring when they
act unilaterally. Moreover, there is little generalizable evidence that presidents' actual unilateral agendas have been affected by their considerations
of these costs. These details are crucially important to understanding the
nature of the constraints on the unilateral president and whether unilateralism threatens to upset the tenuous constitutional balance of power.

We argue that the most important political cost anticipated by presidents is the reaction of the American people. Will the public rally behind
the initiative? Or will executive action erode support for the president and
his policies? Political theorists, pundits, and scholars alike have long argued that presidents face strong incentives to be responsive to popular sentiment. *Federalist 51* is perhaps best remembered for its description of how
the constitutional system of checks and balances pits ambition against
ambition to keep any one office or officeholder from becoming too powerful. But in that same essay, James Madison also discusses the critical importance of public opinion: "A dependence on the people is, no doubt, the

primary control on the government." Institutional checks and balances, while central to the constitutional system, are described as "auxiliary precautions." In *Federalist 72*, Hamilton lauds the president's eligibility for reelection (which was constitutionally unlimited until the ratification of the Twenty-Second Amendment in 1951) as an important inducement toward good behavior. Eager to secure their own reelection or the election of a partisan successor best positioned to defend their policy legacies, presidents remain responsive to public opinion and are reticent to push too far if doing so will engender popular resentment. Since the foundation of the Gallup Poll in the 1930s, the president's public job approval rating has become a ubiquitous shorthand for his reserve of political capital. Moreover, decades of empirical research have shown that low public approval ratings hamper presidents' ability to pursue their policy and political agendas.[63] Presidents, therefore, have strong incentives to guard their standing among the public.

Most political science analyses of presidential unilateralism, grounded in the pivotal politics framework, have focused on the weakness of the institutional constraints checking the president. They pay little if any attention to the potential constraint exercised by public opinion. Instead, our emphasis is most like a provocative argument in the legal literature positing that public opinion has become perhaps the most important safeguard on presidential aggrandizement in a "post-Madisonian" republic. In *The Executive Unbound*, Eric Posner and Adrian Vermeule ask whether any checks remain on the executive in the contemporary administrative state.[64] The legal constraints, as exercised by Congress and the courts, are admittedly weak.[65] The Newtonian system of checks and balances so carefully erected by the Framers is weaker in the contemporary polity than it was in the eighteenth century. However, even an "imperial" president, Posner and Vermeule argue, is constrained by electoral pressures and public opinion: "As long as the public informs itself and maintains a skeptical attitude toward the motivations of government officials, the executive can operate effectively only by proving over and over that it deserves the public's trust."[66] In a discussion of a hypothetical interbranch constitutional showdown, they maintain that the public, not the judiciary, is now the primary arbiter: "Through the mysterious process by which public opinion forms, the public will throw its weight behind one branch or the other, and the branch that receives public support will prevail."[67]

But through what "mysterious process" does the public evaluate contested claims of unilateral authority? Are Americans instinctively skeptical of unilateral power as a threat to checks and balances? Or are they generally permissive of unilateral action? Moreover, do presidents actually consider public opinion when deciding whether to act unilaterally? Under what conditions are they more or less likely to do so?

In the pages that follow, we show that Americans do not assess unilateral action in a vacuum. Perhaps the most important determinant of whether the public rallies behind unilateral action or mobilizes against it is the response of other political actors. In the absence of criticism from political elites, the public will not instinctively oppose acts of unilateralism. Instead, most Americans evaluate executive action by drawing on the same cues—most important, partisanship and policy preferences—that they use when making other political judgments. However, when other actors, especially members of Congress, challenge the unilateral president in the public sphere, they can activate underlying constitutional qualms, sway public opinion, and significantly raise the political costs of unilateral action for the president.

If presidents judge that the benefits of acting unilaterally outweigh even the heightened political costs of doing so, then act on their own initiative they will. But in many cases, presidents determine that the likely political costs of acting on their own are simply too high. The result is that major unilateral actions do occur, but they are relatively rare. Presidents routinely forgo unilateral action to move policy closer to their preferences, even when Congress and the courts could hardly overturn them. The unilateral president is less imperial than often supposed.

PLAN OF THE BOOK

Napoleon famously described public opinion as "the thermometer a monarch should constantly consult."[68] If even the man who chastised Pope Pius VII—reminding him that "your holiness is the sovereign of Rome, but I am its Emperor"—recognized the power of the *vox populi*, surely presidents also consider public opinion when contemplating unilateral action.[69] But how do Americans think about unilateralism?

Chapter 2 examines whether Americans' creedal commitments to liberal values extend to an instinctive rejection of unilateral power. Limited evidence from prior public polling and recent research suggest that popular resistance to presidential aggrandizement will be strong, swift, and spontaneous. Presidents who transgress constitutional mores concerning separation of powers will encounter an inherently skeptical public. We test this argument through a series of nine experiments embedded in nationally representative opinion surveys. The results are unambiguous.

Americans do not automatically oppose unilateral action as a threat to the constitutional system of checks and balances. Rather, the factors driving most Americans' assessment of executive action are the same as those governing other political assessments—namely, partisan ties and policy preferences. Americans largely back executive action when taken by a president of their party; when they approve of the incumbent president; and when that action moves policy in their preferred direction. In each case, they tend to oppose unilateral action when the opposite is true. The public may still turn against the president en masse should he pursue a unilateral policy shift that is too far from the political mainstream. But relatively few Americans will oppose presidential action solely because of the means through which it is achieved.

The public rarely evaluates presidents' unilateral initiatives in a political vacuum, however. Rather, it does so in a hotly contested environment in which competing voices do battle to rally public opinion to their side. When trying to court public support for their unilateral gambits, presidents enjoy the advantages of the proverbial bully pulpit. Of course, they are far from the only actors struggling for support in the court of public opinion. Members of Congress may routinely fail when trying to check the unilateral executive institutionally, but they nonetheless remain relevant because of their capacity to erode public support for executive action. When congressional voices are silent, many executive actions enjoy broad support. When congressional actors push back against administration moves, public support wanes.

To investigate this dynamic, chapter 3 presents a series of eight survey experiments examining public support for unilateral action in both the Obama and the Trump administrations. Americans do not instinctively oppose executive action as a threat to the constitutional balance of power. But they do respond to congressional criticisms attacking presidential unilateralism on both constitutional and policy grounds. Congress plays a critically important role in activating Americans' creedal commitments and mobilizing public opinion against bold and potentially destabilizing assertions of unilateral executive power.

Chapter 4 examines the efficacy of federal courts as a check on presidential power. We do not dispute that courts are at an institutional disadvantage when confronting an increasingly unilateral presidency; yet we note an increasingly assertive judicial response to unilateralism in recent years. Perhaps more important, we argue that past scholarship has overlooked the key indirect role courts may play by shaping popular assessments of executive action. A string of high-profile judicial defeats for the unilateral president—even if they represent exceptions to the general rule—has intensified speculation about the constitutionality of and potential judicial response to a host of executive actions. This speculation, in and of itself, may affect public opinion. Through a series of three survey experiments, we examine the influence of a possible judicial check on public attitudes toward unilateral action. We find that courts need not rule against the White House to undermine popular support for its unilateral initiatives. Rather, even raising the specter of a judicial challenge can undermine popular support for the president.

Public opinion may not instinctively oppose a president's use of his unilateral powers. But if other political actors, especially Congress and the courts, push back and challenge the White House, they can raise the political costs of unilateral action by eroding public support for the president. But are presidents responsive to these political costs? Does public opinion actually impose a check, albeit an informal one, on presidential aggrandizement?

Answering these questions is exceedingly difficult. After all, the main expectation of our argument is that presidents, when contemplating unilateral action, anticipate the likely response of Congress, the courts, and the public. When they anticipate costly pushback and an erosion of public support, they often forgo acting unilaterally altogether. Finding systematic direct evidence of the power of anticipated reactions—that is, identifying executive actions that were contemplated but then abandoned—is almost impossible. Even a thorough sweep of presidential archives would fail to generate a comprehensive list of all considered executive actions and a clear, unbiased view into the precise strategic calculations that led presidents to act, or not to act, in each case. Nevertheless, we look for evidence that public opinion can check unilateral impulses in two ways.

Chapter 5 lays out in greater detail our theory of anticipated reactions and identifies several observable implications that would constitute indirect evidence of a popular check. Most notably, the analysis examines the relationship between the frequency with which presidents issue significant executive orders and their approval ratings. Popular presidents anticipate greater support for their executive actions than do unpopular presidents. They do so because approval is a strong predictor of support for executive action among individual Americans and because popular presidents are less attractive targets for would-be critics in Congress and the courts. As a result, presidents should be more likely to forgo taking major executive action when their approval rating is low. This is exactly what we find.

Using sophisticated statistical techniques, we show that the causal arrow runs from approval to executive action, but not vice versa. Presidents with low approval ratings issue fewer significant executive orders than do their peers with stronger approval ratings. We also empirically test another implication of our theory—most unilateral actions should enjoy broad public support. We find considerable support for this hypothesis in data from the George W. Bush and Barack Obama administrations. By contrast, Donald Trump has consistently pursued executive actions opposed by majorities of Americans. The chapter concludes by examining President Trump's political calculus and whether he is less responsive to political resistance than were his predecessors.

A series of case studies in chapter 6 explores precisely how public opinion and anticipated political costs factor into the president's strategic calculus when contemplating unilateral action. The chapter begins by analyzing three cases of the proverbial dogs that did not bark—cases in which the president considered, but did not take, unilateral action: President Clinton's decision not to issue an executive order allowing gays to serve openly in the military; President Obama's decision not to enforce his "red line" in Syria; and President Trump's decision not to issue a draft executive order to revisit the use of enhanced interrogation techniques and "black site" prisons. In each case, it is clear that the president wanted to act unilaterally and in the first two had all but decided to do so. However, after considering the political pushback unilateral action would entail, all three presidents pulled back and opted against going it alone. Causing presidents to forgo unilateral action altogether is only one way in which political costs influence presidential behavior. In some cases, presidents may fail to anticipate opposition; will act unilaterally; and then reverse course in the face of significant resistance. Finally, as the chapter shows in a pair of additional case studies from the Obama administration, concerns about political costs can also affect both the scope and the timing of executive action.

Chapter 7 summarizes our argument and evidence against popular notions of an imperial president with almost unbridled unilateral power. It then examines three developments in contemporary politics that could weaken the political checks on unilateral power: an erosion of democratic norms; partisan polarization in Congress; and increasing partisan "tribalism" in the mass public. While each of these developments may ultimately pose some threat to the strength of political checks on unilateral power, recent experience suggests that political checks remain robust despite the extreme stresses on each of these dimensions that have defined the Trump presidency.

CHAPTER TWO

How Americans Think about Unilateral Action

Because the institutional checks exercised by Congress and the courts are so weak, public opinion may be the last and most important check on the unilateral president.[1] And because public opinion is so critical to presidents' electoral fortunes as well as to their capacity to move their legislative policy agendas in Washington and to their political capital more broadly, presidents have strong incentives to be responsive to public opinion and avoid taking unilateral action that might erode their store of popular support. Public opinion, therefore, has the potential to constrain executive action. But the strength of this constraint—and whether it will materialize at all—critically depends on how Americans assess presidential unilateral action. To understand the potential strength of this popular check and the conditions under which it might be operative, we must understand, in Eric Posner and Adrian Vermeule's words, the "mysterious process" through which the public decides whether to support or oppose unilateral action.

Somewhat surprisingly, journalists and scholars alike have paid relatively little attention to how Americans think about unilateral action. The last twenty-five years have produced a veritable explosion of scholarship on the unilateral presidency. Analysts have plumbed the constitutional underpinnings of unilateral powers; traced the evolution of their exercise over time; studied the reaction (or, more frequently, the failure to react) of other governing institutions to presidential assertions of unilateral authority; and debated the normative consequences of executive action for democracy. Yet the public's response to presidential unilateralism has largely escaped systematic attention.

However, we do know a great deal about how Americans form their opinions on political questions more generally. Insights from this broader literature can help us generate some testable hypotheses about how the public thinks about unilateral power. Perhaps the single most important and replicable finding from decades of public opinion research is that most Americans possess a shockingly limited amount of information about politics and policy. Survey after survey shows that most Americans fail to grasp even basic facts about American governance and the world around them.[2] The public release of such polls is often greeted with headlines such as *Politico*'s 2015 lede, "Americans Bomb Pew Test of Basic Public Knowledge."[3] Because most Americans lack a deep reservoir of relevant information when forming their political opinions and because acquiring such information is costly, many rationally rely on information shortcuts, or heuristics, to form their political judgments.[4] That is, while a relative few may draw on constitutional or historical knowledge when assessing executive action, many more are likely to rely on the same political cues they use to make political decisions and make sense of political events more generally.

The question, then, is, Which factors will be most important in guiding Americans' assessments of unilateral action? Prior scholarship on public opinion suggests the potential for three forces in particular to drive popular assessments of unilateral action: constitutional concerns, partisan affiliation, and policy preferences. The relative strength of these different explanatory variables has important implications for the nature of any popular check on presidential unilateralism.

CONSTITUTIONAL CONCERNS

Most Americans possess strikingly low levels of political knowledge, and many fail to recall even basic facts about the US government. In a 2014 Annenberg survey, fewer than 40% of subjects could correctly identify which party controlled the House of Representatives or the Senate, and just over a quarter of subjects knew that overriding a presidential veto required a two-thirds majority in both these congressional chambers.[5] Nevertheless, public opinion polls suggest that the Constitution remains widely revered. Although they may not know the particulars, most Americans embrace, or at least claim to embrace, the document's fundamental tenets, including its core commitment to separation of powers.

The Supreme Court has ruled that presidential unilateral initiatives, when exercised pursuant to proper authority, are constitutional and have the force of law.[6] However, the strength of the legal grounds on which presidents justify their unilateral directives varies widely across cases and over time.[7] Thus when evaluating unilateral action, Americans may consider the extent to which it threatens to upset the balance of powers across the branches of the federal government. For example, in 1934 Congress passed a joint resolution authorizing president Franklin Roosevelt to place an embargo on the sale of arms to belligerents in the Chaco War if he should determine that doing so would promote the cause of peace. Roosevelt quickly imposed such a ban via a presidential proclamation, citing the authority delegated to him by Congress in its very first sentence.[8] By contrast, in June 2012 president Barack Obama issued a memorandum to the Department of Homeland Security to create the Deferred Action for Childhood Arrivals (DACA) program that would potentially shield millions of illegal aliens from deportation if they met certain criteria. To justify its action, the administration cited its "prosecutorial discretion" rather than any affirmative statutory authorization from Congress.[9] Indeed, Congress had explicitly considered the Development, Relief, and Education for Alien Minors (DREAM) Act, legislation that would provide many of the very same protections, but ultimately refused to approve it.

Whether President Obama possessed the legal authority to act unilaterally in this case is beside the point. For many Americans, when presidents effect significant shifts in public policy without seeking congressional approval, the process conflicts with common understandings of how policymaking should work under the Constitution. The chief executive is supposed to implement the laws, not make them. If these norms are strongly held, then many Americans may instinctively recoil from efforts by presidents to execute an end run around Congress and change policy on their own through executive action.

In an age when seemingly everything is polled, there is surprisingly little survey evidence on Americans' constitutional attitudes in general and beliefs about unilateral action in particular. However, the data that exist strongly suggest that at least in the abstract, the public is highly skeptical of presidential unilateral power. While the constitutional system of checks and balances may be a cornerstone of civics education, it is also often blamed for the gridlock gripping contemporary Washington. At least since Woodrow Wilson, critics of our constitutional structure have warned that the system of checks and balances is sclerotic and biases the federal government toward inertia. The government's inability to tackle policy problems large and small plainly frustrates most Americans and has greatly contributed to rising popular dissatisfaction with the government writ large. Against this backdrop, one might expect many to support the centralization of power to break through the mess in Washington. But polling data suggest that an overwhelming majority of Americans remains strongly committed to checks and balances. In February 2017, a Pew Research Center poll asked how important "a system of checks and balances dividing power between the president, Congress, and the courts" is to "maintaining a strong democracy." A full 83% of respondents replied that it was very important, versus just 4% who said it was not too or not at all important. Support for checks and balances as a cornerstone of democracy was higher than for either a free press or the protection of unpopular positions.[10]

Most Americans also agree that the greatest threat to checks and balances is the runaway growth of presidential power. The 2007 Constitution and Governance Issues Survey asked Americans how well the contemporary polity reflected the commitment to checks and balances enshrined in the Constitution. Only 13% believed that the constitutional requirements were being met.[11] More concrete questions about unilateral actions taken by individual presidents also reveal widespread unease with the expansion of presidential power. In a December 2014 poll, 68% of Americans said that they were very or somewhat concerned "that Barack Obama's use of executive orders and acting without Congressional approval may be permanently altering our country's system of checks and balances."[12] When the question was asked again in January of 2016, an almost identical 65% expressed concern that Obama's unilateralism threatened to upend the constitutional balance of power.[13]

Finally, even in the realm of war powers, where presidents are commonly held to possess greater authority for independent action, scattered polls suggest widespread public opposition to presidential unilateralism.[14] Since World War II, presidents have routinely dispatched US military forces abroad to pursue a range of missions, even to wage major wars, absent any congressional authorization. Yet despite this repeated practice, surveys consistently show strong support for constitutional checks on presidential war powers. In the fall of 2002, an overwhelming majority of Americans, 70%, believed that president George W. Bush must seek congressional approval before taking military action against Iraq.[15] Similarly, despite the Obama administration's later protestations that US military actions against the regime of dictator Muammar Gaddafi in Libya did not require congressional authorization, fewer than a third of Americans agreed. Instead, most opined that the administration must secure congressional approval to continue military operations beyond the time limit established by the War Powers Resolution of 1973.

While the available public polling data suggest considerable public skepticism toward unilateral presidential power, the findings contain several important shortcomings. The outlets funding the polls tend to ask such questions only when they are particularly salient. As a result, they provide insight into public attitudes in politically charged environments, which renders them unable to tell us whether most Americans automatically oppose unilateral action. In addition, the question wordings vary significantly from poll to poll, and, with few exceptions, these polls do not directly measure attitudes toward unilateral presidential action apart from the use of force.

Overcoming many of these shortcomings, recent research by Andrew Reeves and Jon Rogowski represents one of the first efforts to measure systematically the breadth and depth of public support for unilateral action.[16] To do so, Reeves and Rogowski asked a representative sample of Americans on four separate occasions between November 2013 and January 2015 about their support for or opposition to several aspects of unilateral power. Perhaps most important, they asked subjects to evaluate whether "a president should have the right to enact policies without having those policies voted on by Congress."[17] This question most clearly captures the type of unilateral action that most alarms its critics, as it involves presidents changing public policy on their own initiative without seeking congressional approval. Support for presidential unilateral policy change was both low and remarkably stable. Across the four waves of their panel study, support for unilateral policy change ranged from a high of 27.7% to a low of 23.2%.[18]

But how should we interpret this low level of support for unilateralism in the abstract? Are constitutional concerns really driving many Americans to recoil from presidents acting on their own initiative to change policy outcomes on procedural grounds—that is, because it conflicts with the idea of checks and balances and how government should work? Or is this low level of support driven solely by opposition to the incumbent president, Barack Obama, whose approval rating was mired in the low 40s for much of the period?[19] In analyzing their data further, Reeves and Rogowski argue that constitutional concerns do indeed play an important role in driving opposition to unilateral action. While some of the variation in support for unilateralism can be explained by support for the incumbent president, opposition to unilateralism was most intense among those strongly committed to the rule of law.[20] The more a citizen believes in the key tenets of the objective rule of law, the less supportive he or she is of presidential unilateral action, which cuts against many Americans' constitutional mores.

This interpretation also finds some support in legal scholarship. In a multifaceted investigation into American national identity before and after 9/11, Joseph Margulies argues that public opposition to the Bush administration's conduct of the war was driven not by the ends of the policies themselves but by the unilateral means embraced to achieve them. Bush's claims of unbridled unilateral authority were wholly inconsistent with American values and commitment to the rule of law, and this triggered a popular backlash. "The failure by the Bush administration to recognize this attachment," Margulies concludes, "would prove the president's undoing."[21]

Taken together, this research suggests that many Americans evaluate claims of unilateral presidential authority through a distinctly constitutional lens. While courts have established the constitutionality of unilateral action when taken pursuant to proper constitutional or delegated authority, the image of presidents ordering significant changes in public policy on their own initiative, independent of Congress, conflicts with widely held understandings of the system of checks and balances. If Americans care not only about policy ends but also about the means through which they are obtained, then they should be inherently skeptical of unilateral executive action that appears to contradict both the letter and the spirit of checks and balances.

PARTISAN CUES

Although most Americans publicly express fealty to the Constitution and unflagging support for checks and balances, constitutional concerns are far from the only factors available when citizens assess executive action. Rather, scholars have long shown that partisan affiliation is one of the most important heuristics on which Americans lean when trying to make sense of the political world.[22] Indeed, the influence of partisanship on public opinion formation is truly pervasive. For example, in 2004 the Iraq Survey Group issued a final report on its year-long mission to find and document Iraq's weapons of mass destruction. Contra the White House's preinvasion claims, the group failed to find any stockpiles of WMDs, and it concluded that Saddam Hussein did not have an active WMD program. The matter seemed settled. However, most Americans interpreted these seemingly unambiguous conclusions through partisan-tinted lenses. Many Democrats who read the report of Charles Duelfer, special adviser to the Director of Central Intelligence, concluded that there never were any WMDs and that President Bush had rushed the country to war on false pretenses. By contrast, many Republicans concluded that Saddam Hussein had simply moved or destroyed his stockpiles before they could be found.[23]

Even answers to the seemingly objective question of whether the economy is strong or flailing are often colored by citizens' partisanship and the partisan composition of the incumbent government. Those whose copartisans are running the government in Washington are much more likely to perceive a robust economy, while the administration's partisan opponents are more likely to perceive an economy in trouble.[24] The persistence of partisanship even in economic evaluations is significant because almost all Americans have other relevant information on which to draw: their own pocketbooks.[25] Have their personal economic fortunes increased or decreased in the recent past? Moreover, objective indicators of economic health, such as unemployment and inflation figures or changes in the stock market, are widely available through almost constant coverage in the mass media. Thus if partisan cues significantly influence economic assessments, they are likely to be just as if not more important in shaping assessments of unilateral action for which other relevant information is less accessible.[26]

Finally, there are strong reasons to suspect that partisan cues may be particularly important in shaping public assessments of the president's exercise of unilateral power in the intensely polarized contemporary polity.[27] Beginning with the presidency of Bill Clinton, public assessments of presidential job performance began to polarize along partisan lines to a greater extent than ever before. By the George W. Bush presidency, the divide between Democrats and Republicans in their approval of the president was greater than at the height of the Watergate scandal. Although Barack Obama campaigned as an almost postpartisan leader, popular appraisals of his job in office became even more highly polarized than they had been for his predecessor. Most recently, the partisan chasm dividing Democrats' and Republicans' approval of Donald Trump has smashed records for the first months of a new administration. If partisan cues hold influence on Americans' overall assessments of the president's performance in office, these may similarly dominate their evaluation of the exercise of unilateral power.

Consider the stark partisan divides in public reaction to President Trump's threatened declaration of a national emergency to reprogram funds and build the Mexican border wall after Congress's refusal to appropriate the funds during the shutdown of 2018–19. Within days of Trump first issuing his threat that January, we asked the following question on a nationally representative online survey fielded by YouGov:[28]

President Trump is considering declaring a national emergency to allow him to spend billions of federal dollars to construct a wall on the
Mexican border without legislative approval from Congress. President
Trump argues that this is necessary to secure the border, stop illegal
immigration, and address a humanitarian crisis.

Would you support or oppose President Trump declaring a national
emergency to unilaterally build a wall along the Mexican border?

The results presented in figure 2.1 are broadly consistent with what
we might expect if constitutional concerns drove many Americans' assessments of unilateral action. A strong majority, 63%, of our sample opposed Trump declaring an emergency to build a wall. However, disaggre-
gating the data by partisan affiliation reveals a more nuanced picture. Far
from opposing Trump's brazen gambit on constitutional grounds, 78% of
Republicans supported Trump declaring a national emergency, with 58%
strongly supporting it. Democrats, by contrast, almost unanimously opposed Trump, with 88% strongly disapproving any such declaration. And
finally, independents were somewhat more split, but with a majority
clearly breaking with the president on unilaterally building the wall.

These results coupled with findings from public opinion research gen-

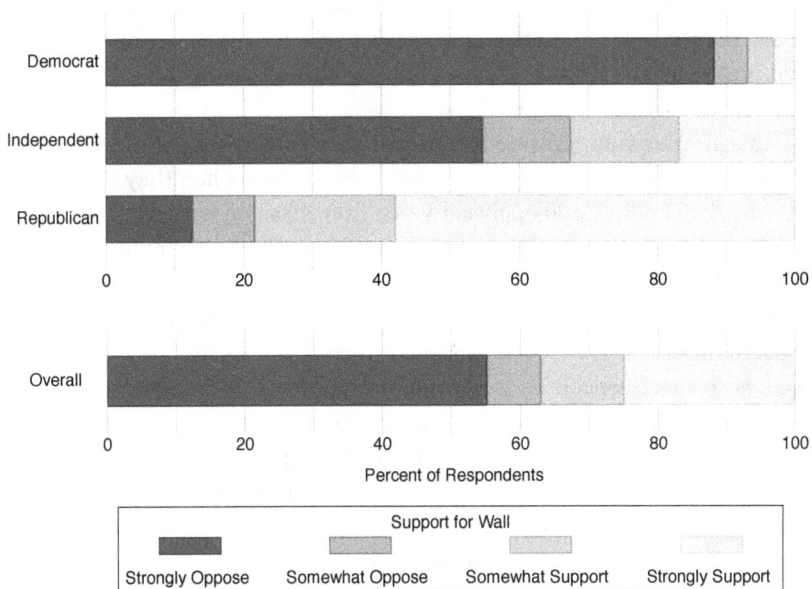

Figure 2.1. Support for President Trump's border wall emergency by party and overall

erally offer strong reasons to think that partisanship will broadly shape
how average citizens judge the unilateral president. If Americans predominantly rely on partisan cues when assessing unilateral action, then citizens will generally support unilateral action when taken by a copartisan
president and oppose unilateral action when initiated by the standard-
bearer of the opposition party.

POLICY PREFERENCES

Finally, Americans may also evaluate presidential unilateral action on its
policy merits and whether it fits their ideas of good public policy. Although
partisanship normally predicts elite support for or opposition to unilateral
action, policy concerns also clearly enter most elites' decision calculus.
For example, while congressional Democrats railed against much of what
President Bush accomplished unilaterally, not all his unilateral maneuvers met with Democratic opprobrium. When the president moved policy
toward the preferences of many congressional Democrats, congressional
pushback was minimal to nonexistent. Democrats voiced no objections
when Bush issued Executive Order 13423, which required the federal government to cut its use of oil-derived fuels by 2% and to increase its use of
renewable fuels by 10% per year. His order forced administrative agencies
to go far beyond the goals established by law in the Energy Policy Act of
2005. Yet congressional Democrats gave a pass to this assertion of unilateral presidential power, as it moved policy closer toward their preferences
regarding environmental policy.[29]

In a similar vein, average Americans may care about policy ends more
than its means. They may support unilateral action when they agree with
the change in policy and oppose it when they disagree with the president's
policy shift. This hypothesis seems intuitive. However, public opinion
scholarship has long minimized the importance of policy concerns in
opinion formation. The main reason for this was alluded to previously.
Most Americans lack even basic political knowledge. This statement
applies to most aspects of governmental policy as well. Americans may
know, for example, that they want government to improve the health care
system. But few possess strong preferences regarding the precise policies
that should be used to achieve this widely held end goal. Decades of survey research have shown that many Americans lack strong, stable policy
preferences on most issues.[30] Instead, there is significant evidence that
policy preferences are often the end result of political judgments rather
than the basis on which citizens make such assessments. Because most

citizens lack much policy-relevant information, they often simply adopt the policy positions of their party or preferred political leaders.[31]

Other studies suggest that many Americans have "sorted" themselves over time to bring their policy preferences and partisan affiliation into alignment.[32] In the contemporary polity, there are many fewer Democrats with conservative policy positions and Republicans with liberal polity positions than in the past. In such an environment, partisan forces and policy preferences may simply reinforce each other. Finally, even in the rare cases in which policy preferences and partisan ties do conflict, prior research suggests that most Americans will rely on the simpler partisan cues and ignore policy information when forming their political judgments.[33]

Nevertheless, recent studies have begun to challenge this conventional view by showing that public opinion may be more responsive to policy concerns than previously supposed.[34] Particularly on highly salient issues, some Americans may indeed hold strong policy preferences that can guide their political assessments. This may be particularly true for those who perceive that they or their family, friends, and neighbors may be directly affected by policy decisions made in Washington.[35]

If policy preferences are another factor from which at least some Americans draw when making political decisions or assessing political actors, then citizens may evaluate executive action at least in part based on its policy consequences. They will support unilateral action that moves policy closer to their preferences, and they will oppose unilateral action that moves policy further away from their preferences.

IMPLICATIONS

Understanding the degree to which each of these three different factors influences Americans' assessments of unilateral action is of more than academic interest. The relative strength of constitutional-, partisan-, and policy-based assessments has important implications for the nature of any popular check on presidential unilateralism. If constitutional concerns are dominant and many Americans recoil from presidents triggering significant changes in policy on their own initiative with no input from Congress, then the popular check on unilateralism should be strong and relatively constant. Bold executive actions will routinely be greeted by a skeptical public, not because of the content of the action, but because the process itself threatens widely held norms about the constitutional system of checks and balances.

By contrast, if most Americans simply evaluate unilateral action through partisan lenses, supporting it when taken by a copartisan president and opposing it when taken by the other party, then the public check will in most cases be a weak one. Contemporary America is often described as a fifty-fifty country almost evenly divided along partisan lines. While this is an oversimplification, it does reflect the intense partisan competition and razor-thin margins of victory and defeat that have defined our politics in recent years.[36] After decades of appreciable stability, for the last thirty years control of at least one chamber of Congress has been at stake in almost every election.[37] Presidential victory-defeat margins have also been incredibly slim—so much so that in two of the last five elections, the candidate who received the most popular votes failed to reach the White House. This would suggest that most unilateral actions will enjoy solid support from a large chunk of the public and steadfast opposition from another large part of the electorate. As long as the president's base holds firm, and independents do not unanimously turn against an executive action, the political pressure generated by public opinion should be limited.

Finally, if most Americans assess unilateral action primarily in terms of whether they agree or disagree with it on the merits of policy, the popular check may be real but contingent. If presidents routinely use their unilateral power to pursue policies opposed by significant majorities of Americans, then they risk incurring both political and ultimately electoral costs. But if presidents keep a finger on the pulse of public opinion and limit their exercise of unilateral power to effecting policy shifts favored by most Americans, they may avoid any significant popular backlash.

DO JUSTIFICATIONS MATTER?

To examine the relative influence of constitutional concerns, partisan cues, and policy preferences on Americans' assessments of unilateral action, we employ a series of nine experiments, all of which were embedded in nationally representative opinion surveys.[38] While simply asking survey questions of representative samples of the public can tell us a good deal about public opinion, there are often limits to the conclusions we can draw from a single question. For instance, if we found that public support for a unilateral action was low, it would be difficult to discern whether this was because many rejected the executive action on constitutional grounds, most simply disapproved of the policy change, or some combination of the two. Instead, survey experiments allow us to manipulate various aspects of a unilateral action and exposure to these variations. By randomly assigning respondents to different unilateral action treatments, we can compare public support for the president across the treatment conditions, which allows us to discern the precise causal effects of the treatments on Americans' evaluations of the unilateral president.

Our first experiment assessed the influence of constitutional concerns and partisan forces on public support for unilateral action by examining whether that support is contingent on congressional inaction being offered as a *justification* for executive action. This experiment was administered to subjects shortly after the 2014 midterm elections.

Subjects were randomly assigned to one of two conditions. Subjects in the control group received the following prompt: "President Obama has aggressively used unilateral executive power to pursue his priorities in both foreign and domestic policy." These subjects received no additional information. Before receiving this same prompt, subjects in the justification treatment were given information about congressional inaction as a justification for presidential unilateral action. These subjects were first told, "The current Congress has been one of the most obstructionist on record and is near historic lows in terms of its legislative productivity. Congress has failed to act on many of the most important issues facing the country." To make the justification argument explicit, these subjects were then told, "As a result of this congressional inaction, President Obama has aggressively used unilateral executive power to pursue his priorities in both foreign and domestic policy." All subjects were then asked the same question, which was adapted from a January 2014 ABC/*Washington Post* poll: "Presidents have the power in some cases to bypass Congress and take action by executive order to accomplish their administrations' goals. Do you support or oppose this approach?"[39]

If Americans' assessments of unilateral action are significantly influenced by constitutional concerns about checks and balances, we should see two patterns. First, support for unilateral action should be low across both conditions. As the question wording makes clear, unilateral action allows presidents to bypass Congress, which directly invokes concerns about checks and balances observed in polling data about presidential power in the abstract. Second, the justification treatment should not increase support for unilateral action. If anything, the justification treatment may decrease support for unilateral action, because it makes the president's decision to sidestep Congress even more explicit. The treatment clearly states that the president did not act unilaterally with Congress's tacit consent. Rather, with his initiatives stalled in Congress, President Obama acted to implement those policies by executive fiat. Because unilateral action in this treatment is in direct defiance of Congress, the challenge to checks and balances is even starker.

Alternately, if partisan forces dominate how citizens assess unilateral action, we should see two different patterns. First, partisan affiliation should strongly predict support for Obama's unilateral course. Second, partisanship should moderate the influence of the justification treatment. Republicans should be unresponsive to the justification of congressional inaction. After all, this treatment reminds them that by acting unilaterally, President Obama was flouting the will of a Republican-controlled Congress.[40] Democrats, by contrast, possessed strong partisan predispositions to back the president's unilateral actions, regardless of whether congressional inaction is cited as a justification. This should mute any influence of the justification treatment on support for the president's initiative.

Instead, the effects of the justification treatment should be strongest for independents who lack strong partisan priors.[41] For these voters, the constitutional concerns raised by the justification treatment could decrease support. Alternately, if the average independent prioritizes breaking the gridlock in Washington over a strict adherence to checks and balances, then the justification treatment could increase support for unilateral action.

A superficial examination of the data casts significant doubt on the hypothesis that constitutional concerns will lead supermajorities of Americans to oppose unilateral executive action. In the control group, only a narrow majority opposed a unilateral approach, with 48% supporting or strongly supporting it. In the congressional inaction justification treatment, support rose, with 56% of respondents backing a unilateral approach. Both the relatively high levels of public support for unilateral action in the abstract and the increase in support observed in the justification treatment over the control group baseline are inconsistent with the hypothesis that constitutional concerns will render most Americans inherently unwilling to back unilateral action.

To probe further, we constructed a pair of statistical models that allow us to examine the influence of the justification treatment—and how its influence varies across Democratic, Republican, and independent respondents—while also controlling for each subject's demographic characteristics.[42] Figure 2.2 illustrates the results by plotting the predicted probability of the median subject in both the treatment and the control group supporting the president taking unilateral action to bypass Congress and pursue their policy goals across the three partisan subgroups.

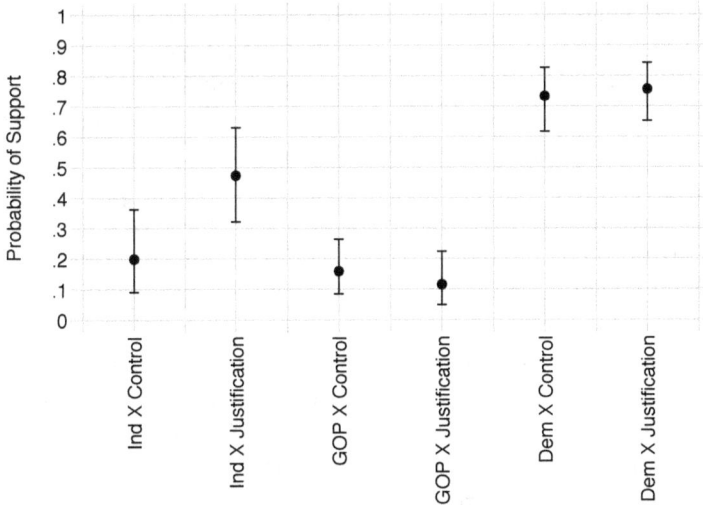

Figure 2.2. Effects of justification treatment on support for unilateral action
Note: Dots present the predicted probability of the median subject in each partisan-treatment subgroup supporting unilateral action (i.e., all other variables set equal to median). I-bars around each point estimate present 95% confidence intervals obtained from simulations.

Two facts are readily apparent. First, partisanship was a very strong predictor of support for unilateral action. With president Barack Obama in the White House, the median Republican was highly unlikely to support executive action, while the median Democrat was highly likely to do so. This result suggests that at least for Democrats in this particular context, partisanship trumped any underlying constitutional concerns with checks and balances. Second, figure 2.2 shows that the justification treatment significantly influenced the opinions of only independents.[43] The median independent respondent in the control group had only a one in five chance of backing presidents taking a unilateral approach.[44] However, the justification treatment more than doubled the predicted probability of the median independent supporting unilateral action, increasing it to just under one in two. Far from worrying that executive initiative threatened the constitutional system of checks and balances, most independents were more willing to support unilateral action when told that it broke gridlock on Capitol Hill than they were in the absence of such justification. By contrast, the justification treatment had no discernible influence on the attitudes of partisans toward executive action. With Obama in the White House, the median Republican was highly unlikely to support presidents acting unilaterally to achieve their policy goals in both the control group and in the justification treatment. Similarly and consistent with partisan cue taking, Democrats had few qualms about backing presidential unilateral action in 2014. The justification treatment did little to increase the probability of the median Democrat supporting unilateral action from its already high level.

The Justification Experiment suggests that most Americans evaluate unilateral action through partisan-tinted glasses. Independents, who lack strong partisan priors, responded to the justification of congressional inaction by becoming more supportive of presidential unilateralism as a means to break legislative gridlock. Partisans were not influenced by the justification treatment. Notably, the data are inconsistent with the hypothesis that most Americans instinctively recoil from unilateral action on constitutional grounds. Instead, subjects' strong reliance on partisan cues when assessing unilateral action echoes the dynamics of opinion formation observed in other polarized contexts.[45]

TWO PRESIDENCIES?

The Justification Experiment informed subjects that President Obama had acted unilaterally to pursue his priorities in both domestic and foreign policy. While scholars still debate the precise constitutional distribution of power across the branches of the US government in foreign affairs, most concede that Article II grants the president greater basis for independent action in the international arena than in the domestic policy realm. More generally, an extensive literature on the "two presidencies" suggests that presidents have greater leverage and leeway in foreign policy than in domestic affairs.[46] Indeed, Aaron Wildavsky's original formulation of the thesis suggests that it may be driven in part because the public looks to the president for leadership in foreign affairs.[47] Because presidents possess greater institutional prerogatives as commander in chief, if constitutional concerns influence Americans' assessment of unilateral action at all, we would expect the public to be more supportive of unilateral action in foreign affairs.

To examine whether support for unilateral action is indeed higher in foreign policy, we fielded a second experiment in the weeks leading up to the 2014 midterm elections. In this experiment, subjects were randomly assigned to one of two groups. Those in the control group read the following prompt: "Presidents have the power in some cases to bypass Congress and take action by executive order to accomplish their administrations' goals particularly in the realm of domestic and social policy." Subjects in the treatment group received the same prompt with one exception. These subjects were told, "Presidents have the power in some cases to bypass Congress and take action by executive order to accomplish their administrations' goals particularly in the realm of *foreign and military policy*."[48] All subjects were then asked the same question: "Is this approach something you support or oppose?"[49]

Contra predictions from the two presidencies thesis, we found no evidence that Americans are more willing to support unilateral action in foreign policy than in the domestic sphere. In fact, the percentage of subjects supporting unilateral action in domestic and social policy (57.1%) was almost identical to that supporting presidential unilateralism in foreign and military policy (56.5%). Despite the president's presumed stronger constitutional prerogatives in foreign affairs, the electorate is no more willing to back unilateralism in military affairs than in the domestic realm.

To explore further, we estimated a more fully specified statistical model of the influence of the foreign policy treatment relative to partisanship and a range of demographic factors on support for presidential unilateralism.[50] As shown in figure 2.3, in the statistical model the foreign policy treatment had no effect on support for unilateralism. Instead, partisanship again was the dominant factor.

The complete absence of any difference in support for unilateral action across foreign and domestic policy was somewhat surprising given the conventional wisdom. One possibility is that our experimental treatment was too subtle and may have been missed by many survey takers. To ensure that our null finding is not simply the result of a weak treatment, we conducted a follow-up experiment in April 2015. In this experiment, all subjects were told, "Presidents have the power in some cases to bypass Congress and take action by executive order to accomplish their administrations' goals." Those in the control group were then asked, "Do you support or oppose presidents taking this approach in domestic and social policy?" Subjects in the foreign policy treatment group were asked, "Do you support or oppose presidents taking this approach in foreign and military policy?" By specifying the policy area in the question itself, we made it especially clear to survey participants that they were being asked about their support for unilateral action in a specific policy realm.

Nevertheless, in this second experiment, we again found no evidence that Americans are more willing to support unilateral action in the international realm than in the domestic sphere. In the aggregate, 53.2% of subjects in the control group supported the president taking a unilateral

approach in the domestic policy realm. In the treatment group, 53.4% of
subjects backed the president taking a unilateral approach in military and
foreign affairs.

A statistical model again shows that partisanship was the predomi-
nant driver.[51] Although President Obama was never named in our experiment, support for unilateral action divided significantly along partisan
lines. Using predicted probabilities calculated from simulations, figure 2.4
shows that the median Democrat was almost certain to support unilateral
action, while the median Republican was almost certain to oppose a unilateral approach; respondents were clearly evaluating unilateral action in
terms of the then current president. Finally, additional analysis shows that
the issue area—whether subjects were asked about foreign versus domestic
policy—had no influence on support for unilateral action among any partisan subgroup. In short, while findings of the two presidencies are prevalent
in political science, such a distinction does not apply to public attitudes
toward unilateral action, which are dominated by partisanship.

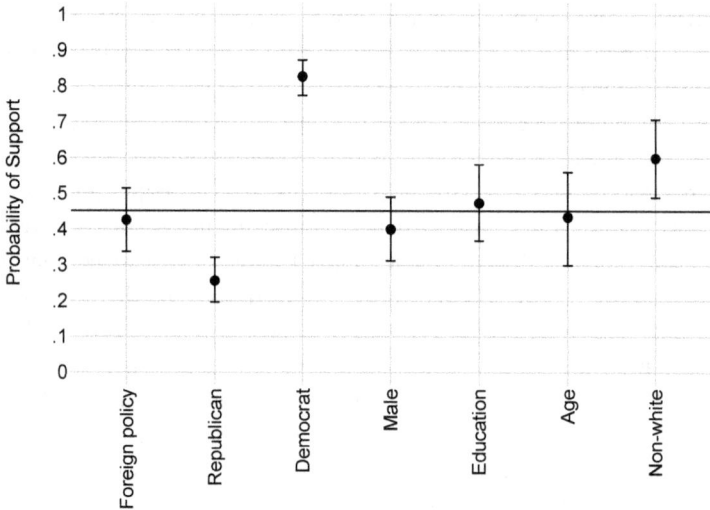

Figure 2.3. Are there "two presidencies" in public support for unilateral action?
Note: Dots present the point estimate for the effect of each factor on support for unilateral
action for the median independent respondent (i.e., all other variables set equal to median). For
binary variables, the figure plots the effect of increasing that factor from 0 to 1. For education
and age, the figure presents the effect of a two standard deviation increase from the median
value. I-bars around each point estimate present 95% confidence intervals obtained from
simulations. The horizontal line at .44 represents the predicted probability of the median
independent respondent in the domestic policy control group supporting unilateral action.

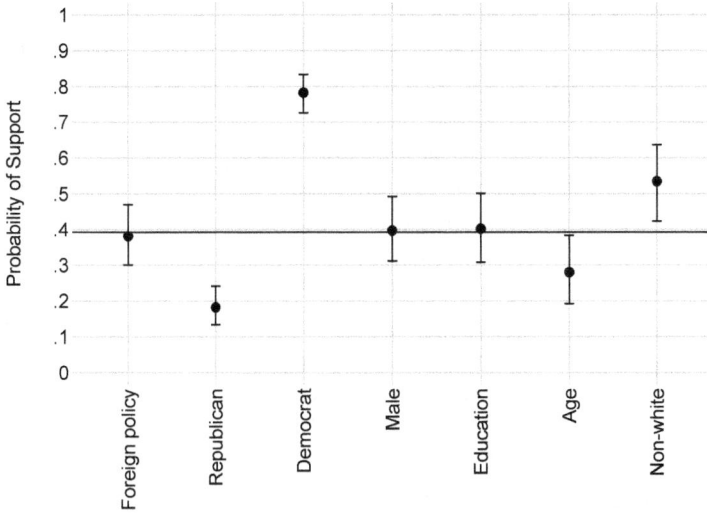

Figure 2.4. Public support for unilateral action in foreign and domestic policy
Note: Dots present the point estimate for the effect of each factor on support for unilateral action for the median independent respondent (i.e., all other variables set equal to median). For binary variables, the figure plots the effect of increasing that factor from 0 to 1. For education and age, the figure presents the effect of a two standard deviation increase from the median value. I-bars around each point estimate present 95% confidence intervals obtained from simulations. The horizontal line at .39 represents the predicted probability of the median independent respondent in the domestic policy control group supporting unilateral action.

REVERSALS OR NEW DIRECTIONS?

As a further test of the importance of constitutional concerns in shaping the public's response to executive action, we examined another type of unilateral action that should raise fewer concerns about threats to checks and balances: when a new president unilaterally overturns executive actions taken by his predecessor. The incumbent president's unilateral record has become a prominent feature of recent presidential campaigns. In 2008, senator Barack Obama (D-IL) repeatedly railed against the unilateral excesses of president George W. Bush, particularly in the context of the war on terror. As president, he swiftly signed a spate of executive actions to reverse policies Bush had implemented unilaterally. For example, Obama revoked a slew of his predecessor's national security orders and required that all interrogations follow the US Army Field Manuals. He ended the moratorium on the federal funding of research involving stem cells, and he tweaked President Bush's order creating the Office of Faith-Based and

Community Initiatives to emphasize the importance of guaranteeing the First Amendment's prohibition on the establishment of religion. Similarly, on the campaign trail in 2016, Donald Trump denounced Obama's exercise of unilateral power, promising to undo many of his predecessor's allegedly unconstitutional actions on day one. Shortly after taking office, Trump quickly reversed a number of Obama's actions, including a restriction on dumping mining waste into rivers and streams, a ban against the mentally ill purchasing firearms, and a requirement that energy companies disclose foreign government payments.[52] If constitutional concerns play an important role in shaping attitudes toward unilateral action, the public should be more supportive of actions that overturn the unilateral policies of preceding presidents than of those that strike out in new directions. The former pose less of a threat to checks and balances than the latter.

To test this hypothesis, we embedded a pair of experiments in a nationally representative survey fielded in March 2017.[53] The first experiment tested whether Americans were more supportive in general of unilateral action if its explicit goal was to reverse prior unilateral policies. Subjects were randomly assigned to one of two experimental groups. Those in the control group were told, "Presidents have the power in some cases to bypass Congress and take action by executive order to enact new policies." Subjects assigned to the treatment group were told instead: "Presidents have the power in some cases to bypass Congress and take action by executive order to *reverse policies that were implemented unilaterally by past presidents.*"[54] All subjects were then asked the same question: "Is this approach something you support or oppose?"

Simply comparing the percentage of subjects supporting unilateral action across the two experimental groups offers some support for the hypothesis. Whereas 58% of subjects in the control group approved of unilateral action, this increased to 66% in the treatment group. This difference could be due to some subjects believing that executive actions reversing prior unilateral directives are less constitutionally suspect than those that simply bypassed Congress to strike out in new directions. However, the baseline figure of almost 60% support for unilateral action is far higher than we would expect if constitutional concerns cause Americans to be instinctively skeptical of unilateralism.

Figure 2.5 illustrates the results of a statistical model examining the effect of the reversals treatment, partisanship, and subjects' demographic characteristics on support for unilateral action. The model estimates that the median independent respondent was approximately 8% more likely to support unilateral action to reverse prior unilateral directives than to

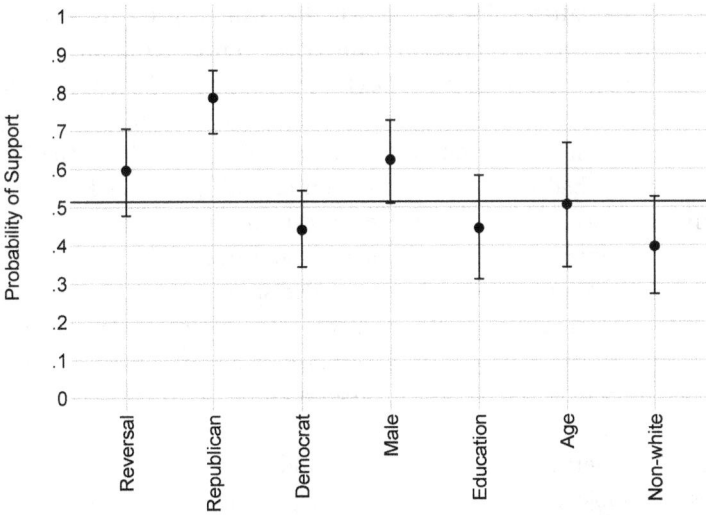

Figure 2.5. Support for unilateral action: new policy versus reversing old policy
Note: Dots present the point estimate for the effect of each factor on support for unilateral action for the median independent respondent (i.e., all other variables set equal to median). For binary variables, the figure plots the effect of increasing that factor from 0 to 1. For education and age, the figure presents the effect of a two standard deviation increase from the median value. I-bars around each point estimate present 95% confidence intervals obtained from simulations. The horizontal line at .51 represents the predicted probability of the median independent respondent in the control group supporting unilateral action.

enact new policies.[55] But the most striking feature of figure 2.5 is the dramatic reversal in Republicans' support for unilateral action. In the three preceding experiments conducted during the Obama presidency, the probability of the median Republican supporting unilateral action never exceeded .3, even if the question made no explicit reference to the incumbent president. By contrast, with Trump in the Oval Office, the median Republican in this survey had a very high probability of supporting unilateral action, approximately .80. The median Democrat was significantly less likely to support unilateral action, though perhaps because memories of the Obama presidency were not too distant they were not nearly as certain to oppose it as Republicans were just a few years prior. Thus, for most Americans even questions about support for the exercise of unilateral power in the abstract are inextricably linked to contemporary political realities.

The preceding experiment found modest evidence that some Americans are more supportive of unilateral action to reverse prior executive actions than to strike out in new directions. Yet even in this more general question, partisanship was the dominant force driving variation in support for unilateralism. To examine whether similar patterns hold in support for a more concrete exercise of unilateral power, we conducted a second experiment exploring public reaction to President Trump's decision to authorize the construction of the Keystone XL and Dakota Access oil pipelines. After a lengthy period of public comment and debate, the Obama administration had blocked construction of both pipelines in 2015/2016. Shortly after taking office, however, President Trump signed an executive memorandum reviving the pipelines, and in March 2017 the administration fully reversed its predecessor's decision and gave them the green light.[56] By crafting an experiment on this issue, we can examine whether public support for Trump's action increases when subjects are explicitly informed that his action simply reverses a previous unilateral move made by President Obama.

In this experiment, subjects were randomly assigned to one of two groups. All subjects received the following prompt: "President Trump has issued an executive order to allow the construction of the Keystone XL and Dakota Access oil pipelines."[57] Subjects in the control group received no further information. By contrast, subjects in the treatment group received additional background information about Trump's action: "Trump's order reverses President Obama's executive action blocking construction of the two pipelines." All subjects were then asked the same question: "Do you support or oppose President Trump's executive order to allow the construction of the Keystone XL and Dakota Access pipelines?" Of course, it is possible that some subjects in the control group know that Trump's action was a reversal of an Obama decision, potentially muting our estimate of the treatment effect. However, given the stark limits on most Americans' political knowledge, we believed that the share of subjects with this knowledge would be relatively small.

Simply comparing the percentage of subjects supporting Trump's action in the treatment and control groups shows no evidence that providing the contextual information about the order increased public support. In the control group, 43% of subjects supported Trump's actions, while only 38% did so in the treatment group informed that Trump's action was not a new policy but rather the reversal of an executive action from the Obama administration.

A statistical model also shows no evidence that informing subjects that Trump's action was a reversal of a previous executive action bolstered support for the maneuver.[58] As shown in figure 2.6, when we move from the abstract to examining public support for a concrete instance of

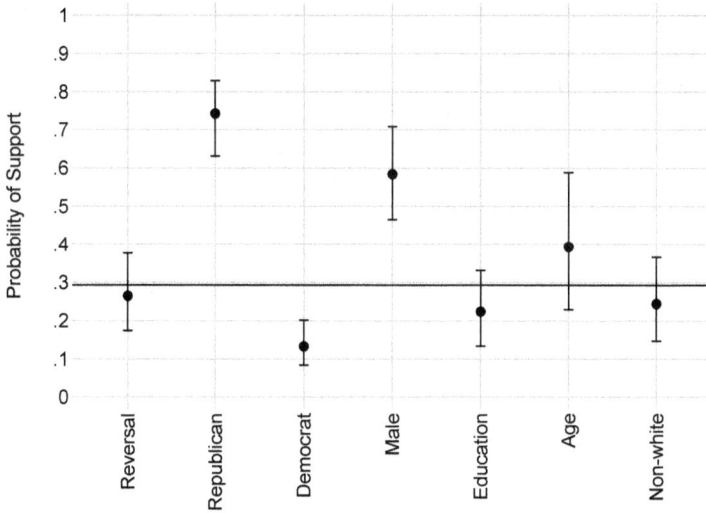

Figure 2.6. Support for Trump's Keystone XL pipeline action

Note: Dots present the point estimate for the effect of each factor on support for unilateral action for the median independent respondent (i.e., all other variables set equal to median). For binary variables, the figure plots the effect of increasing that factor from 0 to 1. For education and age, the figure presents the effect of a two standard deviation increase from the median value. I-bars around each point estimate present 95% confidence intervals obtained from simulations. The horizontal line at .29 represents the predicted probability of the median independent respondent in the control group supporting unilateral action.

unilateral action, whether it was to reverse a prior executive action has no influence on public support. In the case of Keystone XL and Dakota Access, partisanship was again the main driver. The median Republican was highly likely to back Trump's action. The median Democrat was almost certain to oppose it. And the median independent respondent was also skeptical, having roughly a 30% chance of supporting Trump's action.

Taken together, the two Reversal Experiments offer scant evidence that constitutional concerns about checks and balances play a significant role in shaping Americans' assessments of unilateral action. Rather than abstract concerns, partisanship dominates public evaluations of unilateral action.

SAME POLICIES BUT DIFFERENT PARTIES?

When interpreting the results from the preceding experiments, we have argued that they all offer strong evidence for the critical importance of partisanship in shaping popular assessments of unilateral action. In practice, however, it is often exceedingly difficult to disentangle the influence of partisanship and policy preferences. This is perhaps most clear in the Keystone XL pipeline example. Did Republicans overwhelmingly support Trump's executive action and Democrats oppose it because of partisan loyalties? Or did the order move policy toward the policy preferences of most Republicans and away from the policy preferences of most Democrats? The strong correlation between partisanship and policy preference typically hampers our ability to sort out the precise causal effects. Even in our prior questions that queried support for unilateral action in general and showed significant divides along partisan lines, it is all but impossible to know whether these gaps were driven by raw partisanship or more complicated calculations about anticipated policy outcomes.

Another reason that it is often difficult to discern the relative influence of partisan forces and policy preferences on support for unilateral action is that Republican and Democratic presidents often use their unilateral tool kit to pursue very different types of policy change. This significantly complicates comparisons across presidents. Yet the great continuity in foreign policy executive actions from George W. Bush to Obama affords a unique opportunity to explore with strong control whether partisan forces lead many Americans to support unilateral action when it is attributed to a copartisan president and to oppose it when the very same policies are attributed to an opposition party president.[59]

Subjects in this experiment, which was conducted in November 2014, were randomly assigned to one of two treatment groups. Those in the first group received the following prompt: "President Obama has used a variety of instruments, such as executive orders and national security decision directives, to unilaterally expand his power in the war on terror. For example, these unilateral actions have significantly increased electronic surveillance both at home and abroad." The concrete example focused on electronic surveillance because both Presidents Obama and Bush presided over dramatic increases in National Security Agency eavesdropping and data collection programs. In both administrations, revelations of expanded spying caused an uproar and attracted significant media attention. Subjects in this group were then asked the following question adapted from a 2006 Gallup Poll: "Do you think the Obama administration—has gone too far, has been about right, or has not gone far enough—in expanding the power of the presidency and executive branch to combat terrorism?"[60] Subjects in the second treatment group received an identical prompt and question. The only modification was that the prompt and question referenced President Bush rather than President Obama.[61]

Given the serious constitutional questions raised by both presidents' unilateral actions in the war on terror, we might expect strong majorities to believe that both had gone too far in expanding presidential power. This was not the case, however. Only a minority of Americans, 42% and 44%, respectively, believed that Obama or Bush had gone too far. The almost perfect balance across the two experimental groups is also exactly what we would expect if partisan cues are dominant, as different partisans should react to the same treatment in diametrically opposite ways.

To test the importance of partisan cues more directly, we again estimated a statistical model to allow us to assess the effect of the Bush and Obama treatments on different partisan subgroups while controlling for other demographic factors that could also influence support for unilateral action.[62] Figure 2.7 illustrates the magnitude of the effects.

Among independent subjects not affiliated with either of the two major parties, whether the question referenced Bush or Obama had no influence on the probability of a respondent backing presidential unilateral actions in the war on terror. The median independent respondent was unlikely to believe that either president had expanded presidential power too far through his unilateral actions in the war on terror. Given the questionable constitutionality of both presidents' actions, this result among Americans

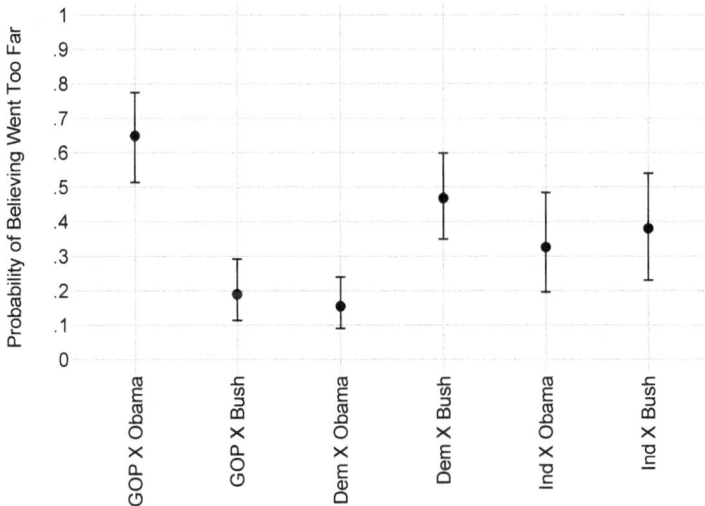

Figure 2.7. Beliefs that president expanded power too far in war on terror
Note: Dots present the predicted probability of the median subject in each partisan-treatment subgroup supporting unilateral action (i.e., all other variables set equal to median). I-bars around each point estimate present 95% confidence intervals obtained from simulations.

without a partisan stake in the fight is another blow to the hypothesis that constitutional concerns and support for the rule of law drive Americans' assessments of unilateral action.

Among Republicans, however, receiving the Bush treatment significantly lowered the probability of believing that the president had gone too far. The median Republican in the Obama treatment group had a very high likelihood, about 65%, of replying that the president had expanded presidential power excessively. By contrast, all else being equal, the same median Republican in the Bush treatment group had less than a one in five chance of believing that the Bush administration had acted too brazenly in expanding presidential power.

Among Democrats the Bush treatment had the opposite effect, significantly increasing the probability of believing that the president had gone too far unilaterally. In the Obama treatment, the median Democrat was very unlikely to believe that Obama had pushed his unilateral authority too far. However, in the Bush treatment the median Democrat had roughly a fifty-fifty chance of responding that the Bush administration had gone too far in expanding presidential power in the context of the war on terror. Considering the vociferous Democratic opposition to the unilateral initiatives of the "imperial" Bush presidency in the late 2000s, this relatively low retrospective figure suggests that a significant share of Democrats may recognize the similarities in the two presidents' conduct of the war on terror.[63] Nevertheless, despite the two presidents pursuing virtually identical policies, Democrats were three times more likely to judge that Bush had gone too far in expanding the powers of the presidency unilaterally than had Obama.

MEANS OR ONLY ENDS?

Thus far, we have found little evidence that constitutional concerns undermine support for unilateral action. Rather than instinctively opposing unilateral initiatives that seem to threaten the constitutional system of checks and balances, most Americans assess executive action through partisan lenses. They support action taken by a copartisan president and oppose unilateral action—even when the policies themselves are all but indistinguishable—when it is taken by an opposition party president.

In the final three experiments, we ask whether citizens care at all about the means, or rather only the ends of the policymaking process. In each experiment, we examine whether the means through which the president pursues a policy objective—unilateral action or legislation—affects support for the president's efforts. We do so across three different policy issues and across two presidents of different parties to ensure that the results do not depend on who is in office or on the degree of general support for or polarization on a particular issue.

STUDENT LOANS EXPERIMENT

Our first experiment examined support for a unilateral action that was limited in scope and nonpolarizing: reducing student loan debt.[64] Subjects were randomly assigned to one of two treatment groups. Subjects in the first group were told, "President Barack Obama has publicly backed legislation in Congress that would cap student loan payments at 10% of a borrower's income, and forgive any remaining debt after 20 years." Subjects in the second treatment group learned of the same White House policy initiative; however, in this treatment Obama pursued his policy goal through unilateral action. Subjects in this treatment were told, "President Barack Obama has issued an executive order to unilaterally cap student loan payments at 10% of a borrower's income, and forgive any remaining debt after 20 years."[65]

A common critique of survey experiments is that they are necessarily artificial and may not accurately reflect politics and the formation of political judgments in the real world. To mitigate such concerns, we consciously chose to examine real policies pursued by the incumbent administration, not hypothetical actions. However, this decision required us to introduce some asymmetry into the two treatments. Specifically, we state in the legislative treatment that Obama "backed legislation," while in the unilateral treatment he "has issued an executive order." Both situations are externally valid, that is, resembling reality. But the former involved only potential policy change, while the latter evoked concrete action. It is possible that if our first treatment read that President Obama had secured congressional passage for his legislation to cap student loan payments, support for his actions would be even higher, though recent research suggests that any increase in support would likely be modest.[66] All subjects were then asked the same question: "Do you support or oppose President Obama's efforts to lower student loan payments?" This question wording was chosen because it applies equally well to both the legislative and the unilateral action pathways.

Does acting unilaterally decrease support for a policy initiative from a higher baseline level when the president pursues the same policy objective through the standard legislative process? Or are public attitudes almost

exclusively a function of citizens' partisan predispositions and policy preferences? If Americans prefer legislative pathways to unilateral ones to effect
policy change, then support for Obama's actions to cap student loan payments should be higher in the legislation treatment than in the executive
order treatment. We found little evidence for this, however. Obama's efforts
to address student loan debt received strong and almost identical levels
of support across the legislative (73%) and the executive order (71%) treatments. This suggests that few Americans cared about the means through
which Obama pursued this popular part of his domestic policy agenda.

To examine the influence of both partisan forces and policy preferences on support for Obama, we estimated a statistical model. To account
for policy preferences, we exploited a question included earlier on our survey that asked, "Do you or does anyone in your household have student
loan debt?" Just under 30% of subjects answered this question in the affirmative. Because these subjects would benefit directly from the policy, we
argue that many will have a strong predisposition to support it.

An additional shortcut on which many Americans may draw when assessing an executive action is whether they approve of the president's overall job performance. Recent research by Andrew Reeves and Jon Rogowski
suggests that while attitudes toward unilateral action and support for the
incumbent president are distinct, the latter is an important predictor of
the former.[67] To examine the influence of presidential approval on support
for Obama's efforts to cap student loan payments, we included a variable
indicating those who either strongly or somewhat approved of Obama's
overall job performance.[68]

The statistical model allows us to examine the influence of the executive order treatment, and each respondent's partisanship, student loan
debt status, presidential approval, and other demographic factors, on his or
her probability of supporting Obama's efforts to provide some relief from
student loan debt. Figure 2.8 illustrates the influence of each factor on the
predicted probability of the median respondent supporting the president's
actions to lower student loan payments.

The horizontal line indicates that the median independent respondent
had a predicted probability of backing the president's efforts of just under
60%. The predicted probability in the executive order treatment is mod-
estly lower; however, the difference is not statistically significant. Instead,
partisanship was the most important predictor of support for Obama's
actions to lower student loan payments. The median Republican was as
likely to oppose the president as to support him.[69] By contrast, the median

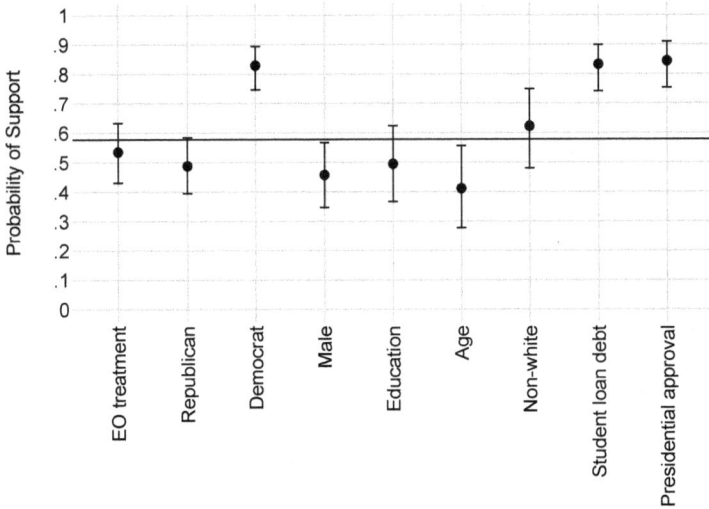

Figure 2.8. Factors influencing support for Obama's
efforts to lower student loan payments

Note: Dots present the point estimate for the effect of each factor on support for unilateral action
for the median independent respondent (i.e., all other variables set equal to median). For binary
variables, the figure plots the effect of increasing that factor from 0 to 1. For education and age,
the figure presents the effect of a two standard deviation increase from the median value. I-bars
around each point estimate present 95% confidence intervals obtained from simulations. The
horizontal line at .59 represents the predicted probability of the median independent respondent in
the lawmaking treatment group supporting Obama's efforts to lower student loan payments.

Democrat was all but certain to support the president's initiative. Presidential approval, which is strongly related to partisanship, also significantly influenced support for Obama's actions. Approving of Obama's job performance increased the predicted probability of the median independent respondent backing his actions on student loans by almost 30%.

Finally, policy preferences also influenced support for Obama's actions. Subjects from families with student loan debt—our proxy for policy preference—were significantly more likely to support Obama than were families without student loan debt, all else being equal. Indeed, for the median independent respondent, having student loan debt in the family increased the predicted probability of supporting Obama's actions by almost 25%. In sum, Americans who supported efforts to cap student loan debt, whether on partisan or on policy grounds, backed Obama's actions, regardless of whether he pursued this policy through legislative or unilateral means.

IMMIGRATION EXPERIMENT

The Student Loans Experiment suggests that few Americans distinguish between legislative and unilateral pathways when assessing presidential policy action. However, President Obama's efforts to address student loan debt is a relatively rare case of a domestic policy issue that is not intensely partisan or politicized. Other more polarizing issues may produce different opinion dynamics.

To address concerns about generalizability, our second experiment examined support for a much broader, higher-profile, and more polarizing unilateral action: President Obama's 2014 memorandum to shield up to 5 million illegal immigrants from deportation. Did Obama's decision to pursue this change unilaterally shape the public's evaluation of his actions? Or would public support for Obama in the immigration arena have looked similar if he had pursued his policy agenda only legislatively?

To answer this question, we embedded another experiment in a nationally representative survey conducted in April 2015. Subjects were randomly assigned to one of two groups. Those in the first were told, "President Barack Obama has publicly backed legislation to give temporary legal status to many undocumented immigrants." Subjects in the second treatment group were told of Obama's unilateral action to liberalize the nation's immigration system. Furthermore, in this follow-up experiment we sought to prime any latent constitutional concerns by using even stronger language in a revised treatment. In the Immigration Experiment, we revised the treatment wording to emphasize that by acting unilaterally, Obama had turned his back on the legislative process. Subjects were told, *"Rather than seeking new legislation from Congress,* President Obama has unilaterally directed the US Department of Homeland Security to give temporary legal status to many undocumented immigrants."[70] All subjects were then asked the same question: "Do you support or oppose President Obama's efforts to give temporary legal status to many undocumented immigrants?"

Even with the stronger treatment emphasizing that by acting unilaterally, President Obama was attempting an end run around Congress, we found little evidence of widespread public unease with a unilateral approach. Indeed, the percentage of subjects supporting Obama's action was slightly higher in the executive order treatment (46%) than in the legislation control group (41%). The president's choice of tactics had little influence on popular evaluations of his actions concerning immigration.

Instead, as shown by another statistical model, partisanship and policy

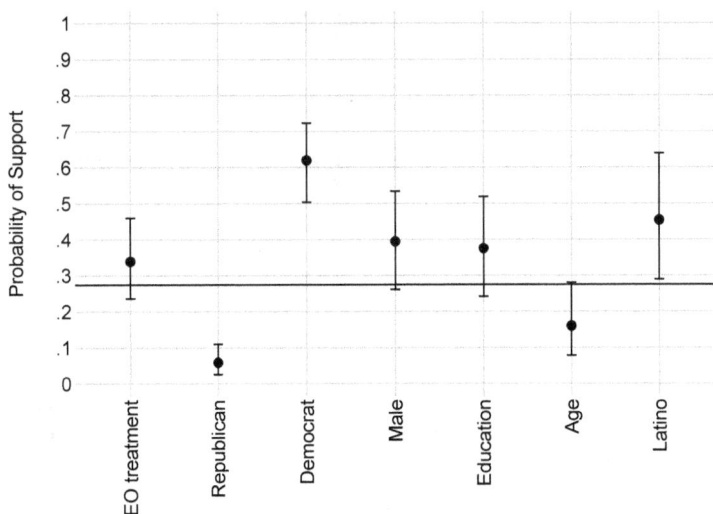

Figure 2.9. Factors influencing support for Obama's efforts to reform immigration
Note: Dots present the point estimate for the effect of each factor on support for unilateral action for the median independent respondent (i.e., all other variables set equal to median). For binary variables, the figure plots the effect of increasing that factor from 0 to 1. For education and age, the figure presents the effect of a two standard deviation increase from the median value. I-bars around each point estimate present 95% confidence intervals obtained from simulations. The horizontal line at .27 represents the predicted probability of the median independent respondent in the lawmaking treatment group supporting Obama's efforts to reform the immigration system.

preferences were the primary drivers of popular reactions to Obama's efforts to liberalize immigration policy. Figure 2.9 illustrates the estimated effects of the experimental treatment, respondent partisanship, and demographic characteristics on the median subject's support for Obama's immigration actions. The horizontal line indicates that the median independent respondent had a predicted probability of backing the president's efforts of about 25%. The predicted probability in the executive order treatment is slightly higher; the difference is not statistically significant, however. Partisanship was the most important predictor of support for Obama's actions to liberalize immigration policy. The median Republican was almost certain to oppose the president's course of action. By contrast, the median Democrat was highly likely to back the president.

Finally, Latinos were significantly more supportive of Obama's immigration efforts than were other subjects. All else being equal, the median Latino was almost 20% more likely to support Obama's immigration efforts than was the median white subject, regardless of whether President Obama pursued this policy shift through legislative or unilateral pathways.[71] Admittedly, this is a somewhat crude proxy for variations in subjects' policy preferences. But from past surveys, there are strong reasons to think that Latinos will be more supportive than non-Latinos of efforts to liberalize immigration policy, all else being equal. This result is again consistent with the argument that policy preferences also shaped support for Obama's actions.

BORDER WALL EXPERIMENT

Our third and final ends versus means experiment again examined public support for presidential efforts to change immigration policy, but of a very different sort: President Trump's initial unilateral efforts in 2017 to follow through on his signature campaign pledge to build a wall along the US border with Mexico. As Trump's recourse to a national emergency declaration in February 2019 made abidingly clear, his January 2017 executive order did not actually provide for the construction of the wall. But it did announce the wall as official administration policy and began the planning process. The Border Wall Experiment allows us to examine whether the same opinion dynamics also hold in the very different context of a new president from a different party in what should be the honeymoon period of a new administration.

The experiment was embedded in a nationally representative survey administered in April 2017. Subjects were randomly assigned to one of two experimental groups. Those in the legislative treatment group received the following prompt: "President Donald Trump has publicly backed legislation in Congress to begin constructing a wall along the Mexican border to reduce illegal immigration." Subjects assigned to the executive order treatment group were told instead that President Trump was pursuing the same policy for reducing illegal immigration, but through executive order: "President Donald Trump has signed an executive order to begin constructing a wall along the Mexican border to reduce illegal immigration."[72] All subjects were then asked the same question: "Do you support or oppose President Trump's efforts to begin building a wall along the Mexican border?"

Simply comparing support for Trump's efforts to build the border wall across the legislative and the executive order treatment groups again offered little evidence that Americans care about the means through which the president pursues his policy goals. In both treatment groups, public opinion was sharply divided, with 46% supporting Trump's efforts to

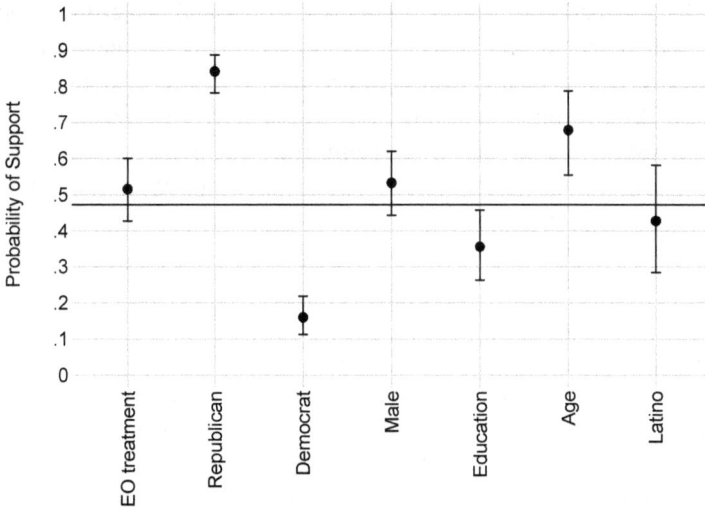

Figure 2.10. Factors influencing support for Trump's efforts to build the border wall
Note: Dots present the point estimate for the effect of each factor on support for unilateral action for the median independent respondent (i.e., all other variables set equal to median). For binary variables, the figure plots the effect of increasing that factor from 0 to 1. For education and age, the figure presents the effect of a two standard deviation increase from the median value. I-bars around each point estimate present 95% confidence intervals obtained from simulations. The horizontal line at .48 represents the predicted probability of the median independent respondent in the lawmaking treatment group supporting Trump's efforts to begin construction of the border wall.

build the wall in the legislative treatment and 48% supporting Trump in the executive order treatment.

A statistical model reveals that partisanship was by far the dominant factor driving attitudes toward Trump and the border wall. As shown in figure 2.10, the partisan split was even greater than that observed in the preceding experiment regarding President Obama's efforts to liberalize immigration policy. The median Republican was all but certain to back Trump's efforts to build the wall, whereas the median Democrat was all but certain to oppose them. The median independent respondent was right in the middle, with just under a fifty-fifty chance of supporting Trump's efforts.

Finally, in contrast to earlier findings from the Obama-era Immigration Experiment, we found no evidence that Latinos were any less supportive of Trump's efforts to build the wall than were other respondents, after controlling for partisanship and other factors. Forty percent of Latinos supported the border wall in our survey, which was only moderately lower than the 48% backing the wall among all other racial and ethnic groups.[73] After controlling for partisanship, the difference in attitudes toward the wall between Latinos and other groups was small and statistically insignificant. Perhaps unsurprisingly given the historically large partisan divide in evaluations of President Trump from the earliest days of his administration, partisanship is far and away the primary driver of attitudes toward the Mexican border wall.

CONCLUSION

Because the formal institutional checks exercised by Congress and the courts on presidential unilateralism are weak, public opinion may serve as the most important remaining check on presidential abuse of unilateral power. It is not unreasonable to expect that Americans instinctively oppose unilateral action on constitutional grounds.[74] If such constitutional concerns are dominant in many Americans' minds, it would suggest a strong and automatic democratic constraint against presidential overreach. When presidents push too far, concern about checks and balances will instinctively encourage many among the electorate to oppose the president's unilateral gambit. Yet the results from this chapter suggest that such opposition may be considerably more conditional than typically supposed.

The survey experiments in this chapter, most of which focus on a range of concrete instances of unilateral action across three presidencies, suggest a weaker and more conditional public constraint on the unilateral presidency. Instead of instinctively recoiling from unilateral action as a threat to our constitutional system of checks and balances, we find that most Americans evaluate unilateral action through the same partisan cues and policy preferences that they use to make other political judgments. In our intensely polarized polity, the dynamics driving public attitudes toward presidential use of unilateral power are remarkably like those driving public opinion on other policy actions.

Across experiments, partisanship was often the most important factor shaping Americans' assessments of the unilateral presidency. Americans commonly supported unilateral action when taken by a copartisan president and opposed it when taken by an opposition party president— even if the unilateral actions in question were substantively the same. If partisanship alone drives public attitudes toward unilateralism, then any popular check would be weak indeed. If the president's copartisans in the mass public stand staunchly by his side, in most cases the political costs to the president will be manageable. Only a massive swing of independents against the White House would raise the political stakes of acting unilaterally in the face of significant public opposition.

However, in several experiments we also found evidence that policy preferences significantly influence Americans' assessments of unilateral action. For example, a strong majority of the electorate supported President Obama's unilateral efforts to reduce the burden of student loan payments for young Americans. And while Democrats remained the president's strongest supporters, more than two-thirds of independents and just under 50% of Republicans also backed Obama's efforts. As long as presidents pursue policy objectives that enjoy broad public support, Americans are unlikely to oppose their efforts if they seek to effect change unilaterally. Interestingly, our results also raise the prospect that if presidents endeavor to pursue highly unpopular changes in policy unilaterally, such actions could risk a public backlash. The results of our experiments thus suggest a much more nuanced and conditional popular check on presidential unilateralism.[75]

From another perspective, the different portraits of public opinion may be complementary. When asked to separate themselves from contemporary politics and evaluate the office of the presidency and its proper place in our governing system, many Americans may be deeply skeptical of presidents circumventing Congress and the legislative process to achieve their policy priorities unilaterally. But when forced to consider concrete examples of unilateral action in the contemporary political arena, partisan forces and policy assessments often all but overwhelm these underlying constitutional concerns.[76] In practice, Americans' partisan demons shout down the better angels of checks and balances they embrace in the abstract.

This does not imply that the public exercises no check on unilateral action. It does suggest, however, that the constraint of public opinion on the unilateral executive is not automatic but a product of political contestation. Because of this, as we explore in the following chapters, Congress and the courts may remain more relevant in shaping the politics of unilateral action than often supposed.

APPENDIX TO CHAPTER 2

Throughout the chapter, we employ a series of graphics to illustrate the effects of our experimental treatments and other factors, including partisanship and proxies for individuals' policy preferences, on the opinions of the median respondent. These estimates are derived from logistic regression models; we then use simulations to estimate the effect of an increase in each variable while holding all other variables constant at their median values. The models used to produce these figures are presented in appendix tables 2.1–2.9 below.

In several model specifications, we look for evidence that the effects of our experimental treatments may be moderated by other factors. For example, in model 1 of appendix table 2.1 the coefficient on the congressional obstruction variable is statistically insignificant. However, model 2 of appendix table 2.1 shows that the effect of the treatment varies considerably by party. Among independents (the omitted baseline category), the treatment justifying unilateral action on the grounds that Congress has

APPENDIX TABLE 2.1. Effect of congressional justification by partisanship

	(1)	(2)
Congressional obstruction	0.30	1.36**
	(0.24)	(0.50)
Congressional obstruction × Republican		−1.79*
		(0.72)
Congressional obstruction × Democrat		−1.26*
		(0.60)
Republican	−1.22**	−0.21
	(0.35)	(0.52)
Democrat	1.74**	2.51**
	(0.28)	(0.46)
Male	−0.11	−0.06
	(0.25)	(0.25)
Education	0.05	0.03
	(0.08)	(0.08)
Age	0.00	0.00
	(0.01)	(0.01)
White	−0.69*	−0.78**
	(0.29)	(0.30)
Constant	−0.27	−0.83
	(0.60)	(0.69)
Observations	440	440

Note: Models are logistic regressions. Robust standard errors are in parentheses. All significance tests are two-tailed.
*p < 0.05
**p < 0.01

APPENDIX TABLE 2.2. "Two presidencies" in
support for unilateral action (2014 CCES)

	(1)
Foreign policy	−0.10
	(0.15)
Republican	−0.87**
	(0.21)
Democrat	1.78**
	(0.20)
Male	−0.20
	(0.16)
Education	0.05
	(0.05)
Age	−0.00
	(0.00)
White	−0.60**
	(0.19)
Constant	0.38
	(0.34)
Observations	998

Note: Model is a logistic regression. Robust standard errors are
in parentheses. All significance tests are two-tailed.
*$p < 0.05$
**$p < 0.01$

resorted to obstruction significantly increased support for unilateral action. By contrast, among Republicans and Democrats it had no net effect
on attitudes toward unilateral action. In appendix table 2.3, we found no
evidence of any partisan split in support for unilateral action in foreign
versus domestic policy. Similarly, in appendix table 2.7, we found no evidence that the executive order treatment significantly decreased support
for President Obama's efforts to lower student loan debt among any partisan group, or among those who had or did not have family members with
student loans. However, as seen in appendix table 2.6 and illustrated in
figure 2.7 in the chapter, partisanship was the most important factor shaping assessments of whether Presidents Bush or Obama had expanded the
powers of the presidency too far in the war on terror despite the prompt
mentioning both having pursued the exact same policies with regard to
expanded electronic surveillance.

APPENDIX TABLE 2.3. "Two presidencies" in support for
unilateral action (April 2015)

	(1)	(2)
Foreign policy	−0.06	0.04
	(0.15)	(0.28)
Foreign policy × Republican		0.10
		(0.39)
Foreign policy × Democrat		−0.32
		(0.37)
Republican	−1.07**	−1.11**
	(0.20)	(0.28)
Democrat	1.74**	1.90**
	(0.19)	(0.27)
Male	0.02	0.02
	(0.16)	(0.16)
Education	0.02	0.02
	(0.05)	(0.05)
Age	−0.01**	−0.01**
	(0.00)	(0.00)
White	−0.58**	−0.58**
	(0.18)	(0.18)
Constant	0.81*	0.75*
	(0.33)	(0.35)
Observations	1,000	1,000

Note: Models are logistic regressions. Robust standard errors are in parentheses.
All significance tests are two-tailed.
*$p < 0.05$
**$p < 0.01$

APPENDIX TABLE 2.4. Public support for
unilateral reversals vs. making new policy

	(1)
Reversal	0.33
	(0.20)
Republican	1.26**
	(0.29)
Democrat	−0.31
	(0.25)
Male	0.45*
	(0.20)
Age	−0.00
	(0.01)
Education	−0.14*
	(0.07)
White	0.50*
	(0.22)
Constant	0.04
	(0.42)
Observations	504

Note: Model is a logistic regression. Robust standard errors are
in parentheses. All significance tests are two-tailed.
*$p < 0.05$
**$p < 0.01$

APPENDIX TABLE 2.5. Support for Trump's
pipelines order

	(1)
Reversal	−0.13
	(0.23)
Republican	1.95**
	(0.31)
Democrat	−1.00**
	(0.27)
Male	1.24**
	(0.23)
Age	0.01
	(0.01)
Education	−0.19*
	(0.08)
White	0.26
	(0.27)
Constant	−1.10*
	(0.47)
Observations	496

Note: Model is a logistic regression. Robust standard errors are
in parentheses. All significance tests are two-tailed.
$*p < 0.05$
$**p < 0.01$

APPENDIX TABLE 2.6. Bush vs. Obama and beliefs that unilateral action has gone too far

	(1)	(2)
Bush treatment	−0.05	0.23
	(0.20)	(0.43)
Bush treatment × Republican		−2.35**
		(0.57)
Bush treatment × Democrat		1.36*
		(0.56)
Republican	0.18	1.37**
	(0.28)	(0.42)
Democrat	−0.18	−0.98*
	(0.27)	(0.41)
Male	0.46*	0.57*
	(0.20)	(0.22)
Education	0.28**	0.31**
	(0.07)	(0.08)
Age	0.01	0.01
	(0.01)	(0.01)
White	0.31	0.35
	(0.26)	(0.27)
Constant	−2.31**	−2.66**
	(0.49)	(0.56)
Observations	445	445

Note: Models are logistic regressions. Robust standard errors are in parentheses. All significance tests are two-tailed.

*$p < 0.05$

**$p < 0.01$

APPENDIX TABLE 2.7. Effect of policy instrument on support for student loan relief

	(1)	(2)	(3)	(4)
Executive order treatment	−0.15	−0.18	−0.23	−0.22
	(0.17)	(0.17)	(0.34)	(0.19)
Executive order × Republican			0.22	
			(0.42)	
Executive order × Democrat			−0.29	
			(0.51)	
Executive order × loan debt				0.25
				(0.47)
Republican	−0.63**	−0.36	−0.48	−0.36
	(0.21)	(0.22)	(0.32)	(0.22)
Democrat	1.89**	1.30**	1.45**	1.30**
	(0.25)	(0.27)	(0.40)	(0.27)
Male	−0.50**	−0.50**	−0.50**	−0.49**
	(0.17)	(0.18)	(0.18)	(0.18)
Education	−0.14*	−0.17**	−0.17*	−0.17**
	(0.06)	(0.07)	(0.07)	(0.07)
Age	−0.02**	−0.02**	−0.02**	−0.02**
	(0.01)	(0.01)	(0.01)	(0.01)
White	−0.34	−0.21	−0.21	−0.21
	(0.23)	(0.23)	(0.23)	(0.23)
Student loan debt	1.27**	1.31**	1.33**	1.19**
	(0.24)	(0.24)	(0.24)	(0.33)
Presidential approval		1.40**	1.41**	1.41**
		(0.25)	(0.26)	(0.25)
Constant	2.45**	2.14**	2.17**	2.17**
	(0.40)	(0.42)	(0.47)	(0.42)
Observations	970	970	970	970

Note: Models are logistic regressions. Robust standard errors are in parentheses. All significance tests are two-tailed.
*$p < 0.05$
**$p < 0.01$

APPENDIX TABLE 2.8. Effect of policy instrument on support for immigration reform

	(1)	(2)	(3)
Executive order treatment	0.32	0.11	0.30
	(0.23)	(0.41)	(0.24)
Executive order × Republican		−0.36	
		(0.68)	
Executive order × Democrat		0.53	
		(0.52)	
Executive order × Latino			0.23
			(0.72)
Republican	−1.85**	−1.71**	−1.86**
	(0.36)	(0.47)	(0.36)
Democrat	1.48**	1.23**	1.48**
	(0.27)	(0.37)	(0.27)
Male	0.56*	0.56*	0.56*
	(0.23)	(0.24)	(0.23)
Education	0.23**	0.23**	0.23**
	(0.08)	(0.08)	(0.08)
Age	−0.02**	−0.02**	−0.02**
	(0.01)	(0.01)	(0.01)
White	0.22	0.21	0.23
	(0.29)	(0.30)	(0.29)
Latino	1.01*	0.97*	0.92
	(0.42)	(0.43)	(0.51)
Constant	−0.99*	−0.82	−0.96
	(0.49)	(0.53)	(0.50)
Observations	486	486	486

Note: Models are logistic regressions. Robust standard errors are in parentheses. All significance tests are two-tailed.

*$p < 0.05$

**$p < 0.01$

APPENDIX TABLE 2.9. Effect of policy instrument on support for building the border wall

	(1)	(2)	(3)
Executive order treatment	0.16	0.26	0.11
	(0.16)	(0.27)	(0.17)
Executive order × Republican		0.00	
		(0.43)	
Executive order × Democrat		−0.24	
		(0.37)	
Executive order × Latino			0.54
			(0.59)
Republican	1.80**	1.80**	1.79**
	(0.22)	(0.29)	(0.22)
Democrat	−1.56**	−1.44**	−1.57**
	(0.19)	(0.27)	(0.19)
Male	0.24	0.24	0.24
	(0.16)	(0.16)	(0.16)
Education	−0.24**	−0.24**	−0.24**
	(0.06)	(0.06)	(0.06)
Age	0.02**	0.02**	0.02**
	(0.00)	(0.00)	(0.00)
White	0.27	0.27	0.27
	(0.24)	(0.24)	(0.24)
Latino	0.07	0.07	−0.18
	(0.35)	(0.35)	(0.45)
Constant	−0.59	−0.63	−0.56
	(0.35)	(0.36)	(0.35)
Observations	1,000	1,000	1,000

Note: Models are logistic regressions. Robust standard errors are in parentheses. All significance tests are two-tailed.
*$p < 0.05$
**$p < 0.01$

CHAPTER THREE

Congressional Pushback in the Public Sphere

The experiments in the preceding chapter suggest it is possible that the public check on rampant presidential unilateralism may not be much stronger than the formal institutional constraints imposed by Congress and the courts.[1] In sharp contrast to existing polling data and prior research, we found no evidence that Americans instinctively oppose unilateral action as a threat to cherished constitutional norms of checks and balances. Instead, most appear to assess actual unilateral actions in the same way that they make other forms of political judgments, above all by relying on partisanship. This suggests that any popular check on wayward unilateralism is highly conditional and—as long as the president can easily maintain support from his political base and independents—fairly weak.

Can anything strengthen the public check? Are the competing visions of public opinion on unilateral action fundamentally irreconcilable? To answer these questions, this chapter explores the potential power of another type of cue that may inform the public's assessment of unilateral action: the reactions of other political elites. While presidents enjoy significant advantages in communicating to the public and shaping media coverage of pressing policy concerns, the president's voice is not the only one that the electorate hears. Although Congress as an institution is all but unable to take action to constrain the president legislatively, individual members can and do battle the unilateral president in the public sphere.[2] And the mass media play a critical role in amplifying the voice of those contesting the presidential position. First and foremost, media outlets are for-profit businesses, and nothing sells like conflict.

In this chapter, we explore how congressional critics can activate citizens' underlying qualms concerning unilateral action and translate them into concrete opposition to policy initiatives. Through a series of eight experiments embedded in nationally representative surveys during both the Obama and the Trump presidencies, we continue to find little evidence that the public instinctively opposes concrete instances of contemporary unilateral action. We do find, however, that members of Congress can erode public support for unilateral action by vocally challenging the administration's actions on both constitutional and policy grounds. Indeed, congressional criticism diminishes popular support for unilateral action across issue areas, both foreign and domestic, and levels of issue salience.

Taken together, our experiments suggest that the popular check on presidential unilateralism may not be as weak as it first seems. Moreover, Congress is far from irrelevant to the politics of unilateral action as the conventional wisdom suggests. Rather, this chapter uncovers a potentially powerful though indirect mechanism through which legislators might influence the strategic calculations of the unilateral executive, even when Congress is unable to overturn such actions legislatively. If presidents anticipate sustained and vocal opposition to a unilateral action from Congress, they may rationally forgo acting unilaterally, fearing that the resulting public backlash could diminish their political capital and prevent them from achieving other aspects of their agenda in the future.

CONGRESSIONAL CRITICISM AND PUBLIC SUPPORT FOR UNILATERAL ACTION

Congress is all but powerless to overturn a unilateral action legislatively. But can it raise the political costs of executive action by turning the public against it? At first blush, it might seem strange to think that members of Congress would have much luck in moving public opinion. After all, Congress has never been overly popular, and its contemporary body has earned the dubious distinction of enjoying record low approval ratings. Nevertheless, despite the public's clear misgivings about Congress as an institution, congressional criticism of presidential policies has proved quite influential on public opinion in other settings. While presidents invest considerable time and energy endeavoring to exploit the bully pulpit and lead public opinion, more often than not presidents of all political stripes—even those like Ronald Reagan and Barack Obama, who are renowned for their rhetorical skills—have struggled mightily to move public opinion to their side.[3] An important reason for such failures is that members of Congress do not stand idly by; rather, they also engage the debate in the public sphere and offer a counternarrative to that advanced by the White House.[4] Indeed, congressional critics of administration policies have even been successful in moving public opinion on questions of war and peace, an area where presidents are traditionally believed to enjoy significant advantages.[5]

Can congressional critics also shape public assessments of unilateral action? There are at least three reasons to believe that they can. First, the previous chapter provided strong evidence that most Americans rely on readily accessible shortcuts or heuristics when evaluating presidential unilateral action. Above all, partisanship guided most views on unilateral power. And in several of our experiments, survey respondents also looked to their own policy preferences when assessing a range of unilateral actions taken by the Bush and Obama administrations in both the foreign and the domestic sphere. Presidential copartisans and those who agreed with a unilateral action on policy grounds mostly supported the president; partisan opponents and those who disagreed with an action on policy grounds largely opposed him. However, partisanship and policy preferences are not the only cues from which Americans can draw when making political assessments. Rather, decades of public opinion scholarship have shown that the public positions taken by other political elites also serve as widely available and highly salient cues that can guide opinion formation on a range of topics. When members of Congress openly criticize an executive action, they provide new information that the public can use to update its assessments of presidential unilateralism. Some Americans—for example, the president's most ardent supporters—may discount and resist congressional criticisms as inconsistent with their partisan or policy priors. But for others, the new information provided by congressional elites may tilt the balance of considerations at the top of their heads against unilateral action.[6]

In addition to simply providing new information, congressional criticism might activate the latent concerns held by many Americans about unilateral action observed in prior research.[7] Our experiments in chapter 2 suggest that constitutional concerns may not be strong enough on their own to turn large majorities of the electorate against presidential unilateral action. However, if these constitutional qualms do exist, it is possible that congressional challenges to unilateral action will resonate with many Americans' innate skepticism of unilateral action and concern that it threatens checks and balances.

Finally, for congressional criticism of unilateral action to be influential, it must reach a wide swath of the mass public. To this end, congressional critics are greatly aided by the mass media.[8] Although presidents enjoy significant advantages in shaping the content of media coverage, an extensive literature on media indexing argues that the media adjust the scope and tenor of their coverage in response to the level of political conflict in Washington.[9] Because journalistic norms of newsworthiness increasingly value political conflict, the media play a significant role in magnifying congressional challenges to presidential unilateral actions.[10] While (bi)partisan support for the president may go unreported, congressional challenges are likely to make the news. Indeed, because conflict sells, media outlets may give disproportionate coverage to those challenging the president, thus heightening the sense of institutional conflict for most Americans.

In sum, there are strong reasons to believe that congressional opposition to a unilateral action can sway the public against the president. However, Congress's capacity to shape public attitudes toward unilateral action may vary substantially across issues and over time. In the analyses below, we examine two potential sources of variation, and we place congressional influence on public opinion in a wider political context.

THE SUBSTANCE OF CONGRESSIONAL PUSHBACK

Does the substance of congressional challenges shape their capacity to influence public opinion? A distinguishing feature of unilateral action is its susceptibility to constitutional challenges. Congressional opponents may simply object that an executive action constitutes an abuse of presidential power without having to battle the president on the merits of the policy itself. Even if constitutional concerns do not automatically trigger widespread opposition to unilateral action, congressional challenges on constitutional or legal grounds may resonate with Americans' underlying unease concerning unilateral presidential power as a threat to separation of powers. As a result, congressional constitutional challenges may significantly decrease public support for unilateral action.

Whereas members of Congress can and do routinely challenge the constitutionality of presidential unilateral initiatives, they can also criticize the president on policy grounds. By engaging the debate over whether a unilateral initiative represents good public policy, Congress can counter the dominant frame offered by the administration. Offering policy critiques of presidential arguments can transform a one-sided information flow dominated by the White House into a competitive information environment, thereby eroding the president's capacity to marshal support for his chosen policy course.[11] In the analysis that follows, we examine the relative efficacy of congressional constitutional versus policy challenges in eroding public support for unilateral action.

GENERALIZABILITY ACROSS ISSUES

While there are strong reasons to believe that Congress can diminish public support for unilateral action in certain conditions, past scholarship suggests that congressional challenges may be more influential regarding some issues than others. We explore two possibilities. First, an extensive literature suggests that presidents enjoy greater leeway in foreign policy than in domestic affairs.[12] In the previous chapter, we found little evidence that the public is more supportive of presidential unilateralism in the realm of foreign policy.[13] However, congressional challenges to executive action may ring hollow in matters of foreign affairs. As a new inquiry into an old debate concerning presidents' alleged advantages in foreign policy, we examine whether Congress is equally able to decrease public support for presidential unilateral action in foreign and domestic affairs.

Second, Congress's capacity to sway public opinion on unilateral action may vary according to both the salience of the issue at hand and the extent to which it polarizes the public. Congressional opposition may have the greatest influence on smaller, less salient, and nonpolarizing unilateral actions on which most citizens lack strong priors. If so, Congress's ability to raise the political costs of executive action for the president would be seriously limited. To test this possibility, we examine the relative efficacy of congressional criticism across a range of unilateral actions that vary in terms of scope, salience, and level of polarization.

SOURCE EFFECTS

Finally, to put Congress's potential opinion leadership in a wider context, we examine whether it is better positioned to influence public attitudes toward unilateral action than are other critics of the unilateral president. There are at least two reasons that Congress may be more influential than other actors in shaping public opinion in this regard. First, congressional criticisms may be more influential simply because they are more likely to be heard by a chronically inattentive public. An extensive literature in political communication documents how the media index the tenor and tone of their coverage to the official debate within Washington.[14] Indeed, a particularly strong variant of the indexing hypothesis argues that critiques not articulated in Washington, especially by legislators, are often system-atically marginalized by the mass media.[15] As such, challenges to presidential unilateral actions levied by members of Congress—interbranch conflict is inherently newsworthy—may be particularly likely to generate the media coverage essential to moving public opinion. Absent congressional criticism, the media may ignore critiques made by other actors. Challenges to the unilateral president that are not widely heard have little chance of swaying public opinion. Thus, the privileged position that congressional critics enjoy with the media affords them important advantages when trying to influence the public.

Apart from the greater media attention received by congressional criticisms, the public may also perceive that challenges to unilateral action from members of Congress are more credible than identical criticisms made by a noninstitutional actor. For example, recent research on congressional investigations shows that charges of executive branch misconduct levied by congressional committees are more influential with the public than are identical charges made by other, nongovernmental actors.[16] This suggests that an institutional credibility mechanism may be at work, giving congressional criticisms of the president more weight with the public. To examine whether such a mechanism also shapes how Americans respond to information about unilateral action, we explore whether criticisms made by congressional actors are more influential than identical critiques of presidential unilateralism made by nongovernmental actors.

A related question concerns whether the efficacy of a congressional challenge depends on the party identification of those challenging unilateral action. Many of the most important unilateral actions in recent years—from domestic initiatives on immigration, gun control, and environmental protection to the authorization of unilateral military strikes in Libya and Syria—have attracted at least some bipartisan pushback from Congress. Yet the most vociferous critiques have often come from the opposition party. Scholars have long emphasized the power of bipartisan elite cues to influence public opinion.[17] Similarly, because copartisan criticism of the White House is politically costly, challenges to unilateral action from within the ranks of the president's own party in Congress should also be influential.[18] By contrast, some may dismiss challenges to unilateral action levied exclusively by opposition party members as mere partisan politicking. But institutional criticisms of unilateral action, even by the partisan opposition, may nonetheless awaken latent concerns that unilateralism threatens separation of powers and therefore erode support for the president's actions. Because they are imbued with institutional credibility, even uncostly challenges to unilateral action by members of the opposition party may resonate with the public. The analysis below will test between these competing hypotheses.

THE BENEFITS OF AN EXPERIMENTAL APPROACH

Decades of public opinion scholarship have analyzed how political elites influence public opinion. However, conclusively proving that elite actions caused an observed shift in public opinion is often exceedingly difficult. For example, both president Bill Clinton's widely anticipated order in 1993 to allow gays to serve openly in the military and president Barack Obama's efforts in 2009 to close the terrorist detention camp at Guantanamo Bay in Cuba provoked an immediate backlash on Capitol Hill. In the face of sustained and withering criticism from lawmakers, public support for both presidential initiatives declined precipitously.[19]

These cases are broadly consistent with decades of scholarship arguing that intense congressional opposition can turn public opinion against the president and his policies. Yet from observational data alone it is all but impossible to say conclusively that the congressional pushback caused the precipitous drop in public support for Clinton's and Obama's policies. The causal arrow may also run, at least partially, in the other direction. Waning public support may have incentivized congressional critics to speak out and challenge the administration. Alternately, a third factor—for example, public expressions of concern from military and other officials—may have influenced both the surge in congressional criticism and the erosion of public support. Thus, observational evidence may often be suggestive of congressional influence on Americans' assessments of executive action, but not conclusive.

To overcome these limitations, this chapter employs a series of eight experiments embedded in nationally representative opinion surveys. Experiments provide great leverage when examining relationships in which causation is difficult to ascertain in practice by affording researchers maximum control. In contrast to observational studies of elite opinion leadership where we cannot be sure who is leading whom, by randomly assigning subjects to different treatment groups that are completely identical except for the nature of the congressional response to the president's unilateral action, we can isolate the causal effect of a congressional position on public support for presidential unilateralism.

CONSTITUTIONAL VERSUS POLICY CRITICISM

Our first experiment both tested our core argument—that Congress has the capacity to erode support for unilateral action—and examined the relative influence of congressional objections on constitutional versus policy grounds. This survey was administered in October 2014 as part of the preelection wave of that year's Cooperative Congressional Election Survey.

Perhaps the most important advantage of an experimental approach is its high internal validity; that is, experiments allow us to precisely identify the causal impact of congressional charges on public support for an executive action. However, this advantage can come at the cost of external validity: the conditions of a controlled experiment may not always reflect how opinion formation takes place in the real world. To minimize such concerns, we first examined the influence of congressional cues for an issue very much in the public eye: President Obama's decision to instruct the Environmental Protection Agency (EPA) to regulate carbon dioxide emissions in order to address the threat posed by global warming.[20] By examining Congress's ability to affect Americans' attitudes toward the president's Clean Power Plan, we begin with a tough case for our argument. If congressional criticism influences public opinion in this highly polarized policy realm, it should be even more influential in other policy areas where citizens possess fewer predispositions and weaker partisan priors.

Subjects were randomly assigned to one of three experimental groups. All subjects received the following prompt: "President Obama has directed the EPA to begin regulating carbon dioxide from coal power plants to reduce greenhouse gas emissions, combat climate change, and improve public health." To bolster the experiment's external validity, the language used was carefully chosen to follow as closely as possible the actual language used by President Obama to describe the plan's goals and by the media in their reporting on the initiative.

Moreover, by ensuring that all subjects receive President Obama's position first, before any information about the opinions of any other political actors, the experiment privileges the president's position. This reflects the White House's advantages in shaping the content of media coverage.[21] In no case do subjects receive a congressional challenge without first receiving an affirmative defense of the unilateral action by the administration on policy grounds. Subjects in the control group received no further information.

After learning of the president's position, subjects in the first treatment group were told that many members of Congress objected to the executive action on constitutional grounds.[22] These subjects were told, "Many members of Congress from both parties, however, oppose the President's decision. They argue that President Obama's actions have overstepped his constitutional authority and that a major change in energy policy requires new legislation from Congress." This treatment did not raise any specific policy objections. It did not challenge the president's frame that the executive action would combat global warming and improve public health. Rather, the congressional criticism in this cue rested solely on constitutional arguments that President Obama had overstepped legal limits on executive power.

Finally, subjects in the second treatment group—after receiving the president's position and policy justification—were told that many members of Congress objected to Obama's executive action on policy grounds: "Many members of Congress from both parties, however, oppose the President's decision. They argue that Obama's actions will increase energy prices and cost jobs." Subsequent experiments will modify this language to vary both the partisan source and the number of members challenging the president.[23] This treatment explicitly primes subjects to evaluate President Obama's executive action from the lens of job creation and pocketbook considerations, two factors that should resonate with many Americans, since they are less arcane and technical than constitutional objections. As such, comparing the effect of this treatment and that of the constitutional objections treatment offers a strong test for the relative influence of constitutional challenges. If the effects are comparable in magnitude, this would suggest that constitutional cues may be even more influential relative to policy critiques that do not involve jobs, dollars, and cents.

After receiving the treatment information, all subjects were asked to indicate whether they supported or opposed "President Obama taking unilateral action to reduce carbon dioxide emissions."[24] To assess the effect of the two congressional criticism treatments on public support for executive action to regulate carbon dioxide emissions, we estimated a statistical model. This allowed us to assess the effect of receiving either the constitutional or the policy-based congressional criticism treatments on support for Obama's unilateral action while controlling for a number of additional factors that might affect support for Obama's move.[25] Most important, the model controlled for subjects' partisan affiliation and approval or disapproval of Obama and included a proxy for their policy preferences: a measure of whether they believe that government action is necessary to combat global warming. The model also controlled for gender, educational attainment, age, and race.[26]

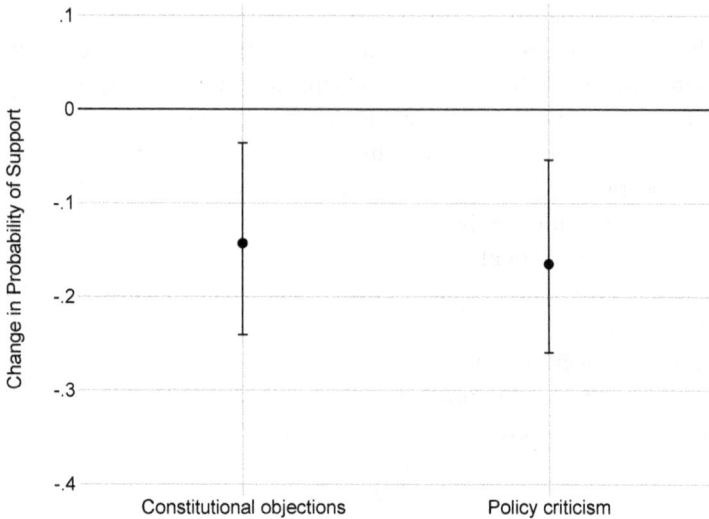

Figure 3.1. Effect of constitutional objections and policy
criticisms on support for Obama's Clean Power Plan
Note: Each dot presents the estimated change in the probability of the median
independent respondent supporting the president's unilateral action. I-bars around each
point estimate present 95% confidence intervals obtained from simulations.

Strongly consistent with our argument, the statistical model found
that congressional criticism significantly eroded public support for President Obama's unilateral push for the Clean Power Plan. Even after controlling for each subject's partisanship and policy preferences, congressional
criticism of Obama's actions on both constitutional and policy grounds
sharply decreased support for the president. Figure 3.1 illustrates the results by showing the estimated effect of both treatments on the predicted
probability of the median subject supporting the Clean Power Plan. When
members of Congress objected that Obama's unilateral action exceeded his
constitutional authority and transgressed on congressional prerogatives, it
decreased the predicted probability of the median subject supporting the
president by roughly 15%. Similarly, when members of Congress rebutted
Obama's arguments about the policy benefits of the plan and claimed it
would increase electricity prices and cost jobs, support also fell. For the
median subject, the policy criticism treatment decreased the predicted
probability of supporting Obama by approximately 18%.[27]

As in the preceding chapter, our statistical model showed that partisanship, presidential approval, and preexisting beliefs (here, concerning
global warming) were the most important predictors of support for Obama.

It is important to reiterate, however, that both congressional treatments significantly decreased support for the unilateral action even after controlling for these traditionally powerful factors. Substantively, a double-digit drop in public support for an executive action could be politically transformative. Moreover, it is important to remember that this is the effect of a single, relatively modest congressional cue critiquing the president's action.

Finally, a common critique of experimental research is that the effects observed in an experimental setting may be much more pronounced than what we observe in the real world. One of the most important reasons for this is that in an experiment, all the subjects in the treatment group receive the treatment. All the subjects in the constitutional objections treatment learned that members of Congress from both parties criticized the Clean Power Plan as an example of presidential overreach and that major changes in environmental policy required congressional action. But in the real world, where many Americans pay only passing attention to happenings in Washington and media coverage of them, even sharp congressional criticism of unilateral action may go unnoticed by some, particularly those who possess low levels of political information.

If low-information subjects, who might be unlikely to learn of congressional criticism in the real world, are driving our results, then we may seriously overestimate the capacity of congressional elites to erode public support for unilateral action. To examine this question, we revised our statistical model to examine whether the treatment effects vary across subjects with high and low levels of political information. The full results of this analysis are presented in the chapter appendix. Easing such fears, we found little evidence that our congressional treatment effects vary across subjects with varying levels of political knowledge.[28] Subjects who closely follow politics and those who lack even basic information about politics both responded to the constitutional and policy criticism treatments in the same way: by becoming less likely to support President Obama's attempt to implement sweeping changes in environmental policy unilaterally.

INFLUENCE ACROSS ISSUES

To examine whether congressional challenges also erode support for unilateral action in two very different policy realms, we embedded a pair of additional experiments in a follow-up nationally representative survey conducted in April 2015. The first examined Congress's capacity to decrease support for President Obama's unilateral decision to launch air strikes against ISIS targets in Iraq and Syria. The second examined the factors driving support for President Obama's executive actions to cap student loan payments.

Along with the Clean Power Plan, the military response to ISIS was among the most consequential and highly salient executive actions taken during the Obama administration. In addition, broadening the scope of our analysis to include important unilateral actions in foreign policy allows us to examine whether the public grants the president more leeway to act unilaterally in foreign affairs. If so, then congressional criticism may be less influential in the context of unilateral strikes against ISIS militants than it was in the Clean Power Plan Experiment.

The student loan memoranda, by contrast, were narrower in scope and attracted considerably less media attention and scrutiny. Moreover, both public polling data and our findings in the preceding chapter suggest that government efforts to help those with student loan debt enjoyed broad popular support. For example, a November 2014 poll found that 84% of Americans supported Congress taking action to improve access to lower-cost student loans and to give borrowers more time to pay off student loan debt.[29] Thus, examining student loans allows us to test whether Congress can erode support for a unilateral action that implements a broadly popular policy change.

Finally, a third factor differentiates this second pair of experiments from the first: the degree to which the policy issues in play polarized public opinion along partisan lines. The Clean Power Plan was, from its very inception, intensely polarizing. Democrats rallied behind it and Republicans largely opposed it. By contrast, prior polling showed little evidence of a significant partisan split in support for strikes against ISIS militants or for government efforts to ease the burden on student loan payments. As a result, this new pair of experiments allows us to examine the opinion dynamics in support for unilateral action on less polarizing policy issues.

In this second set of experiments, we focus exclusively on congressional constitutional objections, which had virtually the same impact on support for unilateral action as policy criticisms in our first Clean Power Plan Experiment. The main advantage of focusing on constitutional criticisms is that it allows us to examine the impact of the same congressional critique—that the president has exceeded his constitutional authority—on unilateral action across very different policy areas. Policy criticisms, by contrast, would almost necessarily differ across issues. As a result, if we observed differences in effects, we would not be able to determine whether

Congress was really less able to sway opinion in one policy than in the other, or if the specific content of one of the policy critiques simply resonated with more Americans.

Half our sample was randomly assigned to an experiment examining support for unilateral air strikes against ISIS militants. Subjects in this experiment were then randomly assigned to one of two groups. All subjects received the following prompt: "As you may know, President Barack Obama has unilaterally launched a series of air strikes against ISIS militants in Iraq and Syria." Subjects in the control group received no further information. Subjects in the treatment group were also told of congressional constitutional objections to the president's actions: "Many members of Congress from both parties, however, oppose the President's decision. They argue that President Obama has overstepped his constitutional authority and that military action requires authorization from Congress."[30] All subjects were then asked whether they "support or oppose President Obama's decision to unilaterally launch air strikes against ISIS in Iraq and Syria."

The other half of our sample was assigned to an experiment examining whether congressional constitutional objections could erode public support for another popular and less polarizing unilateral action in the domestic sphere: President Obama's executive actions to lower student loan payments. All subjects received the following prompt: "President Barack Obama has issued an executive order to unilaterally cap student loan payments at 10% of a borrower's income, and forgive any remaining debt after 20 years."[31] Subjects in the control group received no further information. Subjects in the treatment group were told that many members of Congress believe that Obama has exceeded his constitutional authority: "Many members of Congress from both parties, however, oppose the President's decision. They argue that President Obama's actions have overstepped his constitutional authority and that a major change in student loan policies requires new legislation from Congress." All subjects were then asked whether they "support or oppose President Obama's decision to unilaterally lower student loan payments."

For both experiments, we estimated statistical models that allowed us to assess the influence of the congressional charge that Obama had overstepped the constitutional limits on his power on support for his unilateral action. Both models also controlled for each subject's partisan affiliation, age, gender, educational attainment, and race. Figure 3.2 illustrates the effects of the congressional criticism on support for unilateral action across the two experiments while holding all other factors constant.[32]

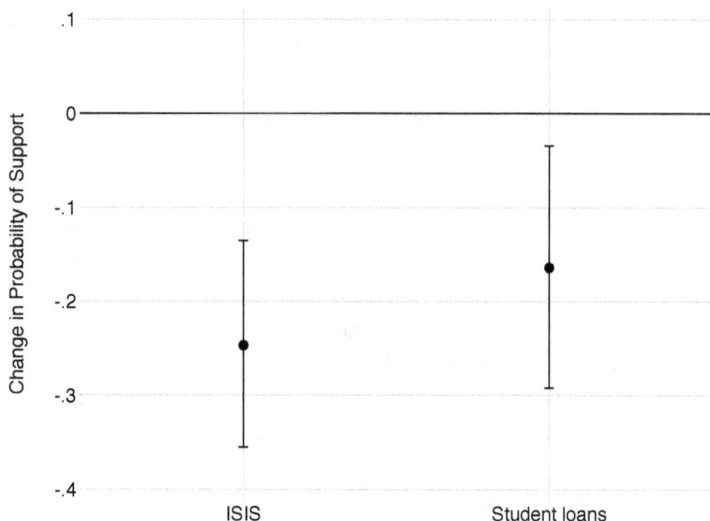

Figure 3.2. Effect of congressional challenges to unilateral
action in foreign and domestic policy
Note: Each dot presents the estimated change in the probability of the median
independent respondent supporting the president's unilateral action. I-bars around each
point estimate present 95% confidence intervals obtained from simulations.

In the ISIS Experiment, when Congress raised constitutional objections to Obama's actions it decreased the probability of the median independent respondent supporting Obama by 25%. Whereas the median subject in the control group had a 65% chance of supporting Obama, that fell to only a 40% chance in the constitutional objections treatment. Indeed, the effect of congressional opposition on support for the ISIS strikes was larger than that for any other factor in the model. This large effect contrasts with what we might expect, given the conventional wisdom that presidents enjoy greater leeway to act on their own initiative in foreign affairs. While a significant percentage of subjects (77%) did back Obama's unilateral strikes in the control group, our ISIS Experiment suggests that this support is far from immune to congressional pressures. Congressional charges that the president has exceeded his powers can significantly erode support for unilateral action.

Congressional constitutional objections also significantly reduced support for Obama's executive actions to cap student loan payments. For the median independent respondent, reading that many members of Congress objected to Obama's actions on constitutional grounds reduced the likelihood of supporting Obama's move by 16%. Even in the context of an uncontroversial, narrowly targeted policy initiative that in the abstract enjoys broad support among the public, a congressional challenge significantly decreased support for unilateral action.

PURELY PARTISAN OPPOSITION

In each of the three preceding experiments, the congressional challenge to unilateral action was a bipartisan one. Even though Washington is an increasingly partisan place, major presidential unilateral action is one of the few things that often unites at least some critics from both sides of the political aisle. On many of the major executive actions taken by both Presidents Obama and George W. Bush, at least a small number of presidential copartisans joined opposition party critiques of executive actions. For example, while most Democrats rallied behind President Obama's Clean Power Plan, a few Democrats from energy-producing states, such as West Virginia senator Joe Manchin, joined with Republicans to criticize the president's initiative as a job killer that would also hurt American consumers.[33] Similarly, in response to President Obama's decision to unilaterally order air strikes against ISIS targets without first seeking congressional approval, Virginia Democrat (and future vice presidential nominee) Tim Kaine joined with Republicans, such as North Carolina's Walter Jones, in criticizing the move on constitutional grounds.[34]

Presidential critics are quick to claim bipartisan support for their position even when joined by only a handful of presidential copartisans. Furthermore, the media, which highlight opposition from presidential copartisans, freely repeat such claims.[35] But given the intense levels of partisan polarization in modern politics, it is important to investigate whether criticisms of unilateral action levied only by members of the partisan opposition can similarly erode support for the president's actions.

To this end, we embedded a revised version of our Clean Power Plan Experiment in another nationally representative survey conducted in April 2015. Subjects in this experiment were also randomly assigned to either a control or to one of two treatment groups. However, instead of varying the content of the congressional criticism, in this experiment we varied the partisan identity of the members challenging the president. All subjects received an initial prompt identical to that in the first EPA experiment describing the basics of Obama's Clean Power Plan. Subjects in the control group received no further information. Subjects in the first treatment group were told that many congressional Republicans objected to Obama's unilateral action on both constitutional and policy grounds.[36]

This treatment combined the constitutional objections and policy criticism of the prior experiment: "Some congressional Republicans, however, oppose the President's decision. They argue that President Obama's actions have overstepped his constitutional authority and that a major change in energy policy requires new legislation from Congress. Moreover, these Republican members of Congress argue that Obama's actions will increase energy prices and cost jobs." Finally, subjects in the second treatment group received an identically worded prompt. However, in this treatment "some congressional Democrats" were identified as the source of the challenge to Obama's action. Thus, the two treatment conditions differed only in terms of the partisanship of the members of Congress expressing opposition. All subjects were then asked whether they supported or opposed "President Obama taking unilateral action to reduce carbon dioxide emissions."

A statistical model allowed us to assess the effects of the same criticism attributed to Democratic and Republican members of Congress while also controlling for each subject's partisanship and other demographic characteristics.[37] As shown in figure 3.3, congressional challenges to a unilateral action on constitutional and policy grounds significantly eroded

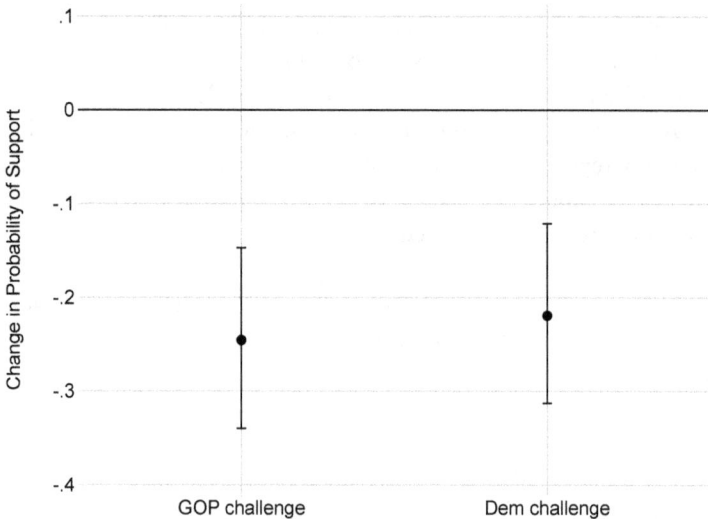

Figure 3.3. Effects of Democratic versus Republican
criticism on support for Clean Power Plan
Note: Each dot presents the estimated change in the probability of the median
independent respondent supporting the president's unilateral action. I-bars around each
point estimate present 95% confidence intervals obtained from simulations.

public support for the president's environmental actions—regardless of the partisan affiliation of the members attacking the administration. Congressional criticism of the president's EPA action decreased the median respondent's likelihood of supporting Obama's move by between 20% and 25% in both partisan treatment groups. These effects are slightly larger than those observed in the first Clean Power Plan Experiment. This is likely the result of the stronger treatments, in which members of Congress criticized the executive action on both policy and constitutional grounds. These treatments also better reflect most congressional challenges to unilateral action in the real world, as members of Congress routinely attack the unilateral president along both dimensions.

In additional analyses presented in the chapter appendix, we found some suggestive evidence that Democrats are slightly more responsive to criticism from congressional Democrats and vice versa for Republicans. However, none of these differences are statistically significant. Instead, our most striking finding is that even opposition levied solely by the opposition party in Congress can be politically costly.

IS CONGRESS UNIQUELY INFLUENTIAL?

Across three very different issue areas spanning both the foreign and the domestic policy realms, the preceding experiments found consistently powerful evidence that congressional challenges to unilateral action undermine public support for the president's exercise of unilateral power. Yet Congress is not the only body capable of bringing criticisms of unilateral action into the public sphere. As a result, we explore whether congressional challenges to unilateral action are inherently more influential with the public than identical charges made by other political actors.

It is important to note that in an experimental setting, a challenge to unilateral action by members of Congress need not be more influential with public opinion than an identical charge made by another actor for Congress to be the most important mover of popular attitudes toward the unilateral presidency. Rather, Congress enjoys significant advantages in terms of ensuring that its criticisms of presidential unilateralism are heard by a large swath of Americans. Research in media politics suggests that criticism of unilateral action from Congress may be particularly newsworthy and enjoy significant advantages in attracting the prominent attention from media outlets essential to influencing public opinion.

Nevertheless, to investigate whether criticisms levied by Congress hold more sway with the public than the same criticisms attributed to other actors, we embedded a modified version of the ISIS Experiment in a nationally representative survey conducted in March 2016. The revised ISIS Experiment differed from the preceding version in four key respects. First, the new experiment contained four treatment groups, the first three of which allowed us to investigate whether the influence of the same constitutional challenge to unilateral air strikes varies depending on the source making the charge.

Second, the wording of the first three treatments was slightly modified from the earlier experiment. Each actor charges that President Obama has overstepped his constitutional authority; however, the final clause asserting that military action requires congressional authorization has been omitted to allow us to examine the relative efficacy of the same critique by each actor without Congress being mentioned in all three treatments. This is important, as it ensures that a reference to Congress and its institutional prerogatives is not included in each treatment, which could potentially confound any effort to identify the importance of the actor criticizing the president.

Third, in the revised experiment the president's position enjoyed even greater privilege, as he gets both the first and the last word. The experiment opened with the president's position and concluded with the president's rebuttal to constitutional challenges to his actions. This dual emphasis on the president's arguments significantly privileged Obama's position and stacked the deck against finding evidence of treatment effects.

Finally, this follow-up survey was conducted in a very different contextual environment, just three days after a terrorist attack against the Brussels airport perpetrated by individuals pledging allegiance to the Islamic State. Media coverage emphasizing the threat posed by ISIS to the West and a rally-round-the-flag dynamic may have rendered many Americans more resistant to constitutional challenges to the unilateral nature of the air strikes. Thus, any treatment effects should be considered conservative.

In the revised experiment, all subjects received the same prompt as before: "As you may know, President Barack Obama has unilaterally launched a series of air strikes against ISIS militants in Iraq and Syria." Subjects were then randomly assigned to one of five experimental manipulations. Those in the control group received no further information. Those in the first three treatment groups were told that "many members of Congress from both parties" or "many law professors at leading universities" or "many newspaper editorial boards, talk radio hosts, and cable news pundits" challenged the president's action on constitutional grounds.

Subjects in these groups were told that the actors in question "oppose the President's decision" and "argue that President Obama has overstepped his constitutional authority."

Subjects in the final treatment group received an expanded version of the congressional opposition treatment identical to that from the preceding experiment: "Many members of Congress from both parties, however, oppose the President's decision. They argue that President Obama has overstepped his constitutional authority and that military action requires authorization from Congress." Comparing this treatment and the shorter treatment in which members of Congress only allege that the president has overstepped his constitutional authority allowed us to investigate whether the additional information asserting that the president has trampled on the institutional prerogatives of the legislature heightens the influence of the constitutional critique on public opinion.

Finally, to address potential objections to our earlier experiments that presidents in the real world are able to respond to critiques by other actors, each treatment concluded with a strong presidential rebuttal: "President Obama rejects this criticism and maintains that his actions are consistent with his constitutional authority as commander in chief." All subjects were then asked whether they "support or oppose President Obama's decision to unilaterally launch air strikes against ISIS in Iraq and Syria."

We constructed a statistical model to assess the effect of each treatment on support for Obama's unilateral air strikes while controlling for respondent partisanship and other demographic characteristics.[38] The effects of each treatment on the opinion of the median respondent are presented in figure 3.4.

Each of the four constitutional challenge treatments decreased the probability of supporting Obama's unilateral strikes against ISIS. However, the two congressional challenge treatments had the largest effects. Moreover, they are the only two effects that were statistically significant.[39]

Less than a week after the terror attack in Brussels, President Obama enjoyed strong support for his unilateral air strikes against ISIS in the control group. Indeed, 80% of subjects in the control backed Obama's unilateral use of force. But this support was not unshakable. Learning of congressional opposition to the strikes and the charge that by acting unilaterally Obama had overstepped his constitutional authority significantly reduced the predicted probability of the median subject supporting the president's actions by 13%. Moreover, it is worth reiterating that this effect was observed even though in this experiment President Obama rebuts the consti-

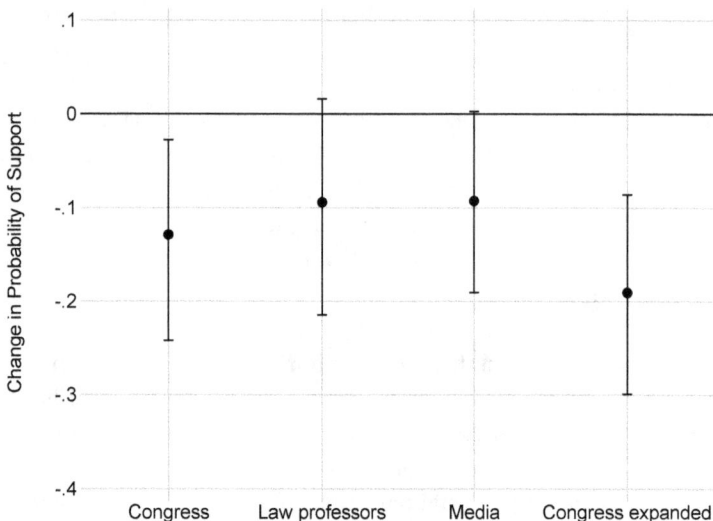

Figure 3.4. Capacity of Congress vs. other sources to decrease support for ISIS strikes
Note: Each dot presents the estimated change in the probability of the median
independent respondent supporting the president's unilateral action. I-bars around each
point estimate present 95% confidence intervals obtained from simulations.

tutional criticism and argues that his actions are fully consistent with his powers as commander in chief.

When the same constitutional challenge is made by law professors or media elites, the estimated effect on support for Obama's action is again negative. However, the effects are not statistically significant. Thus, the results are generally consistent with the hypothesis that a constitutional challenge from Congress is more influential than the same critique made by another political actor.

Finally, the largest effect was observed for the expanded congressional treatment, in which members of Congress both alleged that Obama had overstepped his constitutional authority and argued that in so doing, he encroached on congressional prerogatives, because military action requires authorization from Congress. In this treatment group, the median independent respondent was almost equally likely to support or oppose Obama's unilateral strikes. This represents a decrease of almost 20% from that of the median subject in the control group.

While the difference in effect size across the two congressional treatments is not statistically significant, the greater effect in the expanded treatment is consistent with the hypothesis that the additional constitutional criticism asserting that the president had usurped Congress's legitimate role in war making intensified the influence of congressional opposition.

RAISING THE STAKES: AN EVEN STRONGER PRESIDENTIAL REBUTTAL

In the preceding experiment, President Obama was given an opportunity to rebut the constitutional criticism levied against him by congressional opponents. Even when giving Obama the last word, our experiment showed that congressional criticism continued to significantly erode support for his unilateral action. Yet some might still object that our experiments leave some ambiguity between means and ends. For example, after learning of congressional opposition to the president's decision to act unilaterally, some subjects may be influenced by this and respond that they oppose the president's unilateral action to effect the policy change in question. But would they still oppose unilateral action if it was the only plausible path to effecting policy change? Congressional criticism might heighten subjects' awareness of and sensitivity to process, leading them to prefer a legislative to a unilateral approach. But if faced with the clear choice of policy change via unilateral action versus no policy change without it, would many prefer the former to the latter?

To answer this question, we conducted a revised version of our Clean Power Plan Experiment on another nationally representative survey in December 2016. As in versions of the previous experiment, all subjects received the same initial prompt informing them that President Obama had directed the EPA to begin regulating carbon dioxide emissions in order to reduce greenhouse gas emissions, combat climate change, and improve public health. Subjects assigned to the control group received no further information. Subjects assigned to the first treatment group were told that many members of Congress from both parties opposed the president's action on both constitutional and policy grounds. The treatment language was exactly the same as that used in the Partisan Source Experiment above. Finally, those in the rebuttal treatment received the exact same congressional challenge to Obama's decision to unilaterally implement the Clean Power Plan. However, in this treatment the congressional criticism was followed by a strong rebuttal making clear that without unilateral action there would be no change in policy: "President Obama rejects this criticism and maintains that his actions are consistent with his constitutional authority as chief executive. Because Congress is gridlocked, President Obama argues that without unilateral action there would be no

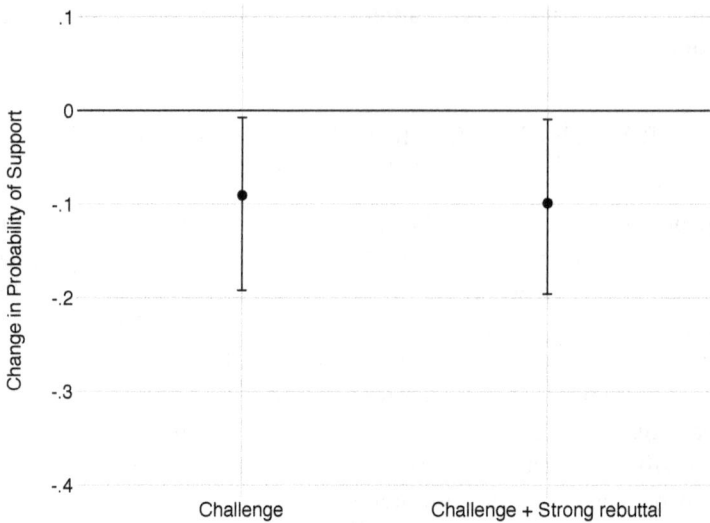

Figure 3.5. Effect of congressional challenge even if no
Clean Power Plan without unilateral action
Note: Each dot presents the estimated change in the probability of the median
independent respondent supporting the president's unilateral action. I-bars around each
point estimate present 95% confidence intervals obtained from simulations.

government policy to reduce power plant emissions." All subjects were then asked whether they supported or opposed President Obama taking unilateral action to reduce carbon dioxide emissions.

A statistical model again allowed us to assess the influence of the two treatments on support for unilateral action while also controlling for each subject's partisanship and demographic characteristics.[40] As in the preceding experiments, congressional criticism significantly decreased support for Obama's decision to unilaterally regulate carbon dioxide emissions. Figure 3.5 shows that for the median subject, this treatment decreased the likelihood of supporting the president's actions by almost 10%.

Moreover, congressional criticism continued to erode support for unilateral action and to almost the same degree when it was followed by a strong rebuttal from the president. Even when presented with Obama's defense of his actions on both constitutional and policy grounds, the median subject became 10% less likely to support the president than in the control group. Congressional criticism does more than simply make Americans prefer achieving a policy goal through a legislative approach rather than through a unilateral one. It also decreases support for unilateral action, even if that is the only viable way to effect policy change in an era of pervasive gridlock.

CONGRESSIONAL INFLUENCE DURING THE TRUMP "HONEYMOON"

Thus far, we have found remarkably robust evidence that members of Congress can erode public support for the unilateral president. Across a range of issues in both foreign and domestic policy, our experiments have shown that congressional criticisms of presidential unilateralism on both policy and constitutional grounds resonate with a large segment of the public. However, an important limitation on our ability to generalize from these experiments is that each involved actions taken by a single president: Barack Obama. We think it very unlikely that public attitudes toward unilateral action by President Obama are somehow particularly susceptible to change in the face of congressional opposition. For example, despite the historic firsts of the Obama presidency, the dynamics driving Obama's job approval rating were similar to those underlying support for his predecessors.[41]

Nevertheless, to further increase confidence that our findings are valid more generally across presidencies, we conducted a final pair of experiments during the first one hundred days of the Trump administration. Scholars and political observers have long considered the opening months of any new presidency to be a honeymoon period, during which the public and members of Congress alike often give the new president additional leeway. As such, the very timing of our final pair of experiments stacked the deck against finding evidence of congressional effects.

BUILDING THE BORDER WALL

The first experiment, which was included in a nationally representative survey fielded in March 2017, examined the ability of congressional criticism to erode public support for President Trump's efforts to unilaterally authorize the construction of a wall along the Mexican border.[42] In terms of structure, the Border Wall Experiment closely followed the first Clean Power Plan Experiment in this chapter and explored the influence of congressional criticism on both constitutional and policy grounds on public support for the president's unilateral action.

All subjects received the following prompt describing Trump's action and his main reason for it—to stem the tide of illegal immigration: "President Donald Trump has signed an executive order directing the Department of Homeland Security to begin constructing a wall along the Mexican border to reduce illegal immigration." Subjects were then randomly assigned to one of three experimental groups. Those assigned to the control group received no further information. Subjects assigned to the constitutional objections treatment received a treatment very similar to that in the earlier experiment: "Many members of Congress from both parties, however, oppose the President's decision. These Republicans and Democrats argue that President Trump's actions have exceeded his constitutional authority and that funding the border wall requires legislation from Congress." Finally, subjects in the policy criticism treatment were told, "Many members of Congress from both parties, however, oppose the President's decision. These Republicans and Democrats argue that the costly wall will add to the national debt and do little to secure the border." All subjects were then asked whether they supported or opposed "President Trump taking unilateral action to begin building the border wall with Mexico."

To assess the effects of each treatment while controlling for each subject's partisanship and other demographic characteristics, we again constructed a statistical model.[43] Figure 3.6 illustrates each congressional criticism treatment's effect on the likelihood of the median independent respondent supporting Trump's unilateral efforts to start building the wall. Our model estimates that both treatments decreased support for Trump. However, the effects of both treatments are substantively small and not statistically significant. Constitutional objections decreased the median independent's likelihood of supporting Trump by only 3%, and the policy objections reduced the likelihood of support by only 5%. Moreover, although consistent with all the prior experiments from the Obama era, the small negative effects may be spurious and the result of random chance.

Syrian Strikes

To explore the question further, in April of 2017 we fielded a second experiment in a nationally representative survey. Rather than examining an issue like the border wall—which was perhaps the centerpiece of Trump's year-long quest for the presidency and on which opinions may have hardened—this experiment examined President Trump's unilateral response to a foreign crisis: his decision to launch a series of missile strikes against Syrian regime targets in response to president Bashar al-Assad's use of chemical weapons against civilians.

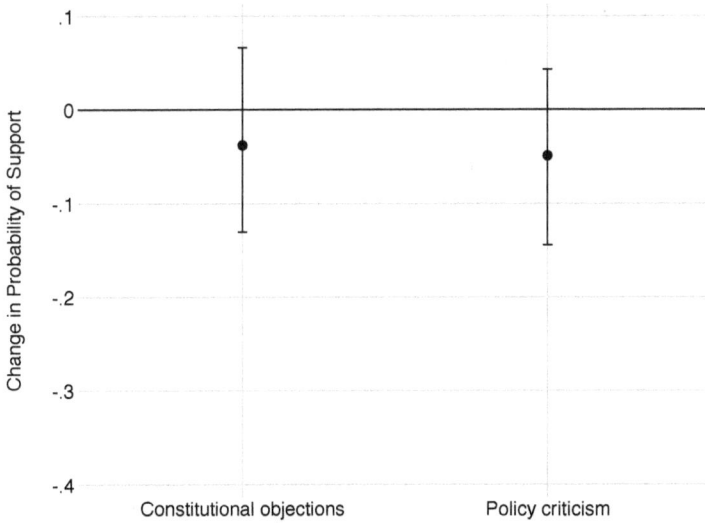

Figure 3.6. Limited congressional influence on support
for Trump's order to build the border wall
Note: Each dot presents the estimated change in the probability of the median
independent respondent supporting the president's unilateral action. I-bars around each
point estimate present 95% confidence intervals obtained from simulations.

Structurally, the Syrian Strikes Experiment followed the same pattern as the Border Wall Experiment. First, all subjects received the same prompt: "As you may know, President Donald Trump has unilaterally launched a series of missile strikes against Syrian forces in retaliation for the Syrian government's use of chemical weapons against civilians." Then subjects were randomly assigned to one of three experimental groups. Those in the control group received no further information. Subjects in the constitutional objections treatment received an additional prompt that was substantively identical to that used in our earlier experiments examining support for President Obama's unilateral strikes against ISIS: "Many members of Congress from both parties, however, oppose the President's decision. They argue that President Trump has overstepped his constitutional authority and that military action requires authorization from Congress." Finally, subjects in the policy criticism treatment were told, "Many members of Congress from both parties, however, oppose the President's decision. They argue that the missile strikes could deepen American's military involvement in the region." All subjects were then asked whether they supported or opposed President Trump's decision "to unilaterally launch missile strikes against Syria."

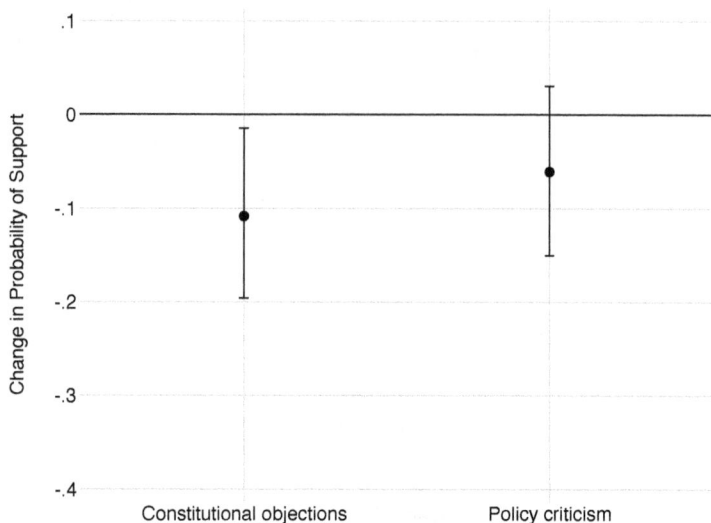

Figure 3.7. Congressional challenges to Trump's unilateral strikes against Syria

Note: Each dot presents the estimated change in the probability of the median
independent respondent supporting the president's unilateral action. I-bars around each
point estimate present 95% confidence intervals obtained from simulations.

A statistical model allowed us to assess the effects of the two treatments while controlling for partisanship and other demographic factors.[44] As shown in figure 3.7, the constitutional objections treatment significantly reduced the likelihood of the median independent respondent supporting Trump's decision to unilaterally retaliate against Syria by 11%. Congressional policy criticism also eroded support for the president's unilateral response. Our model estimates that this treatment decreased the probability of the median independent backing Trump by approximately 8%.[45] Interestingly, these effects are significantly smaller than those observed in the experiments examining Congress's ability to erode support for President Obama's unilateral strikes against ISIS. However, they do show that congressional criticism can decrease public support for presidential unilateralism, even in the honeymoon period when presidents are supposed to enjoy significant advantages.

Making Sense of the Differences

What might explain Congress's greater influence over Americans' support for Trump's unilateral Syria strikes than for his executive order to begin preparations for the border wall? One possibility is that by March

2017, public opinion had simply calcified concerning the latter policy issue. Most Americans lack even basic knowledge of, let alone information about, most of these matters. Trump's border wall may be an exception to this general rule, however. Few issues—or perhaps more accurately, symbols—have been more visible and salient in contemporary politics. Trump launched his campaign in June 2015 with incendiary words highlighting the threat posed by immigration, and he offered a clear solution to protect America from this danger:

> When Mexico sends its people, they're not sending their best. They're not sending you. They're not sending you. They're sending people that have lots of problems, and they're bringing those problems with us [sic]. They're bringing drugs. They're bringing crime. They're rapists. And some, I assume, are good people. . . .
>
> I would build a great wall, and nobody builds walls better than me, believe me, and I'll build them very inexpensively, I will build a great, great wall on our southern border. And I will have Mexico pay for that wall.
>
> Mark my words.[46]

The wall was a centerpiece of Trump's campaign from its very inception, and it remained his most well-known and clearly articulated policy proposal throughout the campaign. Indeed, chants of "build a wall" became routine features of Trump rallies throughout both the primary and general election campaigns.[47] As a result, most Americans may simply have already made up their minds about the wall. If so, then a modest, one-time treatment informing subjects about congressional views on Trump's executive order would be unlikely to hold much sway.

Another difference between the two issues is the base level of support for each. Whereas 63% of subjects in the control group backed Trump's decision to unilaterally launch a series of missile strikes against Syria in retaliation for its use of chemical weapons, just 45% in the control group backed his executive order to build the border wall. Within months of taking office, Donald Trump became the most polarizing president in the history of American polling. While disapproval of the administration has steadily crept up into the mid-50s, Trump continues to enjoy almost unshakeable support from about 35 to 40% of the public—even in the face of a litany of scandals ranging from potential obstruction of justice in the investigation of Russian interference in the 2016 presidential election, to charges of ubiquitous conflicts of interest, to evidence of illegal hush-money payments to a porn star. Because support for Trump's border wall order was so low in the baseline category, the Border Wall Experiment may be evidence of a floor effect. Our best estimate is that congressional opposition to the action decreased support for the wall by roughly 5% from the control; however, given contemporary realities, support for Trump on most issues is unlikely to fall far below the mid- to upper 30s. By contrast, should President Trump take unilateral action that could potentially appeal to a broader swath of the public, the evidence suggests that congressional pushback could significantly erode such support.

CONCLUSION

The conventional wisdom among pundits and scholars alike holds that Congress exercises little constraint on the unilateral presidency. All recent presidents have exploited the presidency's unilateral powers to effect significant changes in public policy that they never would have succeeded in getting from Congress. In only the rarest of cases has Congress successfully enacted legislation to strike down the president's action and restore the status quo. While this correctly captures the significant limits on Congress's legislative power, it overlooks the more informal but nonetheless potentially potent constraint that Congress may exert over the unilateral presidency by mobilizing public opinion against the White House.

When they are deciding whether to take unilateral action, presidents' strategic calculations involve more than estimating the likelihood of Congress enacting legislation over their veto in order to undo an executive action or the probability of the federal courts striking it down. Presidents must also consider how the political costs of unilateral action in one sphere may undermine their capacity to pursue other elements of their agendas in the future. The magnitude of these political costs is significantly shaped by the response of other actors, particularly in Congress, to executive action. Although Congress can rarely overcome the institutional barriers that limit its ability to overturn a unilateral action legislatively, our experiments demonstrate that its members retain an important capacity to increase the political costs of acting unilaterally by mobilizing public opinion against the president and executive action.

Across a diverse range of policy areas in both the foreign and the domestic realms, our experiments suggest that the political costs generated by congressional challenges to executive action on both constitutional and policy grounds may be substantial. Members of Congress enjoy multiple opportunities to voice their displeasure with administration policies and keep charges of presidential abuse of power or reckless policy decisions in the public limelight. Oversight hearings, formal investigations of executive branch misconduct, floor fights over legislation crafted not to pass but to embarrass the president, and appearances on the Sunday talk shows—all afford legislators opportunities to provide the media with that which their norms deem newsworthy: political conflict in Washington.[48] And when they use these tools to challenge unilateral executive action in the public sphere, our experiments consistently show that congressional criticism can erode popular support for the president and his actions.

APPENDIX TO CHAPTER 3

Throughout the chapter, we employ a series of graphics to illustrate the effects of our experimental treatments on the opinions of the median independent respondent. These estimates are derived from logistic regression models that model support for the president's unilateral action as a function of the experimental treatment variables and a series of demographic control variables. The models used to produce these figures are presented in appendix tables 3.1–3.7 below. For each case, the relevant table presents a pair of model specifications, the first without and the second with demographic control variables. All the figures from the chapter are produced from the relevant models with demographic controls and illustrate the estimated effect of each experimental treatment on the median independent respondent.

In two of the appendix tables, we include additional specifications to examine factors that might moderate the effects of our treatments on support for unilateral action. In model 3 of appendix table 3.1, we examine whether the effect of our congressional criticism treatments is moderated by a subject's level of political knowledge and find little evidence of any moderating influence of political sophistication. In model 3 of appendix table 3.3, we examine whether the strictly partisan congressional criticism treatments had differential effects on Democrats and Republicans in our sample. While the coefficients on the interactions are in the expected direction, neither are statistically significant.

APPENDIX TABLE 3.1. Constitutional objections vs. policy criticisms, Clean Power Plan

	(1)	(2)	(3)
Constitutional objections	−0.10	−0.66**	−0.90
	(0.16)	(0.23)	(0.53)
Policy criticism	−0.39*	−0.78**	−1.39**
	(0.16)	(0.24)	(0.52)
Republican		−0.79**	−0.71**
		(0.24)	(0.24)
Democrat		0.81**	0.88**
		(0.27)	(0.28)
Male		−0.40*	−0.34
		(0.19)	(0.20)
Education		−0.04	−0.00
		(0.07)	(0.07)
Age		−0.02**	−0.02**
		(0.01)	(0.01)
White		−0.02	−0.01
		(0.24)	(0.24)
Support action on global warming		2.03**	2.02**
		(0.20)	(0.20)
Presidential approval		1.44**	1.41**
		(0.26)	(0.26)
Political knowledge			−0.16
			(0.08)
Policy criticism × knowledge			0.17
			(0.11)
Constitutional objections × knowledge			0.07
			(0.11)
Constant	0.73**	0.90	1.12
	(0.12)	(0.49)	(0.58)
Observations	996	990	990

Note: Models are logistic regressions. Robust standard errors are in parentheses. All significance tests are two-tailed.

*$p < 0.05$

**$p < 0.01$

APPENDIX TABLE 3.2. Effect of constitutional objections in foreign and domestic policy

	(1) Loans	(2) Loans	(3) ISIS	(4) ISIS
Constitutional objections	−0.43* (0.19)	−0.70** (0.22)	−1.03** (0.19)	−1.02** (0.20)
Republican		−0.85** (0.27)		−0.04 (0.27)
Democrat		1.50** (0.29)		0.99** (0.27)
Male		−0.17 (0.22)		0.28 (0.20)
Education		0.03 (0.07)		0.08 (0.07)
Age		−0.02** (0.01)		0.02** (0.01)
White		−0.33 (0.26)		−0.03 (0.24)
Constant	0.75** (0.14)	1.96** (0.46)	1.21** (0.15)	−0.51 (0.45)
Observations	477	477	523	523

Note: Models are logistic regressions. Robust standard errors are in parentheses. All significance tests are two-tailed.

*$p < 0.05$
**$p < 0.01$

APPENDIX TABLE 3.3. Effect of purely partisan congressional criticism on support for Clean Power Plan

	(1)	(2)	(3)
Republican criticism	−0.57**	−1.00**	−1.17**
	(0.16)	(0.20)	(0.25)
Republican criticism × Democrat			0.41
			(0.48)
Democratic criticism	−0.70**	−0.90**	−0.76**
	(0.16)	(0.21)	(0.23)
Democratic criticism × Democrat			−0.40
			(0.46)
Republican		−1.19**	−1.20**
		(0.20)	(0.20)
Democrat		2.12**	2.13**
		(0.21)	(0.38)
Male		−0.18	−0.17
		(0.16)	(0.16)
Education		0.04	0.05
		(0.06)	(0.06)
Age		−0.02**	−0.02**
		(0.00)	(0.00)
White		−0.20	−0.20
		(0.20)	(0.20)
Constant	0.78**	1.55**	1.54**
	(0.11)	(0.36)	(0.37)
Observations	1,000	1,000	1,000

Note: Models are logistic regressions. Robust standard errors are in parentheses. All significance tests are two-tailed.

*$p < 0.05$

**$p < 0.01$

APPENDIX TABLE 3.4. Relative influence of Congress vs. other
actors on support for ISIS strikes

	(1)	(2)
Congress	−0.55*	−0.58*
	(0.24)	(0.25)
Law professors	−0.35	−0.44
	(0.24)	(0.25)
Media pundits	−0.35	−0.43
	(0.24)	(0.25)
Congress expanded	−0.71**	−0.84**
	(0.23)	(0.25)
Democrat		0.85**
		(0.19)
Republican		0.25
		(0.20)
Education		0.04
		(0.05)
Age		0.03**
		(0.00)
White		−0.46**
		(0.18)
Male		−0.07
		(0.15)
Constant	1.39**	−0.10
	(0.18)	(0.35)
Observations	1,000	1,000

Note: Models are logistic regressions. Robust standard errors are in parentheses. All
significance tests are two-tailed.
*$p < 0.05$
**$p < 0.01$

APPENDIX TABLE 3.5. Effect of congressional challenge even if no policy change without unilateral action

	(1)	(2)
Congressional challenge	−0.25	−0.46*
	(0.16)	(0.22)
Congressional challenge + rebuttal	−0.23	−0.50*
	(0.17)	(0.22)
Republican		−1.77**
		(0.20)
Democrat		1.88**
		(0.26)
Male		−0.42*
		(0.18)
Education		0.05
		(0.06)
Age		−0.02**
		(0.01)
White		−0.53*
		(0.20)
Constant	0.84**	2.68**
	(0.12)	(0.39)
Observations	1,000	1,000

Note: Models are logistic regressions. Robust standard errors are in parentheses. All significance tests are two-tailed.
*$p < 0.05$
**$p < 0.01$

APPENDIX TABLE 3.6. Effect of constitutional objections and policy criticisms on support for Trump's efforts to build border wall

	(1)	(2)
Constitutional challenge	−0.05	−0.16
	(0.16)	(0.20)
Policy criticism	−0.03	−0.20
	(0.16)	(0.19)
Republican		1.49**
		(0.21)
Democrat		−1.54**
		(0.19)
Male		0.47**
		(0.16)
Age		0.01*
		(0.00)
Education		−0.16**
		(0.06)
White		0.28
		(0.19)
Constant	−0.20	−0.28
	(0.11)	(0.33)
Observations	1,000	1,000

Note: Models are logistic regressions. Robust standard errors are in parentheses. All significance tests are two-tailed.

*$p < 0.05$

**$p < 0.01$

APPENDIX TABLE 3.7. Effect of constitutional objections and policy criticisms on support for Trump's unilateral strikes against Syria

	(1)	(2)
Constitutional challenge	−0.45**	−0.45*
	(0.16)	(0.19)
Policy criticism	−0.32*	−0.26
	(0.16)	(0.19)
Republican		1.98**
		(0.23)
Democrat		−0.61**
		(0.17)
Male		0.39*
		(0.15)
Age		0.03**
		(0.00)
Education		−0.17**
		(0.05)
White		0.31
		(0.17)
Constant	0.56**	−0.84**
	(0.11)	(0.32)
Observations	999	999

Note: Models are logistic regressions. Robust standard errors are in parentheses. All significance tests are two-tailed.
*$p < 0.05$
**$p < 0.01$

CHAPTER FOUR

Rethinking the Role of the Courts

The unilateral politics literature has always acknowledged that presidential unilateral power is only as great as other branches of the federal government allow it to be.[1] But the conventional wisdom asserts that the checks placed on the unilateral president are quite weak. Much of the literature has focused on Congress and found it lacking. Even if presidential critics managed to overcome legislative inertia and pass a bill overturning an executive action through both chambers of Congress, the presidential veto pen all but ensures that such efforts will rarely if ever become law.

But what of the courts? Historically, federal courts have played an important role in both legitimizing and policing the exercise of unilateral power. Although they are found nowhere in the constitutional text, the judiciary established that unilateral actions, when taken pursuant to proper constitutional or statutory authority, have the full force of law.[2] Moreover, courts retain the capacity to strike down unilateral actions that exceed the president's inherent authority or that are delegated to the administration by statute. When endeavoring to check presidential overreach, courts enjoy some significant advantages. Justices' life tenure provides considerable insulation from political pressures. Perhaps more important, many of the institutional barriers that cripple congressional attempts to overturn unilateral action are either less significant or irrelevant for the judiciary. For example, only a simple majority is needed to strike down a unilateral action as exceeding delegated or inherent constitutional authority, and collective action dilemmas and transaction costs are also either much lower or largely irrelevant. However, as Alexander Hamilton noted in *Federalist 78*, the courts have no independent means of enforcement. Should the courts strike down a presidential unilateral action, they must rely on the very actor they have just ruled against to implement their ruling.

Precisely because they lack both the purse and the sword, for most of American history the courts have repeatedly and rationally avoided direct confrontations with the executive branch over its exercise of unilateral power.[3] Indeed, the most comprehensive empirical assessment of the strength of the judicial check on the unilateral president paints a dour picture. Between 1942 and 1998, presidents issued more than 4,040 executive orders. Of these, only eighty-three were ever challenged in federal courts. And in these cases, presidents emerged victorious more than 80% of the time.[4]

Moreover, even some of the rare presidential defeats may have paradoxically bolstered presidential power in the long term. Consider, for example, one of the most famous judicial rebukes of the unilateral executive. In *Youngstown v. Sawyer*, the Supreme Court struck down president Harry Truman's executive order authorizing the seizure of the steel mills to resolve a labor management dispute that threatened production during the Korean War. The most remembered and oft-cited part of the opinion is justice Robert Jackson's concurrence, in which he proposes a three-pronged test for assessing the constitutionality of presidential actions. Presidential power is at its zenith when the president acts pursuant both to his inherent Article II power and to specific legislative authority delegated by Congress. Truman's executive order, however, fell into the lowest zone of the typology. He relied primarily on his inherent Article II powers, and the measure that he took—nationalizing private property—was explicitly considered and then rejected by Congress as it drafted the Taft-Hartley Act (which it passed over Truman's veto). When the president's actions directly conflict with statutory intent, presidential power is at its nadir. Yet between these poles, Jackson argued, is a "zone of twilight" in which presidents act pursuant to their own executive authority and Congress is silent. In such cases—which are exceedingly common given Congress's inability to anticipate every possibility and write detailed legislation authorizing some courses of action and explicitly excluding others—courts have largely deferred to the president.[5] In summarizing the feeble nature of the judicial constraint, Eric Posner and Adrian Vermeule provocatively argue that "we live in a regime of executive-centered government, in an age after the separation of powers, and the legally constrained executive is now a historical curiosity."[6]

But is the judicial check on presidential unilateralism as weak as it seems? We tackle this question in two ways. First, we review a series of important judicial defeats suffered by the Bush, Obama, and Trump administrations at the hands of federal courts at various levels. In some cases, federal courts ruled directly against the president and struck down the executive action as exceeding the president's constitutional or statutory authority. In other cases, courts did not explicitly determine that the actions were unconstitutional or in violation of statutes. Rather, they temporarily delayed the implementation of executive actions. These delays, however, effectively killed the presidential initiatives by blocking their implementation until a switch in partisan control of the White House. This largely descriptive analysis suggests an increasingly assertive judiciary in the face of the dramatic expansion of presidential unilateral power after 9/11.

But this increased activism is not the only way that courts may exercise a stronger check on the unilateral president than often supposed. While most executive actions go unchallenged in federal courts, the string of high-profile judicial defeats suffered by recent administrations has had another, broader effect: it has injected public commentary about the likelihood of judicial challenges to bold executive action into the larger political debate concerning unilateral power. In recent years, administration critics, from members of Congress to outside interest groups to specialized legal media commentators, have been quick to raise the possibility that executive actions will be struck down by federal courts. Even raising the specter of judicial defeat—a threat made more credible by a series of recent high-profile administration losses before the bench—may be enough to turn public opinion against the president and raise the political costs of unilateral action.

In sum, the judicial constraint on presidential unilateralism, like the legislative constraint, may be stronger than previously acknowledged. But it, too, may be exerted at least partially through more informal means.

AN INCREASINGLY ASSERTIVE JUDICIARY

Courts have long gone to great lengths to avoid direct confrontations with the executive branch. *Marbury v. Madison* is most often remembered for establishing the principle of judicial review. Yet the strategic motivation behind Chief Justice Marshall's decision to strike down section 13 of the Judiciary Act of 1789 was to avoid a direct confrontation with the Jefferson administration, which had refused to deliver commissions to William Marbury and other Federalist judges appointed by the outgoing president, John Adams.[7] The landmark 1803 case also laid the groundwork for the political questions doctrine, which courts have used repeatedly to avoid ruling on disputes over alleged abuses of executive power.[8]

Yet there is plenty of evidence in recent years that the courts have grown increasingly assertive in checking the unilateral president, in both the foreign and the domestic spheres.[9] While the Supreme Court refrained from confronting broad assertions of unilateral presidential power in the immediate aftermath of 9/11, beginning with *Hamdi v. Rumsfeld* and justice Sandra Day O'Connor's declaration that a state of war "is not a blank check for the President when it comes to the rights of the nation's citizens," the court issued a string of rulings striking down key elements of the George W. Bush administration's conduct of the war on terror. The court in *Hamdi* ruled that the administration could not hold US citizens as enemy combatants and deny them due process and habeas corpus rights. It struck down the military tribunals unilaterally created by the president to try terror suspects as in violation of both the Uniform Code of Military Justice and the Geneva Conventions. And in *Boumediene v. Bush*, the court ruled that all detainees at the terrorist detention facility at Guantanamo Bay, Cuba, regardless of their nationality, were guaranteed habeas corpus rights.

Under president Barack Obama, federal courts were perhaps even more aggressive in thwarting major unilateral initiatives. In the national security realm, several court rulings struck blows against the Obama administration's continuation and expansion of Bush-era electronic surveillance plans. In *Klayman v. Obama*, federal district court judge Richard Leon labeled the National Security Agency's metadata collection program "almost Orwellian," and held that it violated the Fourth Amendment. In 2015, the Second Circuit Court of Appeals ruled in *ACLU v. Clapper* that the implementation of the program exceeded the authority authorized by Congress under the Patriot Act.

Perhaps even more important, court rulings temporarily blocked and ultimately scuttled several of President Obama's most consequential unilateral initiatives in domestic policy. In 2005, the Supreme Court ruled in *Massachusetts v. EPA* that greenhouse gases, including carbon dioxide, are pollutants subject to regulation under the Clean Air Act. This gave the Environmental Protection Agency the authority—and in the assessment of many, the obligation—to regulate carbon dioxide emissions. Under President Bush, the EPA dragged its feet in implementing the ruling. Shortly after taking office, President Obama directed the EPA to begin the process of tightening regulations on greenhouse gas emissions. The first set of EPA efforts strengthened regulations on emissions by cars, trucks, and some industrial sources. These regulations were challenged in court, but mostly upheld in *Utility Air Regulatory Group v. EPA*. However, to make the much more dramatic cuts in greenhouse gas emissions most scientists believe are necessary to address climate change, on August 3, 2015, President Obama announced the Clean Power Plan, a bold set of new regulations that aimed to reduce carbon dioxide emissions from power plants by 32% below 2005 levels by 2030.

The administration anticipated legal challenges, and when crafting the regulations it went to considerable lengths to insulate the plan from critics.[10] Despite these efforts, twenty-seven states filed suit in federal court to block the plan from going into effect. In February 2016, the Supreme Court in a 5–4 decision ordered a temporary stay on the plan's implementation until the legal challenges were resolved. This ruling—although technically not a reversal of the president's executive action—ensured that the Clean Power Plan would not take effect until after President Obama had left office. This, coupled with Donald Trump's surprise victory in the November elections, effectively killed the plan, which initially promised to be perhaps the central component of Obama's environmental legacy. On March 28, 2017, President Trump signed an executive order directing the EPA to review the Clean Power Plan with an eye toward dismantling it before it ever takes effect.

The courts also struck a devastating blow to President Obama's efforts to unilaterally shield millions of undocumented immigrants from deportation. In 2012, after repeated failures to enact the DREAM Act (Development, Relief, and Education for Alien Minors Act), Obama announced the Deferred Action for Childhood Arrivals program, or DACA. While DACA did not provide a pathway to citizenship, it did unilaterally grant up to 1.7 million undocumented immigrants who entered the United States as children a two-year reprieve from deportation, and it allowed eligible youth to secure work permits. Following DACA, Obama initially resisted calls for even more robust executive action to liberalize immigration enforcement, repeatedly stating that he lacked the constitutional authority to go further. However, after the 2014 midterms, which all but extinguished any hope for legislative action in the remainder of his term, the president announced a series of executive actions that expanded DACA eligibility and created a new initiative, Deferred Action for Parents of Americans and Lawful Permanent Residents (DAPA). The 2014 actions were estimated to apply to over 4.9 million undocumented immigrants.

Opponents of the immigration action filed suit in federal court to block the plan's implementation. A federal district court judge issued a preliminary injunction, and the Fifth Circuit rejected the Obama administration's request for a stay in March 2015.[11] In November 2015, the circuit court affirmed the injunction and ordered that the case go to trial. The Obama administration appealed to the Supreme Court, which in a 4–4 decision in *United States v. Texas* affirmed the lower court's ruling, leaving the injunction in place. The continued vacancy of justice Antonin Scalia's position on the high court ensured that the legal challenges to DAPA were not resolved before President Obama left office. As a result, the courts effectively blocked what would have been the most important immigration policy accomplishment of his administration. Moreover, they did this without ever having to affirmatively strike down President Obama's action as unconstitutional. Simply by blocking DAPA's implementation until after the presidential election, the courts essentially killed the program by allowing the incoming Trump administration to preclude it from going into effect. As we discuss in the context of DACA in the following chapter, Trump's task could have been much harder had he been forced to remove recently granted legal protections rather than simply scrapping the plan before it went into operation.

While the Affordable Care Act (ACA) itself has mostly survived several legal challenges to its constitutionality (at least as of 2019), President Obama's signature achievement suffered a significant blow from the courts in the form of a legal challenge to his unilateral implementation of the act. The ACA provided for cost-sharing reduction subsidies that would allow insurers to reduce out-of-pocket costs for low-income Americans by recouping many of the costs in the form of a rebate from the federal government. However, the statute required that the funds for this rebate be appropriated by Congress. In 2014, President Obama requested $4 billion to cover these subsidies, and Congress refused to appropriate the funds. Nevertheless, to fund the rebates the Obama administration took the requisite money from the larger pool that supports premium subsidies. House Speaker John Boehner filed suit in federal court alleging that the president's maneuver was unconstitutional. In May 2016, federal district court judge Rosemary Collyer agreed. In *United States House of Representatives v. Burwell*, Collyer ruled that the Obama administration had overstepped its authority in paying the reimbursement without a congressional appropriation.

In its waning days, the Obama administration appealed the district court ruling, and President Trump reluctantly agreed to continue the subsidy payments for the beginning of his term. But the marked uncertainty over the subsidies and whether they would continue played a major role in several large insurers' decision to exit the exchange marketplace in 2017. Even before President Trump ultimately rescinded Obama's order in October 2017 and stopped making the payments, the uncertainty created by the lower court decision contributed greatly to critics' arguments that the Affordable Care Act was mired in a "death spiral."[12]

Finally, despite the Republican triumph in the 2016 elections, President Obama stood to enjoy one final policy victory in the waning days of his administration through a Department of Labor rule that would extend overtime pay to more than 4 million salaried employees. But on November 21, just nine days before the rule went into effect, district court judge and Obama appointee Amos Mazzant struck down the rule as executive overreach and issued a nationwide injunction against its implementation. With the incoming Trump administration all but certain to drop the appeal, the district court ruling doomed President Obama's boldest action to boost wages.[13] Of course, even without that ruling, President Trump could have endeavored to roll back the regulation after he took office; but the judicial defeat for Obama spared the Trump administration from having to embark on a lengthy process to undo an existing regulation.

This rising tide of increasingly assertive judicial pushback to presidential unilateralism has continued and even accelerated in the early days of the Trump presidency. The transition of presidential power from one party to the next usually produces a flurry of unilateral action, and the fledgling Trump administration is no exception. What is unique is that it took fewer than ten days for President Trump to suffer his first defeat in the federal courts over his executive order banning citizens of seven Islamic countries from entering the United States. As we review more extensively in the following chapter, Trump's first year in office yielded an unprecedented string of judicial defeats. In a series of rulings, federal courts struck down or blocked the implementation of a wide range of his executive actions, including successive travel bans; a ban on transgender Americans serving in the military; an amendment to the implementation of the Affordable Care Act exempting certain employers from the requirement to provide contraceptive coverage; a suspension of the Obama-era rule on emission standards for oil and gas wells; a proclamation to seriously curtail the rights of asylum seekers; and various efforts to deny federal funding to "sanctuary cities."

While the volume and intensity of judicial pushback are impressive and perhaps even unprecedented, this renewed activism may have consequences reaching far beyond the specific defeats suffered by contemporary presidents in the courtroom. This record of recent defeats has broadened the public conversation over a wider range of executive actions to include heated debates about their legality and intense speculation about potential judicial challenges.

AN INFORMAL JUDICIAL CONSTRAINT

The heightened court activity suggests that the formal judicial constraint on wayward unilateralism may be stronger than often believed. It merits mention, though, that simply extending prior research showing the paucity of judicial challenges to executive orders would miss most of the examples cited previously for two reasons. First, most of these high-profile unilateral actions were products not of executive orders but of a range of alternate unilateral tools. Second, many of the key judicial decisions were not outright presidential defeats—rather, they were temporary stays on the implementation of the unilateral action. Many of these in the final months of the Obama presidency prevented policies from taking effect before Trump took office, allowing the Republican successor to more easily block them. More generally, delay in and of itself can be costly, as it allows opposition to mobilize and trigger more political problems for the president.

Nevertheless, we must be wary of pushing the argument too far. Despite the surge in judicial pushback against executive action, most presidential unilateral initiatives are never successfully challenged in court. Yet heightened court activity in recent administrations suggests another, more informal constraint on presidential unilateralism: public speculation about judicial challenges and the constitutionality of presidential actions may significantly erode public support for a unilateral initiative. Previous scholarship has argued that courts respond to public opinion when ruling on the legality of unilateral action; courts are significantly more likely to rule against an unpopular president than one who enjoys a strong reservoir of popular support.[14] But the relationship between judicial action and public opinion may be more complicated than previously supposed. Even the specter of judicial action may decrease support for the president and unilateral policy initiatives. In turn, such an erosion of public support could set the stage for future judicial activism.

The experiments of the preceding chapter demonstrate the potential power of members of Congress to shape public perceptions of unilateral action. Congressional opponents of executive directives routinely challenge the unilateral president in the public sphere.[15] These challenges, on both policy and constitutional grounds, significantly erode support for presidential unilateralism. As a result, members of Congress can raise the political costs of unilateral action for the president—even when they cannot formally block it—by mobilizing public opinion against executive action.

But can judicial action—or even the mere threat of it—similarly sway public sentiment? There are reasons to be skeptical. Most important, in stark contrast to members of Congress, sitting judges almost never offer opinions publicly on the constitutionality of executive actions except when deciding a case pending before them. Nevertheless, other political and media actors routinely speculate that the courts will strike down a unilateral initiative as unconstitutional. For example, in urging the nation's governors to refuse to submit state-level proposals addressing how they would comply with the Clean Power Plan, Senate Majority Leader Mitch McConnell invoked Harvard law professor Laurence Tribe, noting that the liberal legal scholar judged the plan "constitutionally reckless." McConnell argued that if governors carefully examined the plan in detail, they would agree with him that "the EPA's proposal goes far beyond its legal authority and that the courts are likely to strike it down."[16]

For media outlets, conflict in Washington sells product and generates ratings.[17] As the continued popularity of courtroom dramas attests, coverage of high-stakes legal battles holds great appeal in newsrooms for its ratings-boosting potential. Accordingly, it is unsurprising that many media pundits love to speculate about whether courts will hear challenges to the constitutionality of high-profile unilateral actions and how they will rule if they do. When the federal courts at any level take up a case concerning the constitutionality of an executive action, prognosticating journalists are eager to divine the outcome for the public. For example, when the Second Circuit Court of Appeals heard oral arguments on a legal challenge to the National Security Agency's metadata collection program, *Politico* ran with the lede "Appeals Court Chilly to Feds' Argument for NSA Surveillance Program."[18] Even the announcement that the courts will consider a challenge to a presidential order can trigger an avalanche of news coverage and speculation concerning the order's constitutionality. Following the declaration that the Supreme Court would hear a challenge to the constitutionality of President Obama's immigration actions, George Will penned an op-ed in the *Washington Post* in which he openly expressed what he was pining for: "Will the Supreme Court Strike Back at Obama's Overreach?"[19] Similarly, the summer of 2017 was replete with newspaper articles and TV interviews in which legal experts and journalists intensely speculated about whether and how the Supreme Court would resolve the legal battle over President Trump's executive order banning citizens of seven predominantly Muslim countries from entering the United States.

On still other occasions, the courts need not even hear a case to spark media speculation that the judiciary will ultimately strike down a unilateral initiative as unconstitutional.[20] For example, before the ink had dried on President Obama's modest executive actions to tighten the enforcement of federal gun laws, Fox News ran articles by its in-house legal analyst, former New Jersey Superior Court judge Andrew Napolitano, arguing why Obama's actions failed to pass constitutional muster and why the Supreme Court was set to strike them down.[21] In the same way, less than a week into the new Trump administration, Reuters ran an article discussing potential legal challenges to President Trump's executive order targeting "sanctuary cities" that refused to share information on illegal immigrants with federal authorities.[22] And following President Trump's declaration of a national emergency to build the border wall by executive fiat in 2019, Judge Napolitano of Fox News again minced few words in his column "Trump's Brazen, Unconstitutional Overreach."[23]

When the media and other political actors raise the possibility that the courts will strike down unilateral action as unconstitutional, does the specter of judicial intervention have any influence on public opinion? There are at least two reasons to suspect that such speculation may indeed be influential. First, while the public may not automatically oppose unilateral action because it violates deeply held constitutional mores, many Americans are responsive to arguments that unilateralism risks overstepping the legal and constitutional limits on presidential power. The experiments in chapter 3 show that congressional criticism of executive action on constitutional grounds—even when it was devoid of any policy critique—significantly decreased public support for unilateral action. Raising the possibility of a judicial challenge to an executive action on legal grounds might similarly decrease public support for the president.

Second, discussion of a judicial challenge to unilateral action may be particularly influential because of broad public respect for the judicial system itself. Judicial politics scholars have long demonstrated empirically that the judiciary enjoys a depth and breadth of popular legitimacy that is unequaled by other branches of government.[24] This may make the judiciary a particularly influential cue giver. The Supreme Court, in particular, is held in such high esteem because it is seen as above the rough and tumble of everyday politics. Indeed, throughout history the court has taken various steps to reinforce this perception with various symbols (judicial robes, its meeting place in a veritable Greek temple, etc.) that help differentiate it from the executive and the legislative branches.[25] Its unique position was evident recently when the editorial boards of the *New York Times* and the *Washington Post* took umbrage with justice Ruth Bader Ginsburg's public criticism of the presumptive Republican presidential nominee, Donald Trump. Although there is no ethics code that prevents Supreme Court justices from speaking about candidates or elections, legal ethics experts and related media coverage pushed Ginsburg to express regret for publicly expressing her political opinion. Ginsburg quickly apologized: "Judges should avoid commenting on a candidate for public office. In the future I will be more circumspect."[26] Because the judiciary remains the most trusted and respected branch of government, even speculation that the courts might strike down a unilateral action may significantly erode public support for the president.

AN EXPERIMENTAL APPROACH

To examine whether speculation about judicial challenges can erode public support for presidential unilateralism, we embedded three experiments in a series of nationally representative surveys. The first pair of experiments examined public support for two of the most important unilateral actions of Barack Obama's presidency: the Clean Power Plan and the administration's efforts to shield millions of illegal aliens from prosecution and deportation. To ensure that any observed effects did not exclusively apply to the Obama presidency, we then conducted a third experiment in early 2017 examining the ability of speculation about potential judicial challenges to undermine public support for President Trump's efforts to roll back much of the Obama administration's legacy of environmental protection.

An experimental approach is important because it allows us to identify definitively the effects of institutional objections to executive action on public opinion. By contrast, relying on correlations between elite actions and shifts in publicly available polling data risks confusing who is leading whom. Although judges are frequently described as being insulated from public opinion (thereby reducing the prospects for reverse causality), research by William Howell finds that courts are much more likely to rule against unpopular presidents in cases involving unilateral action than they are when the president enjoys strong public support.[27] Randomized treatments allowed us to focus squarely on the effect of speculation about judicial challenges to unilateral action on public opinion.

Each experiment examined the dynamics of popular support for an actual executive action taken by the sitting president. This approach necessarily limited our ability to generalize to other issues and presidents. However, by focusing on a range of current policy issues across two administrations, one Democrat and one Republican, and by using treatments that employ language similar to that used by real political actors to express and defend their positions, we also sought to minimize concerns about external validity.

THE POWER OF THE COURT OVER PUBLIC OPINION

The first experiment tested our main hypothesis—that raising the specter of the Supreme Court striking down a unilateral action as unconstitutional will diminish public support for that action. To do so, we again examined public support for perhaps President Obama's most important executive initiative in the domestic sphere: the Clean Power Plan, which directed the EPA to regulate carbon dioxide emissions as a greenhouse gas. We chose the Clean Power Plan for three reasons. First, as discussed in chapter 3, the Clean Power Plan afforded a critical test of our argument, since it allowed us to examine whether Congress can erode public support for one of the most highly salient, consequential, and polarizing of President Obama's unilateral initiatives. The high salience and intense partisan polarization of public attitudes toward climate change policy in general and the Clean Power Plan in particular stacked the deck against finding treatment effects.[28] Many Americans already know where they stand on whether the government should more aggressively regulate emissions to combat global climate change. Cues anticipating judicial action should be more influential on issues where fewer Americans possess strong priors and public opinion is less calcified. Second, the experiments in the preceding chapter show that congressional criticism of the Clean Power Plan, on both policy and constitutional grounds, eroded support for Obama's initiative. Examining the same issue here allowed us to compare any observed effects for speculations about a judicial challenge with those observed in response to congressional criticism. Finally, in this context our treatment was highly externally valid. In the month before our experiment went into the field, a range of actors, including Harvard law professor Laurence Tribe and Senate Majority Leader Mitch McConnell, publicly argued that the courts were likely to strike down the Clean Power Plan as unconstitutional.[29]

We embedded the experiment in a nationally representative survey conducted in April 2015. All subjects received the following prompt, which was identical to that used in parallel experiments of chapter 3: "President Obama has directed the EPA to begin regulating carbon dioxide from coal power plants to reduce greenhouse gas emissions, combat climate change, and improve public health." Our experiment privileged the president's position by introducing his action and justification first. This reflects the actual advantage of the White House in setting the agenda and generating media coverage.

After learning of the president's position, respondents were randomly assigned to one of two experimental groups. Those in the control group received no further information. Those in the treatment group were provided a strong cue that the Supreme Court may oppose such an action: "Many legal experts warn that such an action could be struck down as unconstitutional by the Supreme Court as an overextension of presidential power. Regardless of the merits of the policy, the Supreme Court is likely to rule that such an action violates our constitutional system of checks and balances."

In some respects, our language—particularly in the final sentence stating that the Supreme Court is "likely" to overturn the executive action—made this a strong treatment. In the chapter's third experiment, we softened our language and said only that the court "could" rule against the president.[30] However, the stronger phrasing used here accords with the usage and claims of those seeking to raise the prospects of a judicial rebuke in the public consciousness. For example, in trying to rally opposition to the Clean Power Plan, McConnell wrote that "the courts are *likely* to strike it down." Similarly, in his *Wall Street Journal* op-ed, Tribe made repeated references to recent precedent to bolster his argument that the Clean Power Plan is unconstitutional and that the courts are *likely* to rule it so.[31] Further, when President Trump sent shock waves through the political system by declaring his support for an executive order that would end birthright citizenship for children of noncitizens, most media outlets featured stories questioning the constitutionality of the move. Much of this coverage openly opined that any such move would rest on shaky legal ground, with headlines such as CNBC's "Trump's Attack on Birthright Citizenship Will *Likely* Hit a Constitutional Dead End."[32]

All subjects in our experiment were asked to indicate their support for "President Obama taking unilateral action to reduce carbon dioxide emissions."[33] To assess the effects of the Supreme Court of the United States (SCOTUS) treatment on support for executive action, we estimated a statistical model. This allowed us to isolate the effect of receiving the speculation that the court might strike down the action as unconstitutional on support for Obama's unilateral action while controlling for several additional factors that might also affect public opinion. Most important, the model controlled for subjects' partisan affiliation and included a proxy for their policy preferences, a measure of whether they believe that government action is necessary to combat global warming. The model also controlled for gender, educational attainment, age, and race.[34]

Strongly consistent with our argument, the statistical model found that even raising the specter of a Supreme Court defeat for Obama significantly decreased public support for the president's unilateral push to implement the Clean Power Plan. Even after controlling for each subject's partisanship, the SCOTUS treatment sharply decreased support for the president. As shown in figure 4.1, the likely judicial challenge treatment decreased support for executive action by almost 20%. Whereas the median independent respondent in the control group had a 65% chance of supporting the Clean Power Plan, this fell to 47% when the respondent was told that the Supreme Court was likely to strike down the action as unconstitutional.

This large drop in support is strong evidence that even the possibility of judicial pushback can prove politically costly to the president. Indeed, the magnitude of this effect is even greater than that produced by con-

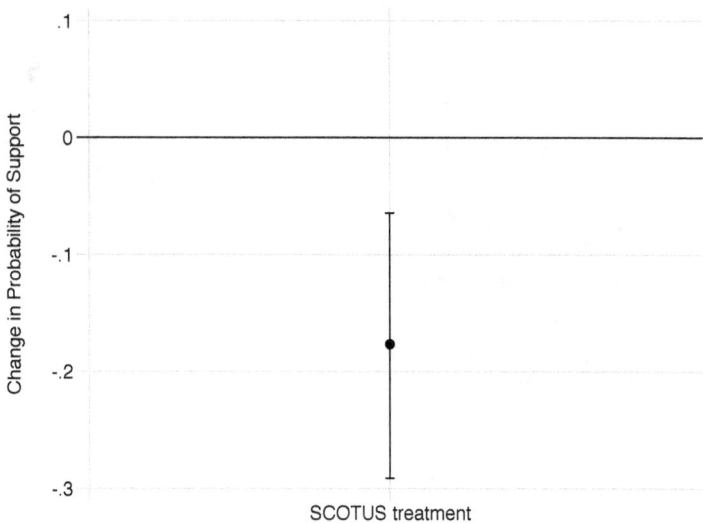

Figure 4.1. Effect of anticipated judicial challenge on support for Clean Power Plan
Note: The dot presents the estimated change in the probability of the median independent respondent supporting the president's unilateral action. I-bars around this point estimate present the 95% confidence interval obtained from simulations.

gressional criticism of the Clean Power Plan on constitutional grounds, observed in the experiments of chapter 3. Even in modern politics, where elites and the public are highly polarized, and even on a highly politicized issue like regulating carbon dioxide emissions, the public responds to cues speculating that the Supreme Court will rule against presidential unilateral action on constitutional grounds. Moreover, it is important to remember that this is the effect of a single, relatively modest cue concerning the likely objection of the Supreme Court to the president's action.[35]

THE IMPORTANCE OF JUDICIAL LEGITIMACY

We hypothesized that cues about the Supreme Court's likely response to a unilateral action would be influential with the public largely because the Court enjoys widespread popular legitimacy. However, while trust in the Supreme Court remains comparatively high in the aggregate, there is considerable variation in the court's perceived legitimacy across individual Americans.[36] Scholars have long shown that cues from "trusted" sources are more influential than identical cues from a source with which the receiver does not share preferences or attachments.[37] Cues from trusted sources are likely to be incorporated into the opinion formation process, while cues from untrusted sources are more likely to be resisted.[38] Thus, while speculation about a judicial rebuke should reduce support for unilateral action in the aggregate, its effects should be strongest among those Americans who hold the Supreme Court in high esteem.

To test this second, more nuanced hypothesis and to examine the influence of speculation about judicial challenges on support for unilateral action in another policy venue, we embedded a second experiment in the preelection wave of the 2014 Cooperative Congressional Election Study. Throughout the summer of 2014, Washington was abuzz with anticipation for a new round of executive actions to liberalize immigration enforcement and shield more illegal aliens from deportation. President Obama ultimately decided to postpone taking the controversial step until after the 2014 midterm elections. Against this backdrop, we constructed an experiment to examine whether informing subjects about speculation that the Supreme Court could overturn Obama's long-anticipated action would reduce public support for a unilateral course.

In important respects, the immigration issue represents perhaps an even more unlikely policy area in which to find evidence of treatment effects. Few Americans lack predispositions on which to base their assessments of immigration-related action. Immigration is one of the most polarizing issues in the contemporary political arena.[39] As a result, partisan cues may simply overwhelm any new information about the likely reaction of other elites, including the Supreme Court. Because public opinion on questions of immigration may already have calcified, the prospects for elite opinion leadership should be smaller here than on other issues on which public opinion is more fluid.

The experiment began by informing all subjects of the basic facts concerning President Obama's anticipated executive action on immigration, which the administration had deferred until after the 2014 midterm elections. All subjects read the following prompt: "Efforts at enacting comprehensive immigration reform have failed in Congress. As a result, President Obama is considering new executive action to give legal status to many undocumented immigrants, and to provide a pathway to citizenship for those who meet certain criteria." Subjects were then randomly assigned to one of two experimental groups. Those assigned to the control group received no additional information. Those assigned to the treatment group received speculation by legal experts that the Supreme Court might strike down the anticipated action as unconstitutional. These subjects were told, "Many legal experts warn that such an action could be struck down as unconstitutional by the Supreme Court as an overextension of presidential power. Regardless of the merits of the policy, the Supreme Court is likely to rule that such an action violates our constitutional system of checks and balances." All subjects were then asked the same question: "Would you support or oppose President Obama acting unilaterally to change the nation's immigration laws?"

Earlier in the survey, we included a series of questions to gauge the public's perception of the Supreme Court's legitimacy. We expected perceptions of judicial legitimacy to moderate the treatment effect: that is, the SCOTUS treatment should be more influential on the assessments of Americans who believe that the court is legitimate than on the judgments of those who question its institutional legitimacy.[40] To measure judicial legitimacy, we used several questions measuring diffuse support for the Supreme Court that are standard in the judicial politics literature.[41] From this battery, we divided our sample into two groups. Consistent with previous polling data showing that the court enjoys widespread legitimacy, 70% of our sample gave the court strong legitimacy ratings. However, 30% of our sample gave the court low legitimacy ratings.[42] We expected the SCOTUS treatment to resonate more firmly with the former group than the latter.

To estimate the effect of the SCOTUS treatment on support for Obama's

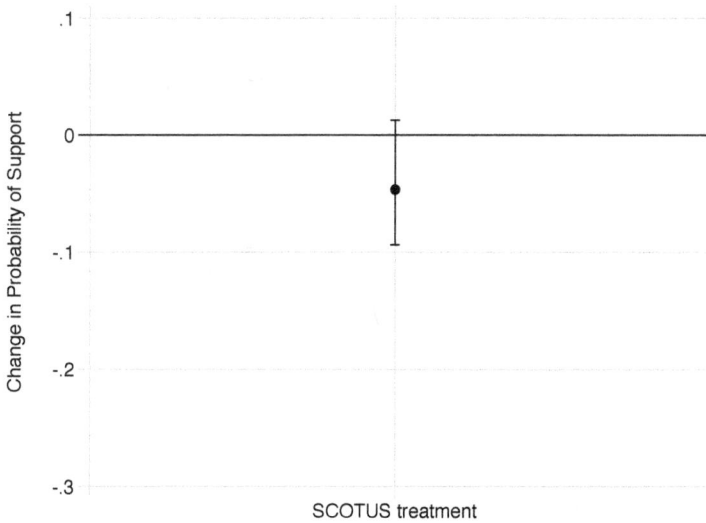

Figure 4.2. Effect of anticipated judicial challenge on support for immigration actions
Note: The dot presents the estimated change in the probability of the median independent
respondent supporting the president's unilateral action. I-bars around this point
estimate present the 95% confidence interval obtained from simulations.

immigration action while controlling for subjects' partisanship, approval
of Obama, and other demographic characteristics, we estimated a pair of
statistical models. We first examined the effect of the SCOTUS treatment
on all respondents, regardless of their views on the court's institutional
legitimacy. As shown in figure 4.2, our model estimated that the SCOTUS
treatment reduced the probability of the median independent respondent
backing Obama's anticipated immigration action by about 5%.[43] Substantively, this estimated effect is relatively modest; it is significantly smaller
than that observed in the preceding experiment examining the Clean
Power Plan.[44]

One reason for the very different estimated effect sizes across the two
experiments may be the much lower base level of support (just 46%) for
President Obama's immigration action.[45] Unsurprisingly, Obama's immigration actions received virtually no support (less than 9%) among Republicans.[46] As such, among a third of our survey sample, support for the president's unilateral action had virtually no room to fall across the treatment
and control groups. Indeed, if we reestimate our statistical model only for
Democratic and independent respondents, we find that the effect of the
SCOTUS treatment is almost a third stronger.[47]

Finally, the SCOTUS treatment resonated strongly with subjects who

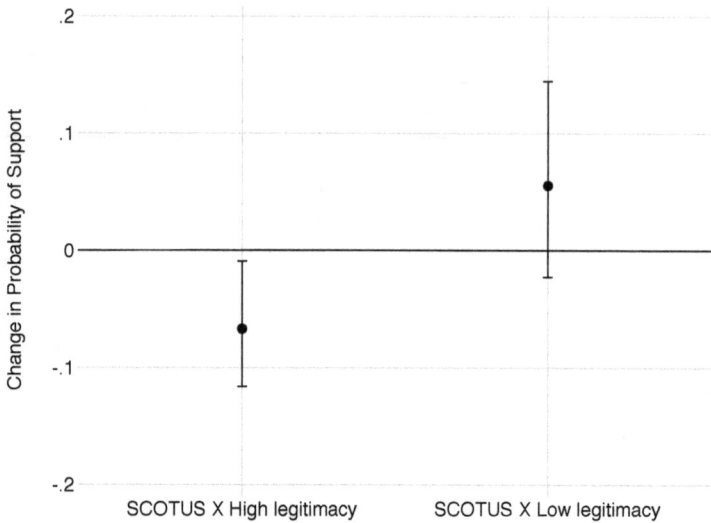

Figure 4.3. Effect of judicial challenge by subjects' assessment of judicial legitimacy
Note: Dots present the estimated change in the probability of the median independent
respondent supporting the president's unilateral action caused by the treatment for
subjects who gave the Supreme Court either high or low legitimacy ratings. I-bars around
each point estimate present 95% confidence intervals obtained from simulations.

esteem the Supreme Court and its institutional legitimacy. In a second
statistical analysis, we modified our model to allow us to estimate the
effect of the SCOTUS treatment on both the 70% of the sample who gave
the court a high legitimacy score and the 30% who gave it a low legitimacy score. Figure 4.3 illustrates the results. For the median independent
respondent who believes the court to be highly legitimate, the SCOTUS
treatment significantly decreased the predicted probability of backing
President Obama's immigration order by about 8%.

By contrast, for the median independent who does not believe that the
court enjoys high legitimacy, the estimated effect of the SCOTUS treatment was actually positive, though not statistically significant. This is at
least suggestive of a backlash effect.[48] Telling subjects who hold the court
in low regard that it was poised to strike down the president's unilateral
action may have paradoxically increased support for the action. While un-
anticipated, this result is consistent with an extensive psychological literature on motivated reasoning and cognitive dissonance.[49] However, we
note that because of the relatively small number of subjects in this subgroup, there is considerable uncertainty about the estimated effect.

TRUMP EPA ROLLBACK EXPERIMENT

To ensure that the specter of judicial rebuke did not shape popular assessments of unilateral action only during the administration of Barack Obama, we conducted a third experiment in the opening days of the presidency of Donald Trump. The design of this experiment was similar to its predecessors; however, it included two important modifications.

First, the strength of the Supreme Court of the United States (SCOTUS) treatment itself was softened. In the previous experiments, subjects were told that the court was "likely" to strike down the unilateral action as unconstitutional. Certainly, those raising the prospects of a judicial challenge often argue that the court is likely to overturn the president's unilateral action. After all, it is precisely the possibility of an interinstitutional showdown that makes such stories attractive to media outlets in the first place. But in this final experiment we explored whether cues arguing that a judicial challenge was only possible, rather than likely, can nonetheless significantly erode public support for unilateral action.

Second, this final experiment took advantage of developments in early 2017 to add a second treatment examining whether reminding subjects of recent judicial defeats further undermines public support for unilateral action. Within weeks of taking the oath of office, President Trump suffered his first major setbacks in court—a string of district and circuit court rulings striking down his executive order banning citizens of seven predominantly Muslim nations from entering the United States. This allowed us to explore whether reminding Americans of recent judicial defeats makes the specter of a future judicial challenge more credible and therefore more influential in decreasing support for unilateral action.

This chapter's first experiment explored whether the specter of judicial pushback eroded support for President Obama's efforts to unilaterally put into effect the Clean Power Plan. Our final experiment examines whether the prospects of a judicial challenge also decreased public support for President Trump's efforts to unilaterally dismantle Obama's environmental legacy. On March 28, 2017, Trump signed a sweeping executive order directing the Environmental Protection Agency to begin the process of rolling back Obama-era regulations designed to combat climate change. Flanked by coal miners at the signing ceremony, Trump declared that the "war on coal" was now over, and he lauded the order as a "historic step to lift the restrictions on American energy, to reverse government intrusion, and to cancel job-killing regulations."[50]

Days later, in April 2017, we embedded an experiment based on this order in a nationally representative survey. All subjects first received a prompt describing the objectives of Trump's executive order and his economic justification for taking action: "President Trump has issued an executive order directing the EPA to weaken environmental regulations on power plant emissions and climate change. President Trump argues that these actions are necessary to help American businesses compete and create jobs." Subjects were then randomly assigned to one of three experimental groups. Those in the control group received no further information. Those in the first treatment group received a treatment similar to those in the preceding pair of experiments; however, in this experiment judicial pushback was described as possible rather than likely. Subjects in this group were told, "Many legal experts warn that this order could be struck down as unconstitutional by the Supreme Court as an overextension of presidential power."

Finally, subjects assigned to the second treatment group received the same cue, but were also reminded of Trump's recent high-profile defeats in court over the Muslim ban. In addition to the treatment language above, these subjects were also told, "Federal courts have already ruled against President Trump's use of unilateral power to ban immigration from seven Muslim countries." It is possible that reminding subjects of a recent judicial defeat will bolster the credibility of our treatment raising the possibility of another judicial rebuke for Trump. If so, then the adverse effect of this treatment on support for Trump's action may be even greater in magnitude than the simpler treatment that does not reference this recent precedent. All subjects were then asked whether they supported or opposed "President Trump taking unilateral action to weaken the nation's environmental regulations."

To estimate the effect of the two SCOTUS treatments on support for Trump's executive order rolling back Obama's environmental legacy, we estimated a statistical model. As in the previous experiments, this model allowed us to estimate the effects of the treatments while controlling for subjects' partisanship and demographic characteristics. Moreover, our statistical model allowed us to include an additional control: support for other Trump unilateral endeavors. The survey included a question asking subjects whether they supported Trump's unilateral efforts to begin building the border wall with Mexico. Support for the border wall should tap into support for Trump more generally, as well as a willingness to support the president even when he acts unilaterally. Because support for the wall was likely to be a strong predictor of support for Trump's environmental order, including it in the model should improve the precision of our estimates.[51]

Most important, the model confirms that even raising the possibility of a judicial challenge significantly eroded support for unilateral action, even in what should have been the honeymoon of the new Trump administration. As shown in figure 4.4, the baseline SCOTUS treatment significantly decreased the probability of the median independent respondent supporting Trump's action by roughly 12%.[52] Interestingly, reminding subjects about Trump's recent defeats in court over his Muslim travel ban order had little influence on the size of the estimated treatment effect. This second treatment decreased the probability of the median independent backing Trump's order rolling back Obama-era environmental regulations by just under 10%. The two treatment effects are statistically indistinguishable from each other.

Taken together, our results suggest that presidents need not suffer recent and high-profile defeats in federal court for the specter of judicial rebuke to be influential with the public. Simply raising the possibility that the Supreme Court might push back against the unilateral president may be enough to strengthen the public check on unilateral overreach.

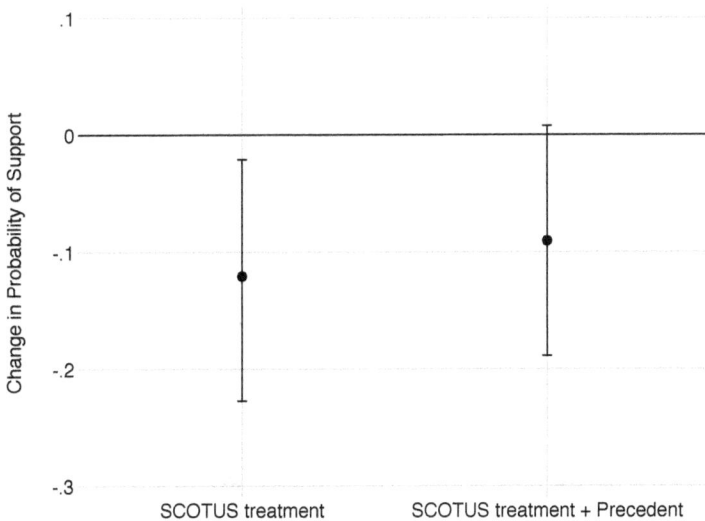

Figure 4.4. Effect of possible court challenge on support for Trump EPA rollback
Note: Dots present the estimated change in the probability of the median independent respondent supporting the president's unilateral action. I-bars around each point estimate present 95% confidence intervals obtained from simulations.

CONCLUSION

Courts, like Congress, possess substantial formal power to check the unilateral president. In practice, however, most scholars and jurists have concluded that the judicial constraint on presidential unilateralism is weak
and highly conditional. Even the surge in high-profile presidential defeats
in recent years should not obscure the broader reality that most presidential unilateral actions are never challenged in courts. And even when
challenges do occur, presidents win far more often than they lose. Legal
doctrines of judicial deference, strategic incentives to avoid potential presidential noncompliance, and the realities of a highly complex administrative state may all combine to limit the courts' capacity to exercise consistently a judicial check on the unilateral president.

Yet the judiciary, like Congress, may remain more relevant in shaping the politics of unilateral action than is often supposed. In an era of
declining trust in national governing institutions, the judiciary stands out
for the breadth and depth of its popular support. When courts speak, public opinion often follows.[53] Perhaps more important, our results suggest
that even the specter of judicial pushback may be enough to rally public
opinion against the president. Legal observers and media pundits routinely
speculate about whether federal courts will hear challenges to highly salient unilateral actions. Our experiments suggest that even raising the
possibility of a rebuke from the Supreme Court can significantly decrease
support for unilateral action, though the impact seems somewhat weaker
and more conditional than that produced by congressional pushback.

Despite the barriers that so often render hapless their formal checks on
unilateral power, both Congress and the courts may nonetheless remain
relevant through their capacity to shape public opinion. When contemplating controversial unilateral action, presidents must anticipate the reactions of the other branches of the federal government. To be sure, in only
rare cases need they worry about formal legislative or legal checks on their
power. However, public criticism or even speculation of it may be enough
to activate many Americans' latent concerns about unilateralism and turn
them against the president's course of action. Anticipating this, presidents
may often decide that the policy benefits of shifting policy unilaterally
may be overwhelmed by its potential political costs.

APPENDIX TO CHAPTER 4

Throughout the chapter, we employ a series of graphics to illustrate the effects of our experimental treatments on the opinions of the median independent respondent. These estimates were derived from logistic regressions that model support for the president's unilateral action as a function of the experimental treatment variables and a series of demographic control variables. The models used to produce these figures are presented in appendix tables 4.1–4.3 below. For each experiment, the relevant table presents model specifications with and without control variables. In appendix table 4.1, the coefficient for the likely legal challenge treatment is negative and statistically significant in both specifications.

In appendix table 4.2, the coefficient for the likely legal challenge treatment is negative and marginally significant in the specification with demographic controls. As seen in model 3, the effect appears to be even stronger among Democrats and independents. This likely reflects a floor effect among Republicans, as support for Obama's actions among the partisan opposition was so low in the control group that it simply had little room to fall further. Finally, as shown in model 4 and illustrated in figure 4.3 in the chapter, the effects of the likely judicial challenge treatment are significantly moderated by subjects' perceptions of the Supreme Court's institutional legitimacy. Those who perceived the court to be highly legitimate were much more responsive to the legal challenge treatment than those who did not perceive it to be highly legitimate.

Finally, in appendix table 4.3 the coefficient estimates for the two Supreme Court challenge treatments in models 1 and 2 are negative, but fail to reach statistical significance. However, both estimates are greater in magnitude, and the first coefficient is statistically significant, $p < .05$, in the final model specification that also controls for subjects' attitudes toward President Trump's border wall. Because this question taps into support for Trump and his policies more generally, including it in the model should yield more precise estimates. As a result, figure 4.4 is based on the results from model 3.

APPENDIX TABLE 4.1 Effect of likely SCOTUS challenge on support for Clean Power Plan

	(1)	(2)
SCOTUS challenge	−0.42*	−0.75**
	(0.19)	(0.24)
Republican		−1.13**
		(0.26)
Democrat		2.07**
		(0.34)
Male		−0.07
		(0.23)
Education		0.04
		(0.08)
Age		−0.02**
		(0.01)
White		−0.59
		(0.30)
Constant	0.83**	2.06**
	(0.13)	(0.53)
Observations	514	514

Note: Models are logistic regressions. Robust standard errors are in parentheses. All significance tests are two-tailed.

*$p < 0.05$

**$p < 0.01$

APPENDIX TABLE 4.2. Effect of likely SCOTUS challenge on support for immigration action

	(1)	(2)	(3)	(4)
SCOTUS challenge	−0.12	−0.32^	−0.41^	0.38
	(0.14)	(0.19)	(0.21)	(0.35)
SCOTUS challenge × Republican			0.48	
			(0.45)	
SCOTUS challenge × legitimate				−0.86*
				(0.42)
Republican		−1.12**	−1.35**	−1.16**
		(0.28)	(0.36)	(0.29)
Democrat		0.80**	0.81**	0.90**
		(0.24)	(0.24)	(0.24)
Male		−0.09	−0.10	−0.09
		(0.19)	(0.19)	(0.19)
Education		0.12^	0.12^	0.11^
		(0.06)	(0.06)	(0.06)
Age		−0.02**	−0.02**	−0.02**
		(0.01)	(0.01)	(0.01)
White		−0.20	−0.20	−0.19
		(0.23)	(0.23)	(0.24)
Believes court is legitimate				0.36
				(0.30)
Presidential approval		2.26**	2.26**	2.20**
		(0.22)	(0.22)	(0.22)
Constant	−0.18	−0.50	−0.47	−0.84
	(0.10)	(0.44)	(0.44)	(0.49)
Observations	884	884	884	859

Note: Models are logistic regressions. Robust standard errors are in parentheses. All significance tests are two-tailed.

^$p < .10$

*$p < 0.05$

**$p < 0.01$

APPENDIX TABLE 4.3. Effect of possible SCOTUS challenge on support for Trump EPA rollback

	(1)	(2)	(3)
SCOTUS challenge	−0.14	−0.18	−0.53*
	(0.16)	(0.20)	(0.25)
SCOTUS challenge + precedent	−0.16	−0.23	−0.41
	(0.16)	(0.20)	(0.24)
Republican		1.61**	0.97**
		(0.20)	(0.25)
Democrat		−1.74**	−1.15**
		(0.21)	(0.25)
Male		0.51**	0.59**
		(0.16)	(0.20)
Age		0.02**	0.01
		(0.00)	(0.01)
Education		−0.15**	−0.02
		(0.06)	(0.07)
White		−0.33	−0.78**
		(0.20)	(0.24)
Supports border wall			3.37**
			(0.24)
Constant	−0.31**	−0.58	−2.02**
	(0.11)	(0.34)	(0.45)
Observations	1,000	1,000	1,000

Note: Models are logistic regressions. Robust standard errors are in parentheses. All significance tests are two-tailed.

*p < 0.05
**p < 0.01

CHAPTER FIVE

A Popular Check on Unilateralism

The preceding three chapters explored how Americans think about unilateral action and how their assessments are influenced by political contestation between the president, Congress, and the courts. But so far, we have said little about whether presidents pay attention to and actually change their behavior in response to pushback, both real and anticipated, from these other actors. Does public opinion—and the political battles in the public sphere that shape it—actually constrain presidents' exercise of their unilateral powers? Has public opinion provided a worthy substitute for Madisonian checks and balances?

The four decades since the publication of Arthur Schlesinger Jr.'s *The Imperial Presidency* have produced a veritable explosion of scholarship on unilateral power. Yet past research offers little systematic evidence that public opinion constrains the exercise of unilateral power. Perhaps the main reason for this lacuna is that the dominant theoretical approach political scientists use to think about unilateral politics affords no role to public opinion. Presidents are strategic in pivotal politics models of unilateral action. However, their strategic calculations focus only on the probability of engendering a formal rebuke from Congress or the courts. If Congress is likely to enact legislation reversing an executive action or the courts are likely to strike it down, then presidents should refrain from going it alone. But these formal institutional constraints are seriously limited by design and empirically infrequent. As such, presidents should rarely anticipate an outright defeat from Congress or the courts, and therefore enjoy an almost free hand when employing the unilateral tool kit to effect significant policy change.

We contend that this dominant theoretical paradigm is incomplete. While it correctly captures the serious limitations on the formal checks exercised by Congress and the courts, it all but ignores the *political costs* that presidents risk incurring by acting unilaterally. When contemplating executive action, presidents do more than simply calculate the likelihood of a formal rebuke from Congress or the courts. They also consider the potentially steep political costs they stand to pay from an ill-advised executive action. Perhaps the most important of these political costs is the risk of alienating public opinion.

A sustained popular backlash to a highly salient and controversial executive action could seriously weaken the president's political position. Critically, the president's public job approval rating is perhaps the most highly visible and ubiquitous measure of his administration's political capital. It signals to other political elites the president's strength or weakness and informs their own calculations of how to respond to presidential requests. Indeed, popular presidents get more of what they want from Congress than unpopular presidents.[1] Thus, executive action to advance one policy priority may prove to be a Pyrrhic victory if it weakens the president's capacity to achieve other important items on his programmatic agenda.

The president's standing among the public also has important electoral ramifications. Popular presidents are more likely to secure reelection for themselves as well as boost the fortunes of a would-be copartisan successor.[2] The latter is particularly critical to defend the president's unilateral policy legacy, as an opposition party president can erase much of it with the stroke of a pen. Moreover, because congressional elections are increasingly nationalized, the president's approval rating casts a long shadow over a host of local races.[3] This could also have major consequences for presidential governing, as the strength of the president's party in Congress is critical to his prospects for legislative success.[4]

Presidents understand these political costs. They anticipate the public's response to a contemplated unilateral action. And they adjust their behavior accordingly. In this way, public opinion—and particularly presidents' anticipations of it—constrains the unilateral presidency.

INDIRECT EVIDENCE OF A POPULAR
CHECK ON UNILATERALISM

Although our argument is straightforward, finding direct empirical evidence of the anticipatory mechanism at its core is anything but. Our theory suggests that much of the influence of public opinion is anticipatory and therefore often not directly observable. Presidents do not wait for the public to turn against them. Rather, they avoid actions likely to trigger popular pushback. To gather direct evidence of our proposed causal logic, we need an unfiltered window on the mind and strategic calculations of presidents as they consider unilateral action. In some cases, we may be able to observe presidents openly worrying about the likely response of the public and the resulting political costs should they act unilaterally. These concerns, in turn, may lead the president to forgo acting alone. We will investigate several such cases in the following chapter. However, many other cases in which presidents are similarly deterred from acting unilaterally leave few readily identifiable traces. Publicly considering executive action but then backing down risks making the president appear indecisive and weak. As a result, presidents have strong incentives to keep their cards close to the chest. Even a thorough combing of presidential archives would fail to recover a comprehensive list of all the times that presidents contemplated taking unilateral action but demurred because of concerns about the public reaction and political costs. In short, it is almost impossible to find systematic direct evidence of the influence of anticipated reactions on presidents' exercise of their unilateral powers.

Nevertheless, we can look for indirect evidence of a political check on presidential unilateralism by examining patterns in the use of unilateral power over time. Specifically, the experimental results of the preceding three chapters examining how Americans assess unilateral action offer important predictions about when the public is likely to rally behind unilateral action and when it is likely to oppose it. These factors should inform presidents' anticipatory calculations and thereby influence both the frequency and the timing of executive action as well as its substantive character.

Presidential Approval and Unilateral Action

We begin our search for evidence that public opinion and anticipations about political costs check presidential unilateralism by examining the relationship between presidential approval and the exercise of unilateral power. Most prior scholarship examining this relationship has focused on a core prediction of the so-called strategic model. This model suggests that presidents are more likely to resort to unilateral action as the prospects for legislative action deteriorate. Politically powerful presidents will logically favor writing their policy preferences into law. Among other benefits, a legislative approach provides presidential victories with significantly greater protection from the meddling of later chief executives. As the protracted battle over the Obama-era Affordable Care Act throughout president Donald Trump's first year in office clearly demonstrated, repealing legislation is difficult. By contrast, reversing a predecessor's executive actions is much easier. However, politically weakened presidents who face an uphill battle on Capitol Hill may increasingly fall back on executive action to advance their programmatic agendas. The strategic model therefore suggests that unpopular presidents should resort to unilateral action more frequently than popular presidents who are better positioned to secure action from Congress.[5]

But while this earlier framework describes how the benefits of acting unilaterally may vary with the president's political position, it fails to consider the potential political costs of executive action. Critically, the president's approval rating should influence the president's anticipatory calculus concerning public response and political cost both directly and indirectly.

Decades of public opinion research show that most Americans have only limited interest in politics and little relevant knowledge about specific governmental policies. Instead, as the experiments of the previous three chapters demonstrate, when most Americans assess executive action they rely heavily on cues or information shortcuts. Some of these shortcuts, while powerful, are unlikely to aid presidents' anticipatory calculations. For example, in chapter 2 one of the strongest determinants of support for executive action was partisanship. Americans are more likely to back executive action taken by a copartisan president. The balance of partisanship is relatively stable, however; as such, a focus on partisan cues affords presidents little insight into popular reaction beyond the reality that it is more difficult to win support for executive action among those who identify with the opposition party.

But other shortcuts do vary over time, and one of the most important of these is presidential approval. Many Americans do not know exactly where they stand on a specific issue; however, they know how they feel about the incumbent president. Those who approve of the president are much more likely to rally behind executive actions than are those who disapprove of his overall performance on the job. Several experiments in the past two chapters plainly illustrate the importance of job approval in shaping assessments of unilateral action.[6] In the Student Loans Experiment in chapter 2, for example, approving of Barack Obama's job performance increased the chance of the median independent respondent backing Obama's executive action to reduce student loan payments by almost 30%.[7] In the first Clean Power Plan Experiment of chapter 3, approving of

Obama's job performance increased the predicted chance of the median independent in the control group backing his action by almost 25%.[8] Finally, in chapter 4 presidential approval was one of the most important predictors of support for President Obama's executive actions on immigration. The median independent who approved of Obama's job performance was more than three times as likely to support executive action as the median independent who did not approve of Obama's job performance (70% vs. 20%).[9] Thus, presidents who enjoy strong approval ratings should anticipate greater support for and less public opposition to their executive actions than presidents with low approval ratings.

Presidential approval also critically influences another factor that drives public opinion on unilateral actions: the response of other political elites. Because many Americans pay relatively little attention to politics and lack extensive political knowledge, many executive actions, if they are relatively uncontroversial, may simply fly under the radar, unnoticed by large segments of the public.[10] But when other political elites publicly contest executive action, they both raise its salience and provide contrasting perspectives to the narrative from the White House. As demonstrated above, elite criticism is therefore critically important in making the public aware of executive action and in shaping its assessment of such action. The experiments in chapters 3 and 4 show that such criticism can significantly erode popular support for unilateral action. A final follow-up experiment shows that institutional criticism can be even more politically costly: not only can it decrease public support for unilateral action, but it can also chip away at the president's overall job approval rating, perhaps the most salient measure of a president's political capital.

In January 2019 as President Trump publicly contemplated declaring a national emergency to build the Mexican border wall, we fielded a final experiment to examine public support for Trump using the emergency power to pursue one of his more broadly popular policy positions—infrastructure.[11] All subjects received the following hypothetical prompt: "President Trump is considering declaring a national emergency to allow him to spend billions of federal dollars on infrastructure projects without legislative approval from Congress. President Trump argues that improving the nation's bridges, roads, and airports will create jobs and grow the economy." Subjects randomly assigned to the control group received no further information. Subjects randomly assigned to the treatment group were told, "Some members of Congress from both parties, however, oppose the President's plan. These congressional Democrats and Republicans argue that President Trump lacks the constitutional and statutory authority

to declare the nation's infrastructure a national security emergency. They
argue that acting unilaterally would be an abuse of power, and that infrastructure spending requires legislation from Congress." All subjects were
then asked whether they would "support or oppose President Trump declaring a national emergency to unilaterally spend federal dollars on infrastructure projects."

As shown in figure 5.1, congressional criticism of this hypothetical
unilateral action decreased President Trump's approval rating by almost
10%.[12] Thus, presidents have a good reason to be wary of taking unilateral actions that could trigger strong resistance from Congress, even if it
cannot reverse the action legislatively. Any significant erosion of presidential approval could have serious consequences at the ballot box and for the
president's broader programmatic agenda.

But other political elites do not decide whether to challenge presidents
in a vacuum. Rather, they are highly strategic and keep in mind both the
benefits and the risks of challenging the president. Central to this calculation is the president's standing among the public. Popular presidents
enjoy a valuable buffer against criticism. Challenging the president could
backfire and cause would-be critics more harm than good. By contrast,

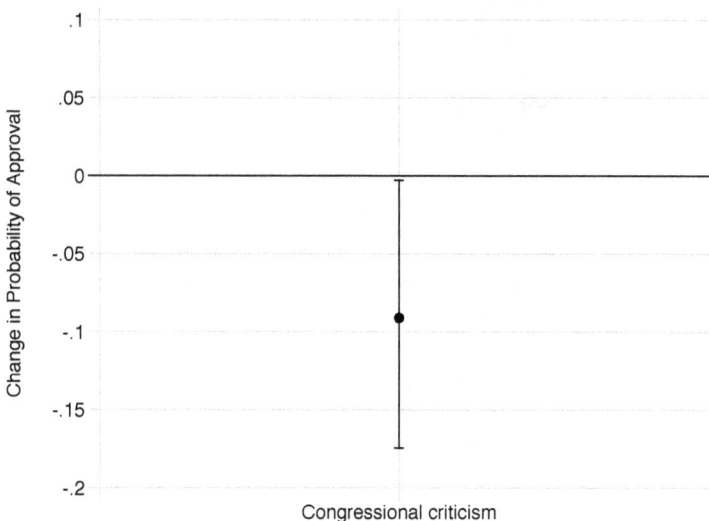

Figure 5.1. Effect of congressional criticism of unilateralism on presidential approval
Note: The dot presents the estimated change in the probability of the median independent
respondent supporting the president's unilateral action. I-bars around this point
estimate present the 95% confidence interval obtained from simulations.

unpopular presidents are much more attractive political targets.[13] Critics may seek to score political points at the expense of an already vulnerable executive, thereby further weakening the administration.[14]

Courts were designed to be insulated from such pressures. However, empirical research has long documented that courts are also more likely to rule against the executive in a variety of cases, including those specifically involving unilateral action, when presidential approval is low.[15] Thus, unpopular presidents anticipate greater institutional pushback, which in turn can further imperil their already low standing among the public.

Consequently, presidents with low approval ratings should anticipate greater pushback and political costs from acting unilaterally than should popular presidents. This generates the first observable implication of our theory of anticipatory action: presidents with strong job approval ratings will issue more significant executive actions than will presidents with weak approval ratings. The other way of thinking about this expectation is that unpopular presidents will be constrained in issuing executive actions.

Our theory of anticipatory action suggests that approval ratings influence presidential decisions to act unilaterally. However, there may also be a reason to think that the causal arrow may run in the opposite direction: presidents' use of unilateral action may affect their overall job approval among the public. Recent experimental work finds that subjects punished a hypothetical presidential candidate for announcing the intention, if elected, to pursue action on key policy priorities unilaterally rather than legislatively.[16] Similarly, the experiments of the last three chapters also show that executive action—in certain conditions—may engender significant public opposition. This raises the possibility that taking executive action could decrease presidential approval.

But if presidents correctly anticipate public reactions and respond accordingly—as implied in our theory of anticipatory action—then we should find little evidence that executive action decreases presidential approval. Most important, presidents can blunt popular pushback by avoiding executive actions that trigger intense institutional opposition; elite criticism is often essential to mobilizing broader opposition from a normally inattentive public. This generates the second observable implication of our anticipatory theory: the frequency with which presidents issue major executive actions should have no effect on the president's job approval rating.

THE POPULARITY OF EXECUTIVE ACTIONS

Our anticipatory theory offers another prediction about the executive actions that presidents do ultimately choose to take: most of these actions should be met with widespread public support. Presidents should act unilaterally only when the policy benefits of executive action outweigh the political costs of doing so. Presidents have clear strategies for minimizing the political costs of executive action. Unpopular presidents can think twice before relying too heavily on unilateral action. Moreover, they can consider preexisting public opinion. Policy preferences are another shortcut on which many Americans rely when assessing unilateral action. They support executive actions that move policy in their preferred direction and oppose orders that do not. On many issues, public opinion may be ill formed and fluid. Yet if there is a prevailing popular sentiment on a policy, presidents should be emboldened to act unilaterally when their move is in accord with popular preferences and reticent to do so when it cuts against the grain.

Of course, in some cases presidents may perceive that the policy benefits of a unilateral action—or perhaps the longer-term costs of *not* acting unilaterally—exceed the short-term political costs incurred by running afoul of contemporary public opinion. For example, shortly after the disastrous 1994 midterm elections, president Bill Clinton confronted a rapidly escalating crisis: the imminent collapse of the Mexican economy. Clinton initially worked with congressional leaders on legislation authorizing $40 billion in loans to Mexico. However, their joint effort was unable to rouse enough votes. On January 31, 1995, with the Mexican government on the verge of default, President Clinton unilaterally authorized $20 billion in loan guarantees. He and his advisers, many of whom strongly warned the president not to act, plainly understood the risks. In his memoirs, Clinton notes that a newly published *Los Angeles Times* poll showed American public opinion running strongly against loan guarantees.[17] Both national security adviser Sandy Berger and Treasury secretary Robert Rubin emphasized the risks. But Clinton replied, "So a year from now, when we have another million illegal immigrants, we're awash in drugs from Mexico, and lots of people on both sides of the Rio Grande are out of work . . . what will I say?" Ultimately, Clinton judged that the long-term risks of inaction exceeded the immediate political risk: "This is something we have to do."[18] In general, though, the anticipated political costs of going against prevailing opinion will cause presidents to forgo acting unilaterally.

Thus, if our theory is correct and anticipatory calculations shape presi-

dents' use of their unilateral power, we arrive at a third observable implication: most of the major executive actions that presidents ultimately take
should receive ample public support.

PRESIDENTIAL APPROVAL AND THE EXERCISE OF UNILATERAL POWER

To assess whether public opinion constrains presidential unilateralism,
we first focus on the frequency with which presidents issue major executive orders. Of course, presidents have the benefit of certain tools in addition to executive orders through which they can advance their policy
agendas unilaterally, including proclamations, memoranda, and national
security directives. Focusing only on executive orders does come at a
cost—it causes us to miss cases in which presidents have pursued significant policy changes through these other instruments. However, this focus
on executive orders does afford several important advantages. First, since
a series of cases in the 1930s the Supreme Court has firmly established
the legal status of executive orders. As such, recent presidents have consistently used executive orders to advance their policy agenda in both the
foreign and the domestic spheres.[19] Second, federal statute requires that all
executive orders be published in the *Federal Register*. By contrast, executive memoranda are published (or not) at the discretion of the president.
This is critically important to ensuring that we have comparable data
across twelve presidents spanning a more than sixty-five-year period. Finally, as political scientist Kenneth Mayer notes, executive orders most
reliably "combine the highest levels of substance, discretion, and direct
presidential involvement."[20]

Examining executive orders thus offers important advantages. Yet most
are fairly routine and consist of technical instructions to departments and
agencies for implementing existing law.[21] Few if any of these orders should
prompt much pushback from Congress or public scrutiny. As such, we do
not expect any strong relationship between the issuance of routine orders
and public opinion. Moreover, routine orders, even if procedurally important, are far from the sort of unilateral maneuvers that trouble normative
theorists concerned about the frailty of contemporary separation of powers. Instead, we endeavor to focus only on the issuance of major executive
orders that strike out in new directions, with material consequences for
politics and policy.

Scholars have devised multiple methods for identifying "significant"
executive orders. Here, we follow one of the most time-tested approaches.[22]

As discussed in chapter 1, we embrace here William Howell's definition of a significant executive order as one that receives even a single mention in the *New York Times* within one year of its issuance. Orders that meet this relatively modest threshold are regarded as significant and included in our monthly counts of major executive orders. Orders not mentioned in the *Times* are coded as insignificant and are excluded from our analysis.

Figure 5.2 presents the monthly count of executive orders mentioned in the *New York Times* from 1953 through 2018. Over this time period, the average month produced just over a single significant executive order, with a standard deviation of roughly 1.5 orders. In most months, the number of significant orders varies somewhere between 0 and 5; however, there are several significant spikes in the data. The biggest spike—a burst of orders relating to the Iran hostage crisis—occurred in the waning days of the Jimmy Carter administration. A pair of additional spikes occurred in John F. Kennedy's second year in office and after 9/11.

To obtain a measure of popular support for the president, we collected all available Gallup Poll presidential approval data from 1953 through 2018.[23] The data plotted in figure 5.3 tell the familiar story of the ebb and flow of such support over this sixty-six-year span. Both Dwight Eisenhower and Kennedy generally enjoyed robust public support, as did Lyndon Johnson early in his presidency. But Johnson's decision to escalate the Vietnam War would slowly and steadily erode his public support and compel him to renounce a reelection bid. Richard Nixon's approval rating cratered after Watergate, and Ronald Reagan's decreased sharply after revelations of the Iran-Contra Affair. George H. W. Bush experienced the highest level of popular approval on record to date after the successful conclusion of the

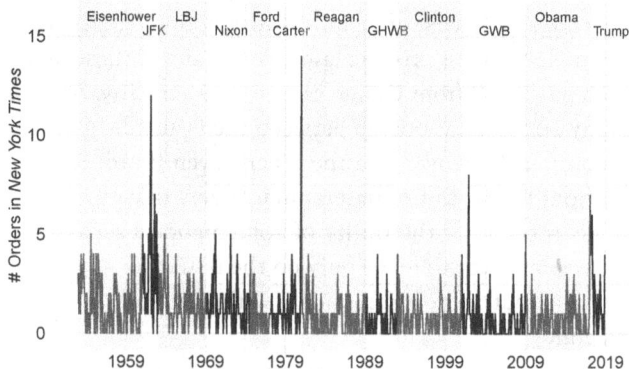

Figure 5.2. Significant executive orders mentioned in the *New York Times*, 1953–2018

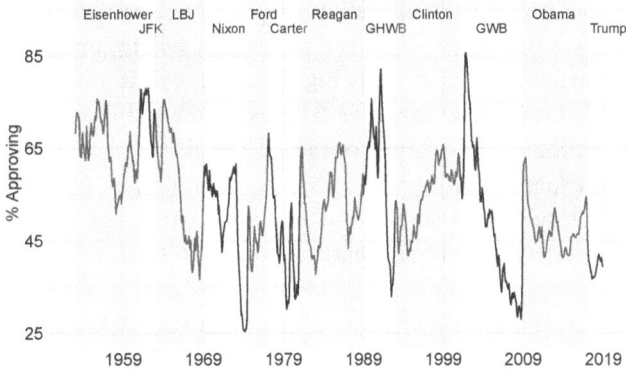

Figure 5.3. Presidential approval, 1953–2018

Persian Gulf War, only to see it plummet with the recession of 1991/1992. Bill Clinton's stewardship of a roaring economy earned him high marks among the public despite salacious scandals and impeachment. The rally-round-the-flag effect after 9/11 vaulted George W. Bush to an approval rating in excess of 85%. However, Bush's popular standing would not last, as the Iraq War eroded his job approval rating as surely and steadily as had Vietnam for Johnson. Overall, the average presidential approval rating during this period was 53%, with significant variation around that mean as indicated by a standard deviation of 12%.

THE DIRECTION OF THE CAUSAL ARROW

Armed with these measures, we can now look for evidence that public opinion actually constrains the unilateral executive. This is no small task methodologically. That is, establishing that changes in presidential approval ratings cause changes in the use of executive action is complicated, because the causal arrow could run in either or both directions. Because they affect presidents' anticipatory calculations, approval ratings may influence the volume of executive action that presidents employ. Yet how aggressively presidents employ their unilateral tool kit may also affect their standing among the public.

Such questions of causality and reverse causality are endemic to all research examining the interactions of political elites and public opinion. Most such relationships are reciprocal, with elites both shaping and being influenced by public opinion, both observed and anticipated. In the previous three chapters, we used experiments to overcome this problem. By randomly assigning survey subjects to carefully manipulated treatments, we could isolate the causal effect of elite actions and arguments on public support for unilateral action. This high internal validity came at the expense of external validity, however. The experimental design allowed us to be sure that our elite treatments caused the observed changes in opinion. But the experimental nature of the studies, despite our best efforts to mimic as closely as possible real-world arguments and conditions, does not perfectly reflect how most Americans make political judgments in the real world.

Using the real-world observational data summarized in figures 5.2 and 5.3 to assess the influence of public opinion on presidential unilateralism insulates us from these external validity concerns. However, an analysis using observational data poses its own challenge: isolating the causal effect of presidential approval on executive order issuance, independent of any reciprocal effect.[24] In the current context, the causal arrow may well run in either or both directions. Simply showing a significant correlation between presidential approval and unilateral executive activity cannot tell us which factor is driving the other, and thus whether we find support for our theory of anticipatory action.

To address this problem, we employed a specific type of time series analysis: a vector autoregressive (VAR) model with complementary Granger causality tests. Full details of our method and a more technical discussion of the results are provided in the chapter's appendix.[25] In brief, this approach allowed us to examine the influence of lagged values of presidential approval on the number of significant executive orders issued in a given month, and vice versa. The subsequent Granger causality analysis allowed us to test and summarize the direction of influence between approval and unilateral action.

The VAR model also allowed us to control for a series of additional exogenous factors that may influence the frequency and timing of executive order issuance and public approval. While prior analyses have examined the influence of a wide range of variables on executive order issuance, several main categories of factors stand out. First, past research has examined whether presidents resort disproportionately to unilateral action when they face intense opposition from Congress. Though the theoretical logic is clear, past empirical analyses have yielded mixed results.[26] Nevertheless, because the situation on Capitol Hill may influence the president's willingness to act unilaterally, our models included an indicator variable identifying periods of divided partisan control of the presidency and at least one chamber of Congress. Many studies have also sought to control for the influence of the larger contextual environment in which the president operates on the exercise of unilateral power. Specifically, past research has often focused on the health of the economy and whether the nation is at peace or at war. To account for these forces, we included a measure of the index of consumer sentiment as well as an indicator variable identifying whether the United States is currently at war.[27] Recently, a number of scholars have shown how executive action may actually complement rather than substitute for legislation.[28] To account for the possibility that trends in significant executive action may be triggered by the enactment of major legislation, we included a control for the number of landmark laws enacted in each month. Finally, previous scholarship has examined whether the propensity to act unilaterally has varied across presidencies. To account for this, our model included a series of presidential fixed effects, which allowed us to model each president's baseline level of significant executive order use.

From Approval to Orders

A feature of almost any type of time series data, such as we have for both presidential approval and significant executive order activity, is that the value of a variable this month is correlated with its value last month and perhaps even with its values in earlier months. Our VAR model accounted for this autocorrelation by modeling executive order activity in month t as a function of its value in the preceding two months, t-1 and t-2, as well as the values of presidential approval in the preceding two months. It likewise modeled presidential approval in the current month as a function of both its values and executive orders in the preceding two months. Two months was chosen as the appropriate lag through a series of tests discussed in the chapter appendix. We then employed a Granger causality test to determine whether past values of each variable influence current values of the other, even after controlling for its own prior values. In this way, we could determine whether changes in presidential approval cause changes in executive order issuance, or if the causal arrow runs in the opposite direction.[29]

The formal results of the Granger causality tests are presented in the chapter appendix. We found strong evidence that the causal arrow runs from presidential approval to executive order issuance. Strongly consistent with the first observable implication of our anticipatory argument, lagged presidential approval ratings are significant predictors of how many significant executive orders presidents issue in each month.

Moreover, we did not find significant evidence that prior levels of executive action systematically influence approval ratings. This is strongly consistent with the second indirect observable implication of our anticipatory logic. Ill-conceived unilateral action may produce a popular backlash against the president.[30] However, if presidents successfully anticipate public reactions and adjust their use of unilateral power accordingly, then we would not expect the frequency or intensity of executive action to systematically influence presidential approval ratings. Although the estimated effect of approval on significant executive order activity is positive in the VAR models, it is substantively small and not statistically significant.

Interpreting the size of the effect of approval on significant executive order activity is complicated by the time series nature of the data. However, we can understand the magnitude of the effect by looking at how an unexpected one-time impulse in one of the variables affects the other variables in the system. In our case, we looked specifically at how approval affects executive orders by shocking approval and tracing out the effect in orders over time. We illustrate these dynamics with two impulse response functions in figure 5.4. The first (the orthogonal impulse response function) illustrates the impact of a sudden surge in approval—an increase of one standard deviation that then disappears and returns to its prior value the following month—on significant executive order activity. The second (the cumulative orthogonal impulse response function) adds the effects of shocks in previous periods, allowing us to examine the influence of a long-lasting or persistent surge in presidential approval on significant executive order issuance over time.

Figure 5.4 illustrates the results from our model of the number of significant executive orders issued in each month. The solid line shows that a one-time standard deviation surge in presidential approval (12%) results in an immediate increase of about .13 in the number of significant executive orders issued by the president the next month. The effect of this one-time spike in approval then diminishes over the next few months until it is essentially zero. To be sure, this represents a substantively small effect. However, it is important to remember that significant executive orders are rare. The average number of orders that merit even a single mention in the *New York Times* is only roughly one per month, with a standard deviation of 1.5. Thus, while the effect from a single short-term shock in approval is small, the effect on executive order issuance is nontrivial given the scarcity of orders meeting even this relatively modest significance threshold.

Such short-term spikes in approval do occasionally occur. Yet what is perhaps more likely and more interesting is the change in presidential use

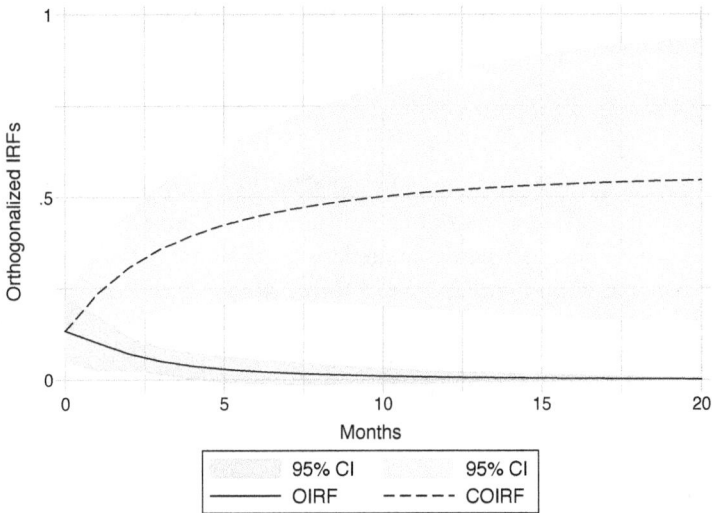

Figure 5.4. Impulse response functions for *New York Times* executive order count
Note: Solid line presents the orthogonalized impulse response function (OIRF) estimates, and dashed line presents the cumulative orthogonalized IRF (COIRF) estimates. Shading around the estimates are 95% confidence bands obtained via the delta method.

of major executive orders given a persistent shift in presidential approval. Presidents who enjoy sustained increases in their approval rating may feel particularly emboldened to act unilaterally. The dashed line plotting the cumulative impulse response function illustrates the effect of just such a scenario. Specifically, the dashed line shows the effect of a one standard deviation increase in approval that is sustained over time. By the fifth month, this persistent surge in approval produces an expected increase of .4 significant orders, and by the tenth-month mark the effect increases to .5 orders before leveling off.

The graphs present the effects of a one standard deviation increase in approval on executive order issuance. However, we can just as easily think about the effect of an equivalently sized decrease in public support. Our model predicts that a president who suffers a one standard deviation drop in approval that persists for a year will issue almost 50% fewer significant executive orders in that time than he would have had his approval not dropped. Thus, the long-term brake of consistently low approval ratings on presidential unilateralism is strong indeed.

The data provide robust support for our argument that public opinion constrains presidential unilateralism. Increasing levels of popular support embolden presidents to take unilateral action in order to advance key elements of their policy agendas. By contrast, declining popular support significantly checks presidents' unilateral impulses.

DOES PRESIDENTIAL SENSITIVITY TO APPROVAL VARY?

We conclude our initial analysis by considering the possibility that presidents may be more responsive to public opinion and give greater weight to their approval ratings when contemplating unilateral action in some political contexts than in others. We examine three possibilities. First, freed from the need to worry about reelection, second-term presidents may be less concerned than first-term presidents with how the public and other institutional actors will respond to executive actions. The logic here echoes Alexander Hamilton's *Federalist 72*: continual eligibility for reelection is the ultimate "inducement to good behavior." Absent this electoral pressure, presidents may be less sensitive to the risks of public backlash to bold unilateral action. However, as noted previously, a serious limitation on the president's unilateral power is the ease with which the next president can dismantle his predecessor's unilateral legacy. Consequently, even second-term presidents may have strong incentives to avoid taking actions that could seriously erode their standing among the public and jeopardize the electoral prospects of a would-be copartisan successor.

Presidential sensitivity to approval ratings could also vary with the political business cycle. The political costs of taking a unilateral action that risks generating a popular backlash may increase with proximity to the next presidential election.[31] The logic underlying this hypothesis is obvious. But here, too, countervailing forces are in play that might equalize sensitivity to approval over time. Approval ratings are a powerful measure of a president's political capital that can affect the president's ability to advance other items on the programmatic agenda as well as his party's electoral fortunes in midterm elections. Thus, presidents should always have strong incentives to anticipate popular reactions when contemplating unilateral action, and the strength of these incentives may vary only slightly with the electoral cycle.

Finally, we explore whether presidents may be more sensitive to anticipatory calculations involving approval in divided versus unified government. Theoretical expectations in this regard are somewhat murky. In unified government, presidents might expect less institutional resistance from Congress should they take bold unilateral action—for example, copartisan majorities could dampen high-profile investigative oversight of executive actions.[32] This, in turn, might reduce the costs presidents with

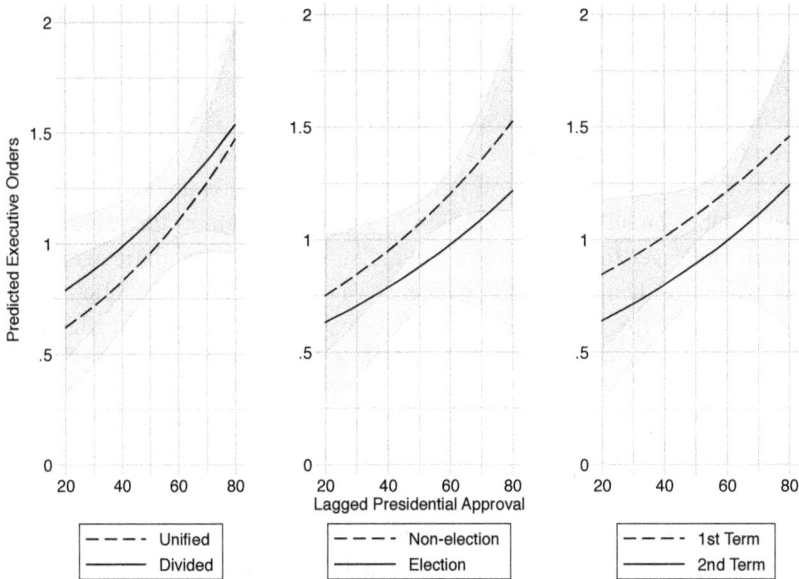

Figure 5.5. Effect of approval on executive orders across contexts
Note: Lines present the expected count of executive orders for each group across the range of presidential approval. Shading around the estimates are 95% confidence bands obtained via the delta method.

lower approval ratings anticipate paying from going it alone. But on the flip side, in facing dour prospects for legislative success on Capitol Hill, presidents in divided government might anticipate greater benefits to acting unilaterally that offset potentially greater costs.

To determine whether presidents are particularly sensitive to approval when taking unilateral action in each of these three political contexts, we estimated a series of event count models that interact presidential approval with one of three indicator variables: a variable identifying second-term presidents; a variable identifying presidential election years; and a variable identifying periods of divided government.[33] Figure 5.5 summarizes the results. In each case, we found no evidence that presidential responsiveness to their approval ratings when contemplating unilateral action varies across political contexts. All three interactions are substantively small and statistically insignificant. In all three panels of figure 5.5, the predicted probability lines are almost perfectly parallel; this shows that the estimated effect of approval on unilateral activity is almost indistinguishable across first and second terms, election and nonelection years, and periods of unified and divided government.

Normatively, these findings are important. While reelection incentives

are an important part of the president's calculus, they are not the only reason that presidents consider the public's likely reaction when contemplating unilateral action. Rather, the president's approval rating is a valuable
political commodity throughout his tenure in office. It affects not just the
president's own reelection prospects but also those of a would-be copartisan successor as well as fellow partisans in congressional and down-ballot
races. More broadly, public opinion is a critically important resource for
presidents eager to advance other items on their programmatic agendas.[34]
As such, presidents have strong incentives to anticipate the public's likely
reaction and the attendant political costs should they act unilaterally
across political contexts and stages of the political business cycle.

THE POPULARITY OF UNILATERAL ACTION

That popular presidents issue significantly more major executive actions
than unpopular presidents is strongly consistent with our anticipatory
theory. The former anticipate significantly less popular pushback should
they act unilaterally than do the latter. A further observable implication
of our argument is that most executive actions that presidents do take
should receive broad popular support.

To test this additional hypothesis, we first searched the holdings of
the Roper Center for Public Opinion Research to identify all polls query-
ing Americans' support for major executive actions taken by presidents
George W. Bush and Barack Obama. Before 2001, polling questions explicitly referencing executive actions were exceedingly sparse. For example,
a search of the Roper Center's holdings yields polling data for only one
additional executive order taken by president Bill Clinton—his 1998 order
to prohibit federal agencies from discriminating against homosexuals.[35]
Notably, this order, in contrast to the Mexican loan guarantees discussed
earlier, received widespread support, with 72% backing Clinton's move
versus only 20% opposing the order.[36]

After 2000, polling outlets began to ask more questions about unilateral action. We found opinion polling data for seven major executive actions taken by President Bush and nine taken by President Obama. Figures
5.6 and 5.7 present the net public approval for each executive action taken
by each president—that is, the percentage of Americans approving of the
action minus the percentage disapproving of the president's action.

With the benefit of hindsight, many Americans may remember President Bush's unilateral actions, particularly those taken in response
to the terrorist attacks of 9/11, as being quite controversial. Indeed, the

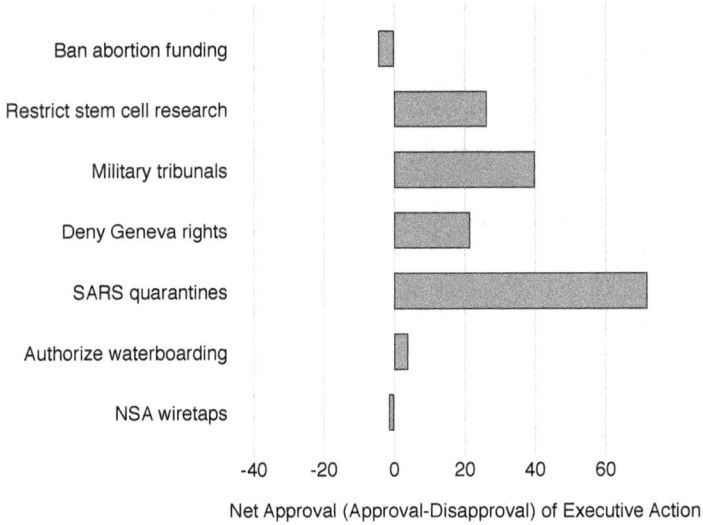

Figure 5.6. Net approval of executive actions taken by George W. Bush

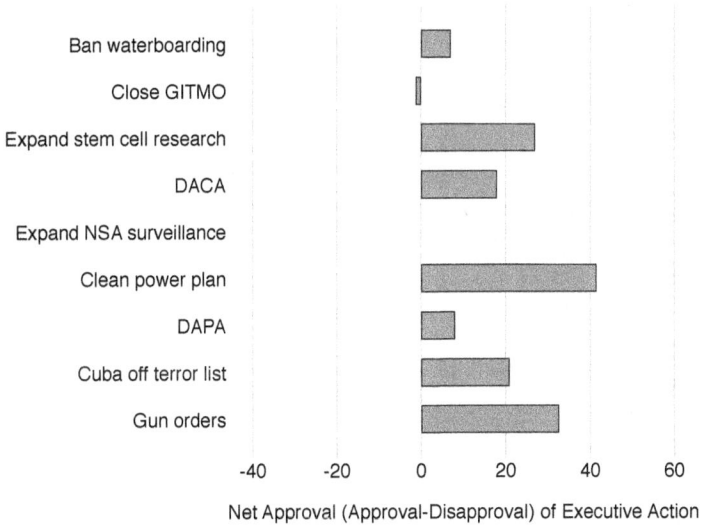

Figure 5.7. Net approval of executive actions taken by Barack Obama

president's most vociferous critics often cited his unilateral directives as evidence of the return of an imperial presidency. But if imperial power implies the ability and willingness to unilaterally effect change opposed by both Congress and broad majorities of the public, Bush was far from imperial. Almost all his highest-profile unilateral actions received considerable contemporary public support. For example, his decision to create unilaterally a new system of military tribunals to try terror suspects outside the civilian court system—tribunals that the Supreme Court later invalidated in *Hamdan v. Rumsfeld* as inconsistent with both the Uniform Code of Military Justice and the Geneva Conventions—were broadly supported by the public at the time. Indeed, 40% more Americans approved of Bush's military order of November 2001 than disapproved of it. Similarly, the president's decision to deny terror suspects their rights under the Geneva Conventions—in legal circles, an incredibly contentious and controversial move—was also backed by a strong majority of the general public. More Americans supported than opposed Bush's decision to authorize "enhanced interrogation techniques," such as waterboarding, against suspected terrorists. Even the shocking revelation of his secret order authorizing the National Security Agency to wiretap certain conversations involving US citizens without a warrant was met with an almost evenly split public. This popular ambivalence reflects the uneasy tradeoffs between security and civil liberties in a time of increased threat.

Perhaps unsurprisingly considering the intense partisan split on the issue, the most controversial of President Bush's executive actions in the data set was his early decision to reinstate the Mexico City policy banning federal funding for organizations that provide abortion counseling or services. Yet even this action received almost as much public approval as disapproval. Moreover, another Bush domestic policy directive widely criticized on the Left—his executive order to place significant restrictions on federal funding for stem cell research—received ample public support in 2001.

Although President Obama campaigned pledging to repudiate the excessively unilateral approach of his predecessor, when in office he, too, made recourse to the presidency's unilateral powers. The data in figure 5.7 show that when Obama acted unilaterally, he did so carefully and almost always when his policy actions received broad public support.[37] For seven of the nine Obama-era executive actions, more Americans approved of the president's move than disapproved. In many cases, popular support for the president's action was overwhelming. For example, both the Clean Power Plan and the president's series of executive actions tightening the enforcement of gun control regulations after the Newtown massacre were supported by more than 60% of the electorate.[38] Fewer than one in three disapproved of Obama's actions. The memoranda for Deferred Action for Childhood Arrivals (DACA) and Deferred Action for Parents of Americans and Lawful Permanent Residents (DAPA), programs protecting millions of illegal immigrants from deportation and perhaps his two boldest unilateral moves, both received considerably greater support than opposition among the public.

Obama's two most controversial executive actions involved his conduct of the inherited war on terror. The first—his quixotic quest to close the terrorist detention center at Guantanamo Bay, Cuba—involved a reversal of Bush administration policy. The second—his expansion of Bush-era warrantless surveillance programs—was an extension of prior policies. Both almost evenly divided Americans.

Critically, none of the major executive actions taken by Presidents Bush or Obama provoked widespread opposition. Rather, when both chief executives resorted to the unilateral powers of the presidency, they routinely did so to effect policy changes that received much public support. This is precisely what we would expect if presidents anticipate the public's likely reaction when contemplating whether to make a significant unilateral move. Of course, in some cases presidents may anticipate popular pushback, but judge that the policy benefits of executive action simply outweigh the political costs. Yet in many if not most cases, those anticipating much public resistance forgo unilateral action. As a result, when presidents do act unilaterally, their actions usually receive broad public support.

"TRUMPIAN" EXCEPTIONALISM?

Since Donald Trump's victory in the 2016 presidential election, pundits, politicians, and political scientists alike have debated whether American politics have been completely transformed under Trump, or whether they have remained remarkably unchanged. Would a brash political neophyte who promised an end to politics as usual adopt a different approach to the exercise of unilateral power?[39] He certainly said so in March of 2016, in lambasting Obama's use of executive orders: "I want to not use too many executive orders, folks. . . . Obama, because he couldn't get anybody to agree with him, he starts signing them like they're butter. So I want to do away with executive orders for the most part."[40]

But Trump's tumultuous campaign suggested competing hypotheses.

On the one hand, he may be less concerned with political costs than most professional politicians. On the campaign trail, he emphasized his outsider status as proof that he would be a man of action, unlike the career politicians who are often paralyzed by concerns for their political futures. In office, Trump has continued to eschew political conventions of all sorts. From his early morning tweet storms to his public feuds with foreign leaders and domestic legislators alike, he has proved to be a veritable iconoclast who governs his way, with seeming disdain for traditional political calculations.

And yet despite his antipolitician persona, throughout the campaign Trump showed himself to have an uncanny knack for keeping his finger on the pulse of the public. Indeed, he revealed an almost unique fascination, bordering on obsession, with public opinion polls.[41] Trump's biographers have stressed how much he craves approval and popularity.[42] In fact, many of his campaign speeches quickly devolved into recitations of his latest poll numbers. Trump's very plasticity in questions of policy—after all, when it proved highly unpopular, he famously called the House Republican health care bill "mean" mere weeks after holding a Rose Garden ceremony to celebrate its passage in the lower chamber—may allow and even encourage him to be uniquely responsive to popular sentiment.

To test between these competing perspectives, we collected all available public polling data on Trump's executive actions during his first two years in office.[43] Testifying to the heightened salience of unilateral action in contemporary politics—and to the prominence of claims that presidential authoritarianism is on the rise!—polling outlets queried public support for sixteen executive actions taken by Trump during this period. This total tally of actions equals that from opinion polling for Presidents Bush and Obama combined over the course of their four terms in office. Figure 5.8 presents the net public approval rating for each of these actions.

The comparison is striking. In stark contrast to Bush and Obama, Trump routinely acted to advance unilaterally policies that most Americans oppose. Only a single Trump executive action—the third version of his travel ban—ultimately received more public support than opposition. And thirteen of his actions were more unpopular than the *least* popular move taken by his two immediate predecessors. On virtually every executive action, polling data show Trump to be underwater, and often significantly so. For thirteen of these, public opposition exceeded support by more than 10%. In five cases, including his initial executive actions

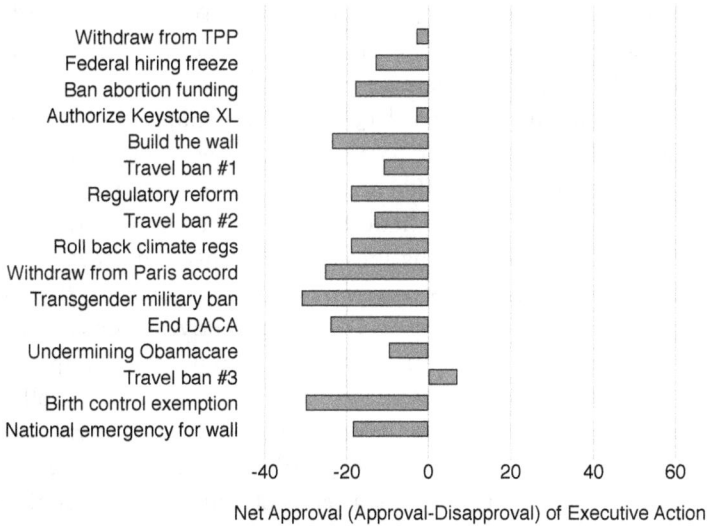

Figure 5.8. Net approval of executive actions taken by Donald Trump

to begin building the Mexican border wall, to withdraw from the Paris climate accord, and to end DACA, opposition exceeded support by more than 20%.

Figure 5.9 summarizes the widely varying levels of public support enjoyed by the nation's forty-third, forty-fourth, and forty-fifth presidents. Despite being two of the most polarizing presidents ever, both George W. Bush's and Barack Obama's average public support for their unilateral actions was in the mid- to upper 50s. Public support for President Bush's executive actions was significantly more variable: a few actions received only minority support, while others were backed by overwhelming majorities of Americans. By contrast, public support for President Obama's major executive actions clustered much more tightly, between 50 and 60%. The clear outlier is President Trump. Just 34% of the electorate, on average, supported the sixteen Trump actions for which public polling data are available. None of Trump's major executive actions received the backing of even 45% of Americans in publicly available opinion surveys.

The data are unambiguous. During his first two years in power, President Trump plainly approached unilateral action from a perspective dramatically different from his predecessors. Whereas Presidents Bush and Obama both took bold unilateral action of significant policy consequence, the policies they pursued unilaterally usually received substantial public support. By contrast, in his first years in office Trump consistently pursued policies that received little support, and indeed engendered significant opposition from the American public.

Before concluding that President Trump has simply been less responsive to (or perceptive of) public opinion, though, we explored an alternate explanation for the sharp differences observed in the data. Do the poll numbers in figure 5.8 actually reflect significant opposition to the policy courses pursued unilaterally by President Trump? Or do they simply reflect Trump's historically low approval rating throughout his first year in office? The variation in opinion on Trump's executive actions already suggests that these polls are capturing something more than simple opposition to Trump's presidency. Moreover, a March 2017 Gallup Poll shows definitively that the strong opposition to many of his unilateral actions is not simply reflective of instinctive opposition to Trump in general.[44] The poll asked respondents to evaluate a series of fourteen policy actions "either taken or proposed by President Trump." Half the statements described actions taken by Trump unilaterally, while the other half described various legislative proposals offered by the president. As shown in figure 5.10, not all policies explicitly linked to President Trump were unpopular. Indeed, Trump's calls to expand paid parental leave and to invest heavily in

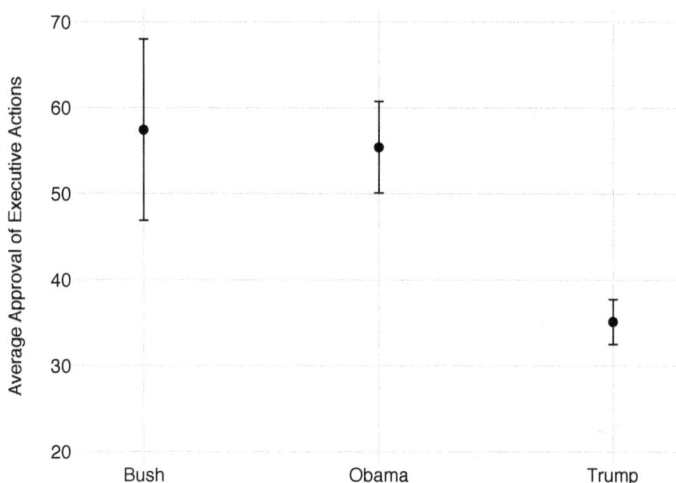

Figure 5.9. Average support for executive actions by president
Note: Dots plot the mean support for executive action by president. I-bars show 95% confidence intervals around each mean value.

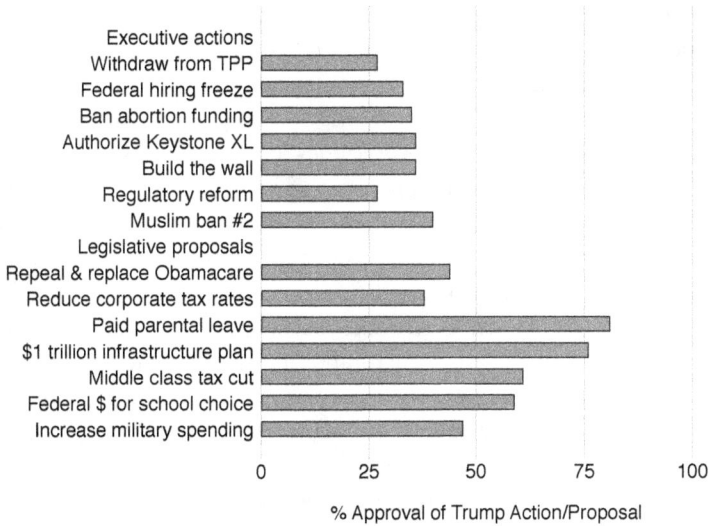

Figure 5.10. Comparison of support for Trump's
legislative proposals and executive actions

upgrading the nation's infrastructure were met with overwhelming public
support. His calls for a middle-class tax cut and for more federal funds
for school choice programs also received considerably more support than
opposition.

Interestingly, only one of Trump's legislative proposals (and ironically
the only one that became law during his first year in office)—his call for a
significant reduction in corporate taxes—was less popular than his most
popular executive action (the second incarnation of the travel ban). In
short, both on the campaign trail and during his first few months in office, President Trump advanced a number of policy proposals that received
widespread support among the public. But he used his unilateral powers to
enact the most widely unpopular elements of his agenda.

A POLITICAL PRICE FOR UNPOPULAR ORDERS?

Our theory of anticipatory action suggests that most executive actions
will be popular because presidents anticipate the likely reaction of both
political elites and the public. Consequently, they often forgo those actions they expect to be politically problematic. The striking unpopularity of many of Trump's first-year executive actions raises important ques-

tions. Did Trump misjudge the likely reaction of other political elites and the general public? Did he simply not care? Has he paid a political price for his brazen use of unilateral power?

To gain greater insight into Trump's strategic calculus, the chapter concludes with a series of four case studies. In the first three cases, the impetuousness with which Trump resorted to his unilateral powers suggests a president with little regard for the political costs of alienating congressional allies and millions of Americans alike. If a president embraces unilateralism without regard for the likely response of other actors, we should expect the resulting orders to provoke marked institutional resistance. In the final case, Trump resisted the temptation to take bold, sudden action. Instead, his extended and even tortured decision-making process plainly shows his awareness of and concern about the political ramifications of executive action.

In each of these cases, Trump's executive actions prompted significant pushback from congressional critics and the courts. Even in cases in which he eventually emerged victorious, the political battle in courtrooms and in front of the cameras weakened his political position.

The Travel Bans

In the late fall of 2015, the West was rattled by two ghastly terrorist attacks. In November, an ISIS-inspired attack at the Bataclan nightclub in Paris claimed the lives of 130 victims. Several weeks later in California, a pair of attackers pledging allegiance to the Islamic State killed fourteen people at the San Bernardino County Department of Public Health's Christmas party. The attacks were widely condemned on both sides of the political aisle. But presidential candidate Trump upped the ante by calling for dramatic action to prevent such attacks in the future. At a campaign stop in South Carolina, he brazenly proclaimed, "Donald J. Trump is calling for a total and complete shutdown of Muslims entering the United States until our country's representatives can figure out what the hell is going on!"[45]

Just one week after taking office, President Trump acted swiftly to follow through on his campaign pledge. On January 27, 2017, he signed Executive Order 13769, banning all citizens of Iraq, Syria, Iran, Libya, Somalia, Sudan, and Yemen from entering the United States for ninety days.[46] The hastily considered order created chaos at airports throughout the country and prompted a bipartisan backlash from Capitol Hill. Democrats quickly and almost uniformly denounced Trump's move as contrary to American values.[47] Senate Minority Leader Chuck Schumer announced his intention to oppose all cabinet nominees who supported the travel ban. And in a break with precedent, former president Obama weighed in publicly, noting that he "fundamentally disagrees with the notion of discriminating against individuals because of their faith or religion."[48]

Perhaps more surprisingly, Trump's order also produced significant pushback from prominent Republicans. Senators John McCain of Arizona and Lindsey Graham of South Carolina quickly issued a joint statement condemning Trump's move as ill-conceived and counterproductive. By implicitly signaling that Americans do not want Muslims in their country, they warned, the travel ban "may do more to help terrorist recruitment than improve our security."[49] While Tennessee senator Lamar Alexander noted his general support for increased scrutiny of travelers from war-torn countries, he lamented that "this vetting proposal itself needed more vetting." He argued that the order as drafted bordered on being a religious test, which would be "inconsistent with our American character."[50]

This swift condemnation from many in Congress was accompanied by simultaneous nationwide demonstrations against the president's actions. Scenes from mass protests at airports filled the airwaves and dramatized the stakes involved for millions of Americans. Opponents of Trump's travel ban acted swiftly not only in the streets but also in the courts, where they filed suit to block the ban's implementation. The day after Trump's announcement, a federal judge in New York granted a temporary restraining order blocking many of the order's provisions after concluding that petitioners had a "strong likelihood of success" in ultimately demonstrating that Trump's ban violates "rights to Due Process and Equal Protection guaranteed by the United States Constitution."[51] The following day, a second federal court in Massachusetts issued a restraining order of its own, barring the government from detaining or removing anyone who had arrived legally from the listed countries. On January 30, acting Attorney General Sally Yates, a holdover from the Obama administration, publicly announced that she was "not convinced that the executive order is lawful," and directed Department of Justice lawyers not to defend it in court.[52] The Trump administration responded by promptly firing Yates. On February 3, a district court judge blocked the implementation of the ban nationwide. Finally, on February 9 the Ninth Circuit Court of Appeals unanimously ruled against the Trump administration's request to reinstate the ban.

The administration seemed to have been caught completely off guard by the flurry of opposition to the travel ban both in Washington and in the country at large. This was almost inevitable given the haphazard and ad hoc manner in which the executive order was drafted. Trump had failed to consult congressional leaders of either party in advance to gauge their reaction before announcing his decision. According to some reports, in rushing to issue the order as quickly as possible the administration even seemed to have skirted the legally required review of the order by the Office of Management and Budget, which would have ensured that relevant departments, including Homeland Security and Justice, had the opportunity to raise concerns and objections before any final decision was made.[53]

A week after the Ninth Circuit ruling, Trump announced his intention to issue a new executive order instituting a limited version of the travel ban. The revised order, issued in March 2017, was tailored to address some of the most vocal criticisms of the first order and to improve its odds of surviving judicial scrutiny. Iraq was removed from the list of countries whose citizens would be temporarily banned from entering the United States; the travel prohibitions would no longer apply to anyone currently holding a valid US visa or green card; and the ban on Syrian refugees was reduced from indefinite to 120 days.

Although Trump's concessions won over many erstwhile Republican critics, Democrats continued to lambaste the president's actions. "A rebranded Muslim ban is still a Muslim ban, plain and simple," concluded New Jersey senator Cory Booker.[54] And like its predecessor, the revised travel ban was dealt a string of defeats in federal court. Only two days after its issuance, the State of Hawaii again sued to block the ban's implementation. On March 15, a federal district court judge agreed and granted a temporary restraining order preventing the ban from going into effect. After a series of additional defeats in district court as well as in the Fourth Circuit Court of Appeals, the Trump administration finally won a partial victory in the Supreme Court. On June 26, the court announced that it would formally take up the case and hear oral arguments in October; however, until then it reversed earlier rulings and allowed the Trump administration to implement the more limited ban.

Yet before the Supreme Court could hear arguments on the second ban, the administration had replaced it with a third version, unveiled in September 2017. This ban, like its predecessors, was defeated multiple times in federal court. However, on December 4 the Supreme Court intervened and allowed the administration to put the ban into effect while the various legal challenges to it continued to work their way through the judicial system. Finally, in June 2018 the Supreme Court upheld the third version of the travel ban on a 5–4 ruling. Thus, the ban's tortuous history illustrates both the president's capacity to shift policy unilaterally and the various limits on the exercise of such power. Trump's moves prompted significant pushback—both formal and informal—which led the administration to considerably modify and scale back its travel bans before the third and final version ultimately survived a legal challenge.

BANNING TRANSGENDER PERSONS FROM THE MILITARY

During his first year in office, president Bill Clinton opened a political Pandora's box when he announced his intention to lift the long-standing ban on homosexuals serving openly in the military. Almost a quarter century later, Donald Trump provoked a similar backlash by unilaterally banning transgender individuals from serving in the armed forces. As was the case with Trump's first travel ban, the decision to bar transgender individuals from military service was not the product of extensive cross-branch consultation or even of a thorough review from within the executive branch. Rather, Trump seems to have decided on the move impetuously, with little anticipation of or regard for the political pushback that would ensue.

Before leaving office, Barack Obama had taken several steps to ease restrictions on transgender individuals serving in the military. Under the new policy announced by defense secretary Ash Carter on June 30, 2016, transgender soldiers already in the military could henceforth serve openly, and the armed services would admit openly transgender new recruits as of July 1, 2017.[55] Then the return of unified Republican control of Congress and the White House afforded conservatives an opportunity to push back against President Obama's policy shift. Specifically, conservatives in the House of Representatives tried to attach an amendment to a Department of Defense appropriations bill that would bar the use of Pentagon funds for gender transition treatments. The amendment was narrowly defeated when a handful of Republicans joined Democrats in voting no. Despite the setback, House conservatives led by Vicky Hartzler (R-MO) reiterated their determination to continue the fight.

Rather than inviting congressional leaders to the White House to hammer out a deal on the narrow issue at hand or simply allowing the controversy to fade away, President Trump threw gasoline on the fire. At 5:55 a.m. on July 26—the fifty-ninth anniversary of president Harry Truman's executive order desegregating the military—Trump tweeted the news: "After consultation with my Generals and military experts, please be advised that the United States government will not accept or allow Transgender individuals to serve in any capacity in the United States military." Trump's decision was so impulsive that defense secretary James Mattis first learned of his decision only the day before.[56]

Trump's policy proclamation by tweet caught most of his own administration off guard as staffers struggled to answer questions about the details of the policy and how it would be implemented. This confusion led Senate Armed Services Committee chair John McCain to criticize the president's language as "unclear." McCain noted that contra Trump's implication, the Defense Department had previously decided to allow transgender persons already serving in the military to remain. He admonished, "We should all be guided by the principle that any American who wants to serve our country and is able to meet the standards should have the opportunity to do so—and should be treated as the patriots they are."[57] While some congressional conservatives welcomed Trump's move, other Republicans joined McCain in decisively breaking with the president. Senator Richard Shelby of Alabama echoed McCain's condemnation and declared that "you ought to treat everybody fairly and give everybody a chance to serve." Similarly, senator Orrin Hatch of Utah told reporters, "I don't think we should be discriminating against anyone," and announced that he stood behind his transgender constituents.[58]

Democrats, whose mobilization in the House of Representatives had defeated the Hartzler amendment, vociferously opposed Trump's move. House Minority Leader Nancy Pelosi lambasted Trump's action as "a cruel and arbitrary decision" designed to humiliate those who volunteered to serve their country. Senator Jack Reed of Rhode Island, the ranking Democrat on the Armed Services Committee, contrasted Trump's move with Truman's, noting that the former "is choosing to retreat in the march toward equality."[59] The ban also triggered a series of spontaneous protests nationwide as thousands of demonstrators took to the streets in defiance of the president's directive.

In the face of this significant pushback both in Washington and across the country, President Trump had little luck in rallying the public to his side. A Quinnipiac University Poll fielded just weeks after Trump's tweet showed that 68% of Americans believed that transgender Americans should be allowed to serve in the military. Only 27% agreed with the president that they should not.[60]

It took the administration a full month to translate Trump's twitter declaration into a formal memorandum directing a change in policy. The final policy followed through on Trump's pledge to block the open recruitment of transgender troops into the military. However, it did not include his promise that transgender persons would not be allowed to serve in any capacity. Instead, the memorandum gave the secretaries of Defense and Homeland Security considerable leeway in setting policy regarding transgender troops currently serving in the armed forces.

No sooner was the ink dry on the new policy than it was challenged in federal court, where the administration quickly suffered a series of significant setbacks. On October 30, 2017, a federal district court judge issued a preliminary injunction preventing the ban from going into effect. Judge Colleen Kollar-Kotelly ruled that the administration's justification for the policy shift "does not appear to be supported by any facts" and likely violated transgender Americans' constitutional rights. In November, a second federal judge in Maryland went even further and issued a preliminary injunction also barring the Defense Department from denying funds for gender transition surgeries.[61]

The Trump administration appealed the injunctions, but its petition for a stay was denied in December 2017. Ultimately, it dropped its appeal pending completion of an ongoing Defense Department review of the policy. As a result, transgender Americans began openly enlisting in the military on January 1, 2018, as the issue worked its way through the courts. The administration issued revised policy guidelines in March 2018. Then in January 2019, the Supreme Court denied Department of Justice petitions to review preliminary district court rulings against the administration, but issued a stay on the district court injunctions; this paved the way for the ban to finally go into effect.[62] The military began implementing the policy in April 2019, almost two years after the initial announcement.

DEFUNDING SANCTUARY CITIES

On July 1, 2015, thirty-two-year-old Kathryn Steinle was killed by a stray gunshot on San Francisco's Pier 14.[63] The bullet had been fired by Jose Inez Garcia Zarate, an illegal immigrant and repeat drug offender. Earlier that year, the US Immigration and Customs Enforcement (ICE) agency had issued a detainer for Zarate. However, because ICE did not serve the sheriff's department with a warrant for Zarate, San Francisco authorities ignored the immigration detainer.

Republican presidential candidate Donald Trump, who only two weeks earlier had announced his campaign by highlighting the threat posed by illegal immigration in stark terms, quickly seized on the slaying to justify his tough talk. "This senseless and totally preventable act of violence committed by an illegal immigrant is yet another example of why we must secure our border immediately," Trump thundered. "This is an absolutely disgraceful situation and I am the only one that can fix it. Nobody else has the guts to even talk about it."[64]

Conservatives in the House of Representatives seized on the tragedy as an opportunity to crack down on sanctuary cities, municipalities that limit their cooperation with federal immigration enforcement efforts. In a bill labeled the "Donald Trump Act" by its Democratic opponents, House Republicans tried to deny federal funding to sanctuary cities. The bill passed the House 241–179, but failed to overcome a filibuster in the Senate.

Within days of his inauguration, President Trump took swift action to punish sanctuary cities. Rather than pushing for new legislation, which would still confront a Democratic filibuster, Trump acted on his own. On January 25, 2017, he signed Executive Order 13768, barring sanctuary cities from receiving federal grant funding. The reaction on Capitol Hill split along partisan lines. Democrats strongly objected to Trump's order, while congressional Republicans rallied behind the president. The most vociferous reaction to his move would come from sanctuary cities themselves. Officials from cities large and small, from New York to Los Angeles and Syracuse to Austin, railed against the order. New York mayor Bill de Blasio declared, "We're going to defend all of our people regardless of where they come from, regardless of their immigration status." Chicago mayor Rahm Emanuel, former Obama administration Chief of Staff, was equally defiant when he said, "I want to be clear: We're going to stay a sanctuary city." In Boston, mayor Marty Walsh pledged to use City Hall itself if necessary to protect anyone unjustly targeted.[65]

Municipal leaders across the nation quickly filed suit, alleging that Trump lacked the legal authority to curtail grant funding as punishment for failing to participate in federal immigration programs. Ironically, perhaps the most salient precedent was chief justice John Roberts's decision that crippled the Medicaid expansion under the Affordable Care Act (ACA). To encourage states to agree to expand Medicaid to include citizens earning up to 138% of the poverty level, the ACA employed both a carrot and a stick. The federal government would cover the complete cost of the expansion through 2016; this contribution would then slowly decrease to 90% and remain at that rate from 2020 forward. If a state refused the expansion, it risked losing some of or even all its current Medicaid funding. In *NFIB v. Sebelius*, the Supreme Court ruled that this last provision was "unconstitutionally coercive," because it denied states a genuine choice of whether to comply with the federal program. In the sanctuary city suits, attorneys for plaintiff municipalities argued that threatening to withhold federal grant funding to force compliance with federal immigration programs was similarly coercive and therefore unconstitutional.

In April 2017, a federal district judge sided with plaintiffs and issued a preliminary injunction to prevent the ban from going into effect. Judge William Orrick ruled that Trump's unilateral ban violated the separation of powers; only Congress has the constitutional authority to place restrictions on eligibility for federal funds. Moreover, Orrick ruled that the ban, which was not limited to grant programs specifically related to immigration programs, was far too broad and therefore failed to meet the test established by *NFIB v. Sebelius*.[66]

Responding to the defeat in district court in May, Attorney General Jeff Sessions issued a guidance memorandum "clarifying" President Trump's executive order. More specifically, it narrowed the scope of the original order significantly. Whereas the January 25 missive opened the possibility of cutting off all funding to sanctuary cities, the new memorandum specified that only grants from the Justice Department and the Department of Homeland Security could be denied to state and local entities that failed to comply with section 1373 of the United States Code.[67]

Having issued the narrowly tailored implementation memo, the Department of Justice appealed to the district court to reconsider its ruling. However, in July Judge Orrick denied the department's request, and the injunction remained in place.[68] Within days of Orrick's decision, the department rolled out a new, even more narrowly tailored policy regarding uncooperative sanctuary cities that it hoped might survive legal scrutiny. This time, it focused narrowly on Byrne/JAG grants for state and local law enforcement, which were exempt from the district court's injunction because they already required recipients to certify compliance with various immigration laws. The new Justice Department policy required recipients to allow federal immigration authorities access to municipal jails and to give federal authorities forty-eight-hour notice before releasing any illegal immigrant wanted by federal officials.[69]

The City of Chicago immediately filed suit, arguing that even this more targeted program exceeded executive discretion. In September, a federal district court judge agreed with petitioners and ordered a halt to the program's implementation nationwide. In November, the Trump administration suffered yet another setback in federal district court, when Judge Orrick made his preliminary injunction a permanent one after ruling that Trump's executive order was "unconstitutional on its face."[70] As of 2019, the administration's losing streak on the issue has continued, with the most recent defeat occurring in the Third Circuit Court of Appeals in Philadelphia.[71] The president's policies remain blocked in court.

DACA and the Fate of the Dreamers

In the three preceding case studies, President Trump seemed all but impervious to any serious consideration of the political costs of unilateral action. And as a result, his ill-conceived actions received little support from the mass public and provoked significant pushback from Congress and the courts. Nevertheless, at least one important case suggests that Trump is not completely immune from calculations concerning political costs: the tortured path to his decision to revoke President Obama's Deferred Action for Childhood Arrivals (DACA) program. Yet after finally taking action to end DACA, Trump has again doubled down and provoked fierce institutional resistance.

The Trump presidential campaign was widely derided for failing to articulate clear positions on a host of issues of national import. However, on one policy Trump's position was abidingly clear: illegal immigration. Indeed, he made a tough line on immigration the substantive focal point of his campaign from the day he rode the down escalator at Trump Tower to address a gaggle of curious reporters. In his very first speech, Trump vehemently denounced the influx of immigrants from Latin America as the main driver of the nation's crime and drug problems. To protect America from these ills, he promised to build "a great wall on our southern border" and to reverse Obama-era policies that were soft on illegal immigrants. Specifically, Trump pledged to end DACA and Deferred Action for Parents of Americans and Lawful Permanent Residents (DAPA): "I will immediately terminate President Obama's illegal executive order on immigration."[72]

Trump's anti-immigration rhetoric helped catapult him past his rivals to win the Republican nomination. As his focus shifted from the primaries to the general election contest against Democratic nominee Hillary Clinton, he did not pivot to the center and back away from his promises to end Obama's unilateral moves on immigration. Instead, he doubled down. At a campaign rally in Arizona in August 2016, Trump roared to a frenzied crowd, "We will immediately terminate President Obama's two illegal executive amnesties, in which he defied federal law and the constitution to give amnesty to approximately 5 million illegal immigrants."[73] These "deadly" policies, he warned, "allow thousands of criminal aliens to freely roam our streets."[74]

Yet almost immediately after securing his election win, President-Elect Trump began to take a softer line on DACA. In an interview with *Time* for its issue naming him Person of the Year, he talked not about immediately scrapping DACA but about finding a permanent solution to the Dreamers' legal status. "We're going to work something out that's going to make people happy and proud," Trump declared. Gone was language denouncing illegal aliens as "rapists," "murderers," and not their home countries' "best." Instead, Trump expressed genuine sympathy for the Dreamers and their plight: "They got brought here at a very young age, they've worked here, they've gone to school here. Some were good students. Some have wonderful jobs. And they're in never-never land because they don't know what's going to happen."[75]

Trump echoed this radically transformed view in an interview with ABC News *World News Tonight* anchor David Muir several days after the inauguration. Muir reminded Trump of his harsh campaign rhetoric and asked whether many Dreamers were right to fear deportation under his administration. The president forcefully dismissed such concerns. "They shouldn't be very worried," he emphasized. "I do have a big heart. We're going to take care of everybody."[76] In February, the *Los Angeles Times* reported that White House staffers had drafted an executive order to scrap DACA; however, the president refused to sign it.[77]

What can explain Trump's epiphany on DACA and the Dreamers? It is impossible to know for sure. However, the president's tightrope act throughout 2017 on the question of DACA suggests that he understood full well the almost intractable political situation in which he found himself. On the one hand, many in his base expected him to follow through on his pledge to terminate DACA, uphold the law, and deport all illegal immigrants, regardless of their merits or circumstances. But at the same time, Trump clearly perceived significant political risks should he end DACA unilaterally. DACA and the Dreamers received overwhelming public support, with polls consistently showing roughly three out of four Americans in favor of allowing the Dreamers to stay. Moreover, the underlying policy established by DACA if not Obama's action itself received considerable support from within the president's own party in Congress, particularly in the Senate. If Trump ended DACA, he would invariably invite criticism from members on both sides of the aisle. In addition, he would force congressional Republicans to deal with an issue with no clear winning formula. To extend DACA, Republican leaders would have to rely on Democratic votes and break the Hastert Rule—that Republicans in the House of Representatives would allow to the floor only bills that were supported by a majority of the Republican caucus. The alternative, allowing DACA to expire without a legislative replacement, could be even more costly. The inevitable images of deported Dreamers would reinforce the party's reputation for being callous and unreasonable on immigration, further undermining its appeal to nonwhite voters.

In a February press conference, President Trump offered an almost stream-of-consciousness window on his thinking on the matter. "DACA is a very, very difficult subject for me," he admitted. He called many of the Dreamers "incredible kids" who came here through no fault of their own and who deserved compassion. Yet he argued that existing immigration law is "rough," and that he finds it "very, very hard doing what the law says exactly to do." Trump again pledged to "deal with DACA with heart," but seemed to suggest that doing so would ultimately require a legislative solution. The president noted that to fix the situation, he must "deal with a lot of politicians" and "convince them that what I'm saying is right."[78]

In June, Trump officially ended another Obama-era immigration initiative, Deferred Action for Parents of Americans and Lawful Permanent Residents (DAPA). Because an evenly divided Supreme Court in a June 2016 ruling left in place a lower court's preliminary injunction against DAPA, the program never went into effect before Obama left office.[79] At the time, Trump had praised the decision for "block[ing] one of the most unconstitutional actions ever undertaken by a president."[80] However, even as Trump rescinded Obama's memorandum establishing DAPA, Homeland Security secretary John Kelly emphasized that there would be no immediate change to DACA.

While the ultimate death of DAPA cheered many on the Right, it was not enough to silence the most outspoken critics of illegal immigration. In July 2017, officials from ten states led by Texas Attorney General Ken Paxton sent President Trump a formal memo calling on him to end DACA, or face lawsuits challenging its constitutionality. In July, Paxton wrote an op-ed for *USA Today* publicly calling on Trump "to fulfill his campaign promise and make our nation safer by enforcing federal immigration laws."[81]

Paxton and other immigration hardliners had a powerful ally within the administration: Attorney General Jeff Sessions. Sessions was unequivocal in his view that DACA was unconstitutional, and in late August 2017, he informed Trump that neither he nor the Department of Justice would defend the program in court.[82] A week later, Trump rescinded DACA.

In the president's September 5 statement announcing his decision, he endeavored to couch his action as an inescapable result of Obama's failings. Trump claimed that his objection to DACA was based solely on procedural, not policy grounds. In a pointed jab at his predecessor, he noted that while Obama famously said "I can't just do these things by myself," in issuing DACA through an executive memorandum, that was precisely what he did. In so doing, Trump claimed that Obama had made "an end run around Congress and violat[ed] the core tenets that sustain our republic."[83] For this reason, he announced his decision to end DACA within six months, and he encouraged Congress to find a legislative solution to the Dreamers' fate.

The decision produced an immediate backlash from many on Capitol Hill. Democrats uniformly panned it. Despite Trump's bragging about his "great heart," senator Tim Kaine (D-VA) charged that the president's action revealed he is "heartless." House Minority Leader Nancy Pelosi chided Trump for his "act of political cowardice." Many Republican supporters of DACA instead focused on the need for legislative action. However, senator John McCain (R-AZ) publicly blasted the president's move. McCain said that while he disagreed with Obama's decision to issue DACA unilaterally, "rescinding DACA at this time is an unacceptable reversal of the promises and opportunities that have been conferred to these individuals."[84]

That evening, Trump took to Twitter to respond to his critics and muddied the waters in the process. "Congress now has 6 months to legalize DACA (something the Obama Administration was unable to do)," he tweeted. "If they can't, I will revisit this issue!"[85] Trump's tweet plainly conflicted with the logic of his earlier statement that he had no choice but to revoke the immigration program because it was unconstitutional. However, the tweet suggests that he anticipated political costs should DACA expire without a legislative deal, and that he wanted to reserve unilateral options to avoid them if possible.

In January 2018, the battle over the future of Deferred Action for Childhood Arrivals contributed to the first government shutdown during a period of unified government in American history. As of early 2019, DACA's fate remains uncertain. Congress has repeatedly failed to pass legislation protecting the Dreamers, largely because the president himself backed out of a deal to save DACA in exchange for increased funds for border security.[86] The administration's six-month deadline came and went. And yet, DACA remains in force thanks to yet another string of defeats for the Trump administration in federal courts.[87]

Ultimately, President Trump faced a politically parlous choice on DACA. He could rescind the program via executive action. Or he could keep it in place until explicitly ordered to end it by a federal court. His waffling on the subject suggests a strong sensitivity to the political costs—of both acting and not acting—in the DACA case. Whether this case is unique or evidence of an evolution in Trump's approach to unilateral action remains unseen.

⟨∞⟩

The historic unpopularity of many of President Trump's unilateral actions has consistently triggered significant backlashes from other institutional actors. In the first three case studies, Trump took bold unilateral action seemingly with little thought to the political consequences of doing so. Falling prey to what Richard Neustadt labeled "the hazards of transition," the new president rushed each order without soliciting input from congressional leaders or even from key officials within his own administration. As a result, he was repeatedly caught off guard by the ferocity of the political pushback, and his own subordinates were often left in the dark, undermining their ability to defend the administration. In the DACA case, Trump proceeded much more cautiously, but ultimately found himself forced into a political minefield over that program's future. In each case, battles with Congress, local officials, and mass demonstrators caused the administration to quickly lose control of the news cycle and put the White House on the defensive. This institutional resistance almost certainly contributed to the strikingly low levels of public support for Trump's actions. Although the fate of these unilateral actions remains pending, each action has been dealt an embarrassing defeat in federal courts, delaying implementation of the president's wishes and frequently making him appear both isolated and weak.

CONCLUSION

Chapter 1 began with a puzzle: If the formal legislative and judicial checks on unilateral action are so weak, why do presidents resort to such action so rarely? Presidents have long found their formal constitutional powers wholly insufficient to meet the expectations and demands placed on them. The rising tide of polarization and increasingly tribal partisanship in Congress have rendered almost Sisyphean the challenge of building legislative coalitions behind meaningful policy change. Hence the temptation to rely instead on the presidency's unilateral powers is great indeed. Yet presidents routinely forgo opportunities to move policy unilaterally closer to their position, even in cases in which Congress and the courts are all but powerless to stop them. The varied analyses in this chapter offer the first systematic evidence that public opinion constrains presidential unilateralism.

When contemplating unilateral action, presidents consider more than simply the likelihood of being reversed by Congress or overturned in the courts. They also consider the backlash that acting unilaterally might provoke and the political costs it might entail. The president's standing among the public fundamentally shapes the nature of these cost-benefit calculations. Those chief executives who enjoy little support among the public are in a precarious position. Americans who disapprove of the president's job performance are also likely to oppose his executive actions. Moreover, unpopular presidents are attractive targets for their political foes and must anticipate significant pushback from other elites. By contrast, popular presidents are both less attractive targets for would-be critics of unilateral policies and better positioned to weather the storm should it arise. As a result, popular presidents issue more significant executive actions than do unpopular presidents. However, even popular presidents do not promulgate significant unilateral directives with wanton abandon; upticks in approval lead to modest, not extreme, increases in executive order issuances and significance.

We also found no evidence that the frequency of major executive actions systematically influenced presidential approval ratings. This is precisely what we would expect if presidents routinely forgo unilateral action when the political costs it would provoke are likely to be high. If presidents anticipate public reactions successfully, most executive actions, far from being inherently controversial, should also receive broad public support. Analyzing all available public polling data from the presidencies of George W. Bush and Barack Obama provided strong support for this hypothesis. Presidents push policies opposed by strong majorities of Americans at their political peril. As a result, most presidents pursue major unilateral action only when they anticipate that it will receive widespread support. Opinion polls from President Trump's first years in office, however, suggest a president who either cannot anticipate or does not care about the aggregate public response to his unilateral moves.

Perhaps it should come as no surprise that the most iconoclastic and polarizing president in recent memory has embraced a different view of executive action. Deliberations concerning what would appeal to his base and not to most Americans seem to underlie much of Trump's strategic calculus. This strategy may ultimately prove politically sustainable. After all, Trump became president by ignoring the myriad of pundits who declared that his base was insufficient to gain first the Republican nomination and then the White House. He won the election with the base in 2016, and he may well do so again in 2020 if it remains motivated and steadfastly in his corner. However, consistent with our argument, Trump's repeated willingness to pursue unpopular policies unilaterally has come at a cost: virtually unprecedented levels of institutional resistance.

To be sure, both Bush and Obama occasionally issued directives that prompted some criticism from Congress and even setbacks in federal court. But the institutional pushback to many of Trump's early unilateral actions has been great and extraordinarily consistent, capped by a dizzying rate of defeats in federal court. On these dimensions, Trump has certainly fulfilled his promise to divert from politics as usual. Yet his unilateral achievements have almost certainly come at a great political cost.

The economy's upward trajectory since the Great Recession, which began under Obama, has continued through Trump's first two years. Indeed, in October 2017, the index of consumer sentiment surpassed 100 for the first time in more than a decade, and in May 2018 the unemployment rate fell to an almost fifty-year low. A booming economy has historically translated into ebullient approval ratings for the incumbent. Between 1953 and 2016, presidents in office during an index of consumer sentiment rating greater than 100 have enjoyed an average approval rating of 62%. The incumbent's approval never dipped below 52% during this period. By contrast, Donald Trump's approval ratings for almost his entire first two years in office have been mired in the high 30s to low 40s, with most Americans disapproving of his job performance.[88] Of course, a myriad of other factors—from Russiagate to trade wars to tweetstorms to Stormy Daniels—have contributed to Trump's low popular standing. It is likely, however, that his highly unpopular executive actions and the intense institutional resistance they provoked have contributed to his lackluster approval ratings. This in turn, by weakening the president's political capital, also almost certainly contributed to Trump's failure to make much headway on his legislative agenda despite Republican control of both houses of Congress. Trump's low approval ratings also almost certainly fueled the Democratic gains in the 2018 midterms, which handed Nancy Pelosi the speaker's gavel.[89] Even his modest unilateral successes have come at a significant price politically.

APPENDIX TO CHAPTER 5

Regression Results for Effects of
Congressional Opposition on Approval

The results of the logistic regression models used to produce the estimated
effects of congressional opposition to a hypothetical unilateral action by
President Trump to declare a national emergency for infrastructure are
presented in appendix table 5.1. The estimates in figure 5.1 are based on
model 2 of that table with demographic controls.

APPENDIX TABLE 5.1. Effects of congressional unilateralism
criticism on presidential approval

	(1)	(2)
Congressional opposition	−0.36**	−0.42*
	(0.13)	(0.17)
Republican		1.99**
		(0.21)
Democrat		−1.80**
		(0.24)
Male		0.38*
		(0.17)
Age		0.02**
		(0.01)
Education		−0.00
		(0.06)
White		0.01
		(0.19)
Constant	−0.17	−1.35**
	(0.09)	(0.34)
Observations	1,000	1,000

Note: Models are logistic regressions. Robust standard errors are in parentheses. All
significance tests are two-tailed.
*p < 0.05
**p < 0.01

Additional Methodological Details on
Vector Autoregressive Model

Because the relationship between presidential approval and significant executive order issuance is potentially endogenous, we utilized a vector autoregressive (VAR) model to explore the opinion-action relationship. A VAR system contains a set of variables, each of which is expressed as a linear function of lags of itself and of the other variables, plus an error term:

$$y_t = \alpha + \phi_1 y_{t-1} + \ldots + \phi_p y_{t-p} + \Theta X_t + \epsilon_t.$$

In the VAR expression above, y_t is an $(n \times 1)$ vector of the potentially endogenous variables, presidential approval and executive orders. ϕ is an $(n \times n)$ matrix of coefficients relating lagged values of the two endogenous variables to their current values, and Θ is an $(n \times m)$ matrix of coefficients relating the exogenous variables to the endogenous ones. α denotes an $(n \times 1)$ vector of intercept terms, and ϵ_t represents an $(n \times 1)$ vector of disturbance terms. Unlike structural equation models, the VAR does not impose structural relationships a priori, which reduces the likelihood of omitted variable bias and misspecification.[90] The VAR also allows for the specification of strictly exogenous variables. As described in the chapter, our models all included presidency fixed effects to account for different propensities to act unilaterally across administrations; a measure of economic performance, the index of consumer sentiment; a dummy variable indicating periods of divided partisan control of the White House and at least one chamber of Congress; and a dummy variable indicating whether the country was at war.

Prior to the estimation of the VAR, we noted that both the count of significant executive orders and presidential approval are all stationary according to unit root tests, such as the Dickey-Fuller (-23.457, $p = 0.000$; -3.049, $p = 0.031$, respectively) and Phillips-Perron (-24.362, $p = 0.000$; -4.136, $p = 0.001$, respectively). We determined the appropriate lag length with a series of selection statistics. Likelihood ratio, final prediction error (FPE), Akaike's information criterion (AIC), Schwarz's Bayesian information criterion (SBIC), and the Hannan and Quinn information criterion (HQIC) all select two lags. Post-estimation, we noted that the VAR specifications satisfied the stability condition, with all eigenvalues inside the unit circle. Analysis of the residuals using Jarque-Bera, skewness, and kurtosis tests suggested normally distributed disturbances in both cases.

APPENDIX TABLE 5.2. Granger causality tests

| | New York Times executive orders | |
	χ^2	df
Approval equation		
Orders	2.149	2
Orders equation		
Approval	8.611*	2

*$p < .05$

We employed Granger causality tests to examine the relationships between approval and significant executive orders as specified by their cor-
responding VAR models. The concept of Granger causality is based on
prediction such that a variable can be said to "Granger-cause" another
variable if the former's past values help predict those of the latter, beyond
what its past values do alone.[91] The results of the Granger causality tests
are presented in appendix table 5.2. Here we computed Wald tests that the
coefficients on all the lags of an endogenous variable are jointly zero. Thus,
for each equation we tested the null hypothesis that the other endogenous
variable does not Granger-cause the dependent variable of that equation.

In the first equation, we tested whether the coefficients on the two lags
of executive orders in the equation for approval are jointly zero. The null
hypothesis that executive orders do not Granger-cause approval could not
be rejected. In the second equation, we tested the potential for approval to
affect executive orders. Here, in line with our hypothesis, we could reject
the null hypothesis that the two lags of approval do not Granger-cause executive orders. In sum, while approval ratings affect significant executive
orders, there was little evidence of the reverse.[92]

ROBUSTNESS CHECK: EXCLUDING THE FIRST
QUARTER OF NEW PRESIDENCIES

To check the robustness of the results in the face of new presidential terms
that upset the alignment between the approval and executive order time
series, we dropped the first quarter of new presidential terms and re-ran
the same models used to produce the Granger causality tests reported

APPENDIX TABLE 5.3. Granger causality tests, excluding first quarter of new presidents

	New York Times executive orders	
	χ^2	df
Approval equation		
Orders	0.049	2
Orders equation		
Approval	6.013*	2

*$p < .05$

in appendix table 5.2. Because the VAR models executive order issuance as a function of both lagged presidential approval and two-month-lagged presidential approval, in the opening months of a new administration the model uses the prior president's approval rating to predict the new president's executive order activity. Moreover, because some new presidents do not have an approval rating until February or even March of the first year, predictions for these months could be influenced at least in part by the approval rating of the prior president. Thus, dropping first quarter ensured that we examined only the influence of the current president's approval ratings on his level of significant executive order activity. As shown in appendix table 5.3, we arrived at the same conclusions as we did when looking at the entire time series (see appendix table 5.2): we can reject the null hypothesis that presidential approval does not Granger-cause an increase in executive order issuance and significance.

COUNT MODELS INVESTIGATING POTENTIAL MODERATING FACTORS

Our analysis concluded by examining whether presidential sensitivity to approval ratings when contemplating unilateral action varied across different political contexts. The event count models used to produce the estimates presented in figure 5.5 are in appendix table 5.4 below.

APPENDIX TABLE 5.4. Event count models of effect of approval on orders by context

	(1)	(2)	(3)
Lagged orders	0.05	0.05	0.05
	(0.03)	(0.03)	(0.03)
Lagged approval	0.01	0.01*	0.01*
	(0.01)	(0.00)	(0.01)
Lagged approval × second term	0.00		
	(0.01)		
Lagged approval × election year		−0.00	
		(0.01)	
Lagged approval × divided government			−0.00
			(0.01)
Second term	−0.32		
	(0.51)		
Election year		−0.15	
		(0.54)	
Divided government	0.20	0.15	0.31
	(0.14)	(0.14)	(0.46)
Kennedy	0.80**	0.81**	0.80**
	(0.21)	(0.21)	(0.21)
Johnson	0.03	0.13	0.08
	(0.25)	(0.25)	(0.24)
Nixon	−0.21	−0.16	−0.17
	(0.23)	(0.23)	(0.22)
Ford	−0.64*	−0.54*	−0.51
	(0.28)	(0.27)	(0.27)
Carter	−0.20	−0.11	−0.12
	(0.23)	(0.23)	(0.23)
Reagan	−0.33	−0.29	−0.28
	(0.17)	(0.17)	(0.17)
Bush 41	−0.94**	−0.84**	−0.83**
	(0.24)	(0.23)	(0.23)
Clinton	−0.30	−0.26	−0.24
	(0.18)	(0.18)	(0.18)
Bush 43	−0.70**	−0.71**	−0.73**
	(0.24)	(0.23)	(0.23)
Obama	−0.75**	−0.76**	−0.79**
	(0.25)	(0.25)	(0.25)

(continued)

APPENDIX TABLE 5.4. (*continued*)

	(1)	(2)	(3)
Trump	0.55	0.62*	0.66*
	(0.31)	(0.31)	(0.31)
Index of consumer sentiment	−0.02**	−0.02**	−0.02**
	(0.01)	(0.01)	(0.01)
War	0.23	0.26	0.28
	(0.18)	(0.18)	(0.17)
Significant laws	−0.01	−0.01	−0.01
	(0.04)	(0.04)	(0.04)
Constant	0.94*	0.87	0.78
	(0.47)	(0.46)	(0.54)
Observations	791	791	791

Note: Models are negative binomial regressions. Robust standard errors are in parentheses. All significance tests are two-tailed.

*p < 0.05

**p < 0.01

CHAPTER SIX

Pathways of Political Constraint

By examining the relationship between the frequency with which presidents issue important executive orders and presidential approval ratings over time, the previous chapter established a clear linkage between public opinion and presidents' willingness to use the unilateral tools at their disposal. Presidents with low approval ratings anticipate greater popular and institutional pushback should they effect a major shift in policy unilaterally. As a result, presidents who enjoy little public support issue fewer major executive orders than do popular presidents. Of course, the unilateral power of the presidency itself is constant. Both popular and unpopular presidents possess the same capacity to change policy unilaterally. However, this empirical pattern suggests that the exercise of unilateral power is significantly constrained by *political* calculations.

Although they provide important and varied indirect evidence of an informal political constraint on unilateral action, the analyses of the previous chapter are limited in some respects. First, because of data limitations, the empirical analysis focused primarily on the relationship between presidential approval and the frequency and intensity of unilateral action. Approval is a major determinant of both how Americans assess executive action and the probability of that action receiving pushback from Congress or the courts. It is not the only factor entering such presidential calculations, however. Even popular presidents may perceive significant political costs to implementing unilaterally a change in policy that majorities of Americans are inclined to oppose on policy grounds. Presidential anticipatory calculations are considerably more complex and can vary significantly across cases. Yet the preceding analyses examined only a single pathway through which anticipatory calculations about public response and political costs influence the politics of unilateral action: by encouraging presidents to forgo executive action altogether. In what follows, we explore strategies that exist for unilateral action beyond simply acting or not.

Carefully chosen case studies can illuminate precisely how these political dynamics unfold. By unpacking the politics driving presidential decision-making in a series of cases involving actual or intended unilateral action, we can trace the processes through which presidential calculations about public opinion and anticipated political costs constrain the use of unilateral powers in line with our theory and earlier analyses. Case studies also allow us to explore alternate pathways through which political checks shape the decision-making of the unilateral president. Yes, presidents often contemplate but ultimately defer acting unilaterally when they anticipate costly political pushback from Congress, the courts, and the public. However, in other cases anticipated costs may not forestall unilateral action altogether, but rather influence its timing and scope in ways that materially affect the content of public policy.

FORGOING UNILATERAL ACTION

Exploring the politics that lead presidents *not* to issue significant executive orders requires us to find the proverbial dogs that did not bark. It can be extremely difficult to identify such cases, let alone examine them closely, precisely because the result we observe is the absence of presidential action. If presidents anticipate pushback from other institutional actors and an erosion of public support, they will rarely publicize their preference to act unilaterally but then ultimately refrain from doing so. This would make a president appear weak and ineffective. In such situations, chief executives have incentives to hold their cards close to the vest, rendering it all but impossible for the public to know how often they would have liked to act unilaterally, but opted against doing so, in order to avoid provoking politically costly opposition.

It is precisely because of these difficulties that indirect analyses, such as our statistical models in chapter 5, are so useful. Because we cannot identify every time that a president wished to take unilateral action but ultimately did not, we instead looked at variation in presidents' use of their office's unilateral powers over time as political conditions changed. This affords a window on how informal political checks constrain the unilateral president.

Yet in some cases, presidents miscalculate. They may publicly declare their intention to act unilaterally, but as opposition mounts, they reevaluate their position and ultimately defer taking the action. In other cases, nascent plans for unilateral action get leaked to the media before a final decision has been reached. If significant opposition materializes, presidents may reverse course and pull back from going it alone. The case studies that follow explore three such instances. The first involves a newly elected president who pushed too far too fast before recognizing the full extent of the costs he risked incurring should he move forward and change policy with the stroke of a pen. Ultimately, the president backed down and never issued his promised executive order. The second case examines a seasoned second-term president who, at the last second, reversed his intended course of action to avoid congressional pushback and its corrosive influence on public opinion. The final case involves a draft executive order that was leaked to the press, triggering an avalanche of criticism from key members on both sides of the political aisle, and then stopped dead in its tracks.

GAYS IN THE MILITARY

In October 1991, shortly after the forty-five-year-old governor of Arkansas had announced his long-shot bid for the presidency, Bill Clinton attended an open forum at Harvard University's Kennedy School of Government. During the question and answer period, a student asked Clinton whether, as president, he would lift the ban on homosexuals openly serving in the US armed forces. The question caught Clinton slightly off guard. After all, the issue of homosexuals openly serving in the military was far from the national spotlight in the fall of 1991, and the fledgling campaign had no official position. But Clinton responded off the cuff, saying he would end the ban if given the opportunity to do so.[1] As the campaign unfolded, he formalized this response into a firm pledge.

A week after his electoral victory, Clinton publicly reaffirmed his commitment to lifting the ban on gays openly serving in the military. While pledging to consult and work with military leaders about "the mechanics of doing it," he reiterated, "my position is we need everybody in America that's got a contribution to make that's willing to obey the law and work hard and play by the rules."[2] Unlike many of his campaign's major promises—including first and foremost his proposal to remake the health care system in a way that significantly expanded access and lowered costs—delivering on the pledge to lift the ban on gays in the military was relatively easy. It did not require bridging the divide between the Democratic Party's liberal and conservative wings in Congress or overcoming a Republican-led filibuster. Rather, President Clinton could repeal the ban simply by signing an executive order to bar discrimination in the armed forces based on sexual orientation. Indeed, there was clear precedent for taking such a course; Harry Truman had ended racial segregation in the military via executive order almost a half century earlier.

But even before the new president took office, opponents of Clinton's pledge had begun to mobilize on multiple fronts. Most of the military's top leadership strongly opposed lifting the ban, and they refused to keep their professional opinions private. In November 1992, General Colin Powell, chairman of the Joint Chiefs of Staff, publicly warned that lifting the ban "would be prejudicial to good order and discipline."[3] Before Clinton's inauguration, Powell went further in a January 1993 speech in Annapolis, where he publicly lobbied against any change in current policy. He explicitly rejected any parallels between ending discrimination against gays and President Truman's decision to desegregate the armed forces via executive order. "Homosexuality is not a benign behavioral characteristic such as skin color," Powell argued. Rather, in his view homosexuality "goes to the core of the most fundamental aspect of human behavior."[4]

There were also ominous signs of simmering opposition on Capitol Hill. The powerful chair of the Senate Armed Services Committee, Sam Nunn, strongly opposed lifting the ban, as did a number of other prominent Democrats. President Clinton later recalled former Senate Majority Leader Robert Byrd arguing vehemently against lifting the ban. Not only did Byrd tell the new president that he personally considered homosexuality a sin, but he also echoed the military's views that it was corrosive to martial discipline and cohesion. He even went so far as to blame homosexual conduct in part for the collapse of the Roman Empire.[5]

This quick crystallization of opposition to the plan opened a fissure within the administration itself. Some White House advisers argued that Clinton must fulfill his pledge and stay the course. However, many of the president's political advisers, led by Paul Begala and Clinton's pollster Stanley Greenberg, urged an about-face before it was too late. According to Begala, the political winds had shifted too much, and the political risks were too high to move forward. "It wasn't a big thing in the campaign," he noted. "We clearly had no appreciation of the offense that would be taken at a Presidential directive ending the ban."[6] And Clinton was keenly aware that he was a minority president. He had received only 43% of the vote in the three-way contest with incumbent president George H. W. Bush and Texas billionaire H. Ross Perot. Republicans, led by senator Robert Dole of Kansas, had already emphasized his paltry popular vote share to insist that the new president possessed no mandate for his policy vision.[7] Winning over Perot voters was essential if Clinton hoped to be reelected in 1996. In economic policy, this imperative dictated a significant programmatic shift. On the campaign trail, candidate Clinton had supported a middle-class tax cut to ease the economic pain of recession and get the economy moving again. But just several months later as president, he abandoned such plans and instead focused squarely on the raison d'être of Perot's campaign—the deficit—which the administration would reduce through a package of painful spending cuts and tax increases.

This pivot toward winning over Perot voters would also influence the fledgling administration's approach to social policy. A Gallup Poll conducted a week after the election showed the overall American public split roughly fifty-fifty on the question of whether gays should be allowed to serve in the military. But Perot voters opposed a shift in policy, with 55% saying gays should not be allowed to serve versus only 41% saying that they should.[8] Moreover, a mid-November Gallup Poll suggested that the main arguments advanced by military and congressional opponents of lifting the ban resonated with many Americans. When asked whether Clinton should delay lifting the ban "if there are strong arguments that this action will produce serious morale and readiness problems," 61% of Americans said yes versus only 29% who said no.[9]

The day after the inauguration, White House communications director George Stephanopoulos publicly affirmed the administration's commitment to lifting the ban through executive action. When pressed for more details by veteran reporter Helen Thomas, Stephanopoulos replied that he expected an executive order lifting the ban to be announced within the next week.[10] Even as Stephanopoulos spoke, however, defense secretary Les Aspin was crafting a compromise proposal to delay action on lifting the ban pending a formal six-month review by the Department of Defense. During this six-month period, Aspin wanted the military to suspend asking new recruits any questions regarding their sexual orientation and to cease discharging any soldier on the grounds of homosexuality. Despite the concessions, Senator Nunn rejected Aspin's proposal.

While Nunn supported the basic idea of a six-month delay, he demanded that military commanders be given greater flexibility over reassigning soldiers accused of homosexuality during the interim period.[11] His position was markedly strengthened by the growing momentum on the other side of the political aisle for legislation that would tie Clinton's hands and limit his authority to lift the ban unilaterally. While some

senior Republicans, including Arizona senator Barry Goldwater, backed
Clinton's decision, Minority Leader Dole rallied most Republicans behind
an effort to attach a rider to one of the president's top domestic priorities,
the Family Medical Leave Act. Dole's rider would write the extant ban on
homosexuals serving in the military into law, which would put any effort
by Clinton to change policy via executive order on shaky legal grounds.
Winning Nunn's support was crucial to securing enough Democratic votes
to block Dole's gambit.

While the new president faced this potential revolt in Congress, he
also had to grapple with quickly evaporating popularity. Internal polls by
Stan Greenberg showed Clinton having lost twenty points in favorability
ratings in two weeks, a drop Greenberg largely attributed to Clinton's unpopular stand on gays in the military.[12] In his memoirs, Clinton frankly
admits the role that public opinion and political calculations played in his
reversal. "While all this was going on," he writes, "I saw a poll showing
that by 48 to 45 percent the public disagreed with my position." While a
roughly even split was not too bad for a controversial issue, these top-line
numbers belied a more significant gap in the intensity of public preferences: "Only 16 percent of the electorate strongly approved of lifting the
ban, while 33 percent very strongly disapproved."[13] Clinton reasoned that
many in Congress would yield to this intense opposition, rendering his
political situation tenuous at best.

Unwilling to incur such costs and risks, Clinton caved. He scrapped
his earlier plan to sign an executive order shortly after the inauguration;
agreed to a six-month postponement of a final decision; and offered further concessions to Senator Nunn. While the military would temporarily
suspend asking new recruits about their sexual orientation, it could continue to take measures against those already in the armed services and accused of homosexuality. Moreover, Clinton agreed that Nunn could hold
his own hearings on the matter while the Defense Department conducted
its review.

Nunn accepted the compromise and rallied enough Democrats to table
Dole's amendment to the Family Leave Act. However, the Senate Armed
Services Committee chair did not sit quietly through the next six months
while the Defense Department conducted its own policy review. Rather,
he convened a series of public hearings to examine the issues in play. In
addition to hearing from members on both sides of the issues, the committee heard testimony from a range of experts on the effects of homosexuals'
service on military unit cohesion. On May 11, all eyes on the commit-

tee and in the press were focused on the probe's highest-profile witness: the victorious Gulf War commander, General H. Norman Schwarzkopf. When asked by Idaho Republican Dirk Kempthorne whether lifting the ban would "jeopardize the military's ability to defend this Nation," the revered general minced few words: "I think it will have a serious impact upon the quality of our armed forces. I think in fact we will end up with a second class armed force for quite some time in the future."[14]

The steady public criticism of lifting the service ban, culminating in Schwarzkopf's emphatic rejection of such a policy shift, had a devastating effect on public support for President Clinton's original position. A poll fielded in the days immediately following Schwarzkopf's testimony found that by mid-May 1993, only 36% of Americans supported Clinton's plan to lift the service ban, while 55% opposed it. Among Perot voters, the split was even worse, with only 29% in favor and 63% opposed.[15]

As the end of the review period approached, Rep. Barney Frank (D-MA) proposed a new compromise. Gay service members must be closeted while on their military base. However, when off the base they would be free to live openly as homosexuals, protected from any military investigation of their private lives.[16] President Clinton publicly voiced support for the proposal at a televised town hall meeting. He expressed his hope for a compromise solution and seemed to endorse the basic elements of Frank's plan. Clinton reiterated his belief that gays serving in the military should be allowed to answer truthfully if asked their sexual orientation without being discharged, as long as other service members are "not forced to confront it."[17]

But Senator Nunn and other conservatives on the issue were having none of it and rejected further efforts at compromise. Faced with their implacable opposition, Clinton capitulated to their demands. In this environment, his administration calculated that the political costs of more aggressive action to end discrimination against homosexuals in the military were too extreme. Not only would stronger action run in the face of prevailing popular sentiment, but it also risked antagonizing key members of Congress on whom the administration would depend to enact its other legislative priorities.[18] On July 19, 1993, the White House announced a new policy that hewed closely to Nunn's demands. It described the policy as "don't ask, don't tell, don't pursue," but history would remember only the first two clauses. Administration officials tried to put the best spin possible on their reversal, calling the policy "an honorable compromise" and arguing that although it would not allow gays to serve openly, it would respect service members' right to privacy. "We must and will protect unit cohesion and troop morale," Clinton said as he announced the policy. "But this is an end to witch hunts that spend millions of taxpayer dollars to ferret out individuals who have served their country well."[19]

Yet no amount of presidential sugarcoating could obscure the reality that Clinton had backed down from his pledge to repeal the ban and allow homosexuals to serve openly in the US military. He could have fulfilled his promise with the stroke of a pen on day one of his administration. By changing policy unilaterally, he would have forced opponents of the change to compile supermajorities in both chambers of Congress in order to pass legislation restoring the status quo over a presidential veto. Conceivably, such efforts could have succeeded. But moving any legislation through Congress's procedural gauntlet is difficult. Compiling supermajorities to override a presidential veto when both chambers are controlled by the president's copartisans is even more so. In short, had Clinton acted, his policy likely would have prevailed. Nevertheless, he believed that the political costs of acting unilaterally outweighed the benefits of immediately and decisively fulfilling his campaign pledge.

SYRIA AND THE "RED LINE"

Even before assuming the presidency, Barack Obama had adopted an ambivalent posture toward the use of military force. He built his national political persona in large part on his opposition to the Iraq War—a position that clearly differentiated him from his most important rivals for the 2008 Democratic presidential nomination, senators Hillary Clinton of New York and John Edwards of North Carolina; both had voted to authorize the use of force against Iraq in October of 2002. Yet Obama did not run as a pacifist. Instead, he sought to draw a clear distinction between the "good" war in Afghanistan and the "bad" war in Iraq. Once in office, he pulled the troops from Iraq, but he also ramped up military operations in Afghanistan, tripling the number of troops on the ground and dramatically expanding the drone program in Central Asia. And yet, despite his best efforts to disentangle the United States from a seemingly intractable military situation in the Middle East, events and the eruption of political unrest across the region presented the Obama administration with a host of new policy challenges and calls for military action.

On December 17, 2010, a Tunisian street vendor set himself on fire to protest abuses by the police forces of his country's dictator, Zine el-Abidine Ben Ali. The shocking act triggered a wave of protests that culminated in the collapse of the Ben Ali regime in January of 2011. The dictator's dramatic fall kindled pro-democracy movements across much of the Arab world, including serious threats to autocratic rule in Egypt, Libya, and Syria.[20] That same month, demonstrators flooded Cairo's Tahrir Square to protest Egyptian president Hosni Mubarak. After eighteen days of clashes, the military turned on Mubarak, and Egypt's defiant pharaoh stepped down.[21]

By February, the Arab Spring had spread to Libya as demonstrators protested the more than forty-year reign of dictator Muammar Gaddafi. A rebel army from Benghazi headed west across the desert and by March threatened the capital of Tripoli itself. However, Gaddafi rallied his troops and turned the tide on the rebels, driving them back to their eastern stronghold. On March 17, he issued a chilling warning to the rebels in Benghazi: "The moment of truth has come. There will be no mercy. Our troops will be coming to Benghazi tonight."[22] In a desperate effort to prevent the slaughter of innocents, the United Nations Security Council passed Resolution 1973, calling for a cessation of hostilities; authorizing the establishment of a no-fly zone; and empowering member states to take "all necessary measures" to protect civilians. To enforce the resolution, a coalition of countries including the United States began a lengthy air campaign that included scores of attacks on Libyan military targets.

Also in March, demonstrations began in Syria against the oppressive regime of its president, Bashar al-Assad. When the regime brutally cracked down on the demonstrators, more widespread conflict erupted, which eventually spiraled out of control into a full-fledged civil war. As the fighting intensified in the summer of 2012, the body count also soared. By that August, the United Nations estimated that more than 20,000 people had died, including 1,600 in the month's final week alone. A quarter million had fled into neighboring countries.[23] As the Obama administration grappled with how to respond to the carnage, secretary of state Hillary Clinton and CIA director General David Petraeus championed a covert plan to vet rebel groups and provide arms and training to moderate forces fighting the regime. The plan was backed by both defense secretary Leon Panetta and Joint Chiefs of Staff chairman Martin Dempsey. However, President Obama and other top administration officials feared that the weapons could ultimately end up in the wrong hands. With the 2012 election only a few months away, Obama vetoed the Clinton-Petraeus initiative.[24]

While the president resisted covert US involvement in the fighting, he openly worried about the prospect of the Assad regime using chemical weapons if its position on the ground deteriorated further. In July,

the Syrian government confirmed international suspicions that it possessed stockpiles of chemical weapons when it threatened to use them,
not against its own people but against any foreign forces that might intervene on behalf of the rebels.[25] That same day, President Obama issued
a veiled warning to Assad not to use chemical munitions: "Given the regime's stockpiles of chemical weapons, we will continue to make it clear
to Assad and those around him that the world is watching and that they
will be held accountable by the international community and the United
States should they make the tragic mistake of using those weapons."[26] A
month later during an August 20 news conference, Obama went further
and declared that the use of chemical weapons constituted a "red line" for
the United States:

> But the point that you made about chemical and biological weapons is
> critical. That's an issue that doesn't just concern Syria, it concerns our
> close allies in the region, including Israel. It concerns us. We cannot
> have a situation where chemical or biological weapons are falling into
> the hands of the wrong people. We have been very clear to the Assad
> regime, but also to other players on the ground, that a red line for us is
> we start seeing a whole bunch of chemical weapons moving around or
> being utilized. That would change my calculus. That would change my
> equation.[27]

In early 2013, the US government began to receive initial reports that
chemical weapons may have been used by the Assad regime in an attack
against the rebel stronghold of Homs on December 23, 2012. Throughout
the following spring, the intelligence community gathered additional evidence of a series of small-scale potential chemical weapons attacks.[28] On
April 25, 2013, the White House sent a formal letter to senators John Mc-
Cain (R-AZ) and Carl Levin (D-MI) in response to their concerns about
the use of chemical weapons in Syria. The letter, widely circulated in the
American press, acknowledged that "our intelligence community does assess with varying degrees of confidence that the Syrian regime has used
chemical weapons on a small scale in Syria, specifically the chemical
agent sarin." However, wary of repeating the George W. Bush administration's mistakes in prewar intelligence regarding Iraq and its nonexistent
weapons of mass destruction, the Obama administration emphasized the
need for more concrete proof: "Our standard of evidence must build on
these intelligence assessments as we seek to establish credible and cor-
roborated facts."[29]

The death toll continued to mount as fighting intensified and Assad's forces gained ground in the summer of 2013. A report in June by the United Nations Human Rights Office estimated that almost 93,000 people had died in the Syrian war between March 2011 and April 2013.[30] Despite the war's ghastly toll, the Obama administration continued to resist calls for military intervention in Syria. However, the president's extreme reluctance to intervene seemed to evaporate in August when unimpeachable evidence of a large-scale chemical weapons attack emerged. Images of the August 21 attacks, including video clips showing victims struggling to breathe after inhaling poison gas, quickly pervaded the media.[31] Three days later, President Obama met with the National Security Council to consider options for a US military response. By all accounts, the president decided to order unilaterally a limited series of military strikes against the Assad regime in retaliation for its use of chemical weapons.[32] In setting the stage for a military strike, on August 30 the White House released an official assessment concluding that the Assad regime had indeed used chemical weapons in the August 21 attack that killed 1,429 people, including at least 426 children.[33]

As a result, when President Obama strode into the White House Rose Garden on August 31, 2013, his words took many by surprise. He began predictably enough by informing the American people that he had decided the United States should take military action to punish the Assad regime for its use of chemical weapons. However, what he said next caught even many administration officials off guard:

> But having made my decision as Commander-in-Chief based on what I am convinced is our national security interests, I'm also mindful that I'm the President of the world's oldest constitutional democracy. I've long believed that our power is rooted not just in our military might, but in our example as a government of the people, by the people, and for the people. And that's why I've made a second decision: I will seek authorization for the use of force from the American people's representatives in Congress.[34]

The reversal stunned most political and legal observers.[35] Only two days prior, secretary of state John Kerry had denounced Assad as "a thug and a murderer," leaving little doubt in the minds of most that a US military response was in the offing.[36] But in the twenty-four hours preceding the Rose Garden address, Obama had changed his mind.[37]

President Obama did not reverse course because he believed that a unilateral strike was unconstitutional. In 2011, the Office of Legal Counsel in the Department of Justice had provided the administration with a sweeping opinion that the president possessed independent constitutional authority to intervene militarily in Libya without congressional approval. The reason given was that the mission was tied to the national interest—even if the crisis in Libya plainly did not involve an actual or imminent threat to the United States itself.[38] Administration lawyers reached similar conclusions in the case of Syria. Because the United States possessed "important national interests" in enforcing international norms against the use of chemical weapons and in bringing stability to Syria, the president had the constitutional authority to act independently of Congress.[39] Indeed, in the Rose Garden address itself, Obama, like other post-1945 presidents before him seeking congressional authorization, emphasized that he possessed the requisite constitutional authority to act unilaterally absent any congressional approval.

Rather, his reasons for going to Congress were political, not constitutional: "While I believe I have the authority to carry out this military action without specific congressional authorization, I know that the country will be stronger if we take this course, and our actions will be even more effective."[40] While many factors, including the legitimacy of a unilateral strike as perceived by domestic and international observers alike, undoubtedly entered the president's calculations, Obama's reversal is best explained as an effort to avoid the political costs of another unilateral military strike in the Arab world.[41]

Opinion polls plainly showed that the American public had little appetite for a new military intervention in the Middle East. As shown in figure 6.1, between early 2012 and June 2013, eight surveys asked Americans whether "the United States has a responsibility to do something about the fighting in Syria between government forces and anti-government groups." No more than 31% of the public ever backed military intervention in these polls. Other polls using slightly different question wordings painted the same picture: most Americans opposed military action in Syria and believed that it was unlikely to improve the situation on the ground.

Against this backdrop of widespread public skepticism, a growing chorus in Congress called on Obama to first seek legislative authorization before any use of force in Syria. As of August 29, 2013, 140 members, including twenty-one Democrats, had signed a letter stating that unilateral presidential military action in Syria would violate the separation of powers outlined in the US Constitution.[42] The overwhelming majority of the American public agreed. An NBC News poll conducted between

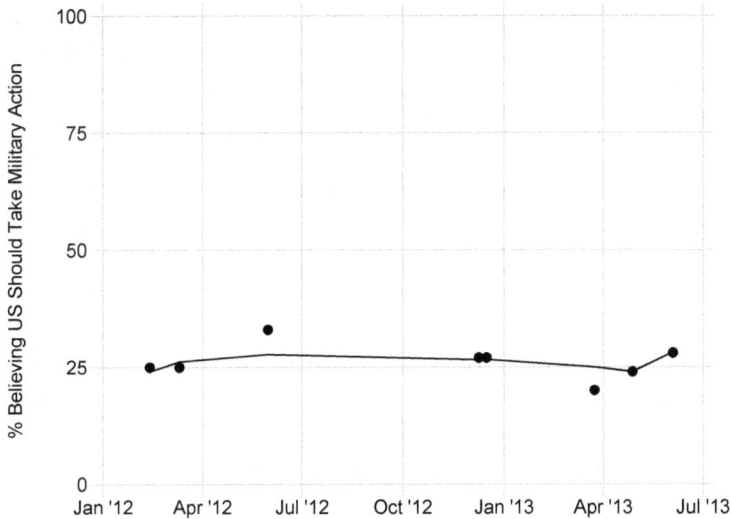

Figure 6.1. Support for American military intervention
in Syria, February 2012–June 2013

Note: Figure plots the percentage of Americans agreeing with the statement "The US should take
military action to help stop the killing of civilians." Line indicates smoothed time trend.

August 28 and 29, 2013, asked, "Do you think that President Obama should or should not be required to receive approval from Congress before taking military action in Syria?" An impressive 79% said that the president should be required to seek prior approval.[43]

Thus, Obama faced a dual risk when contemplating acting unilaterally to strike back at Syria for the Assad regime's use of chemical weapons. First, the policy response under consideration was not overly popular. For years, strong majorities of Americans believed that Syria was not their fight. Even the gruesome images of the aftermath of Assad's chemical attack did little to bolster the public's willingness to use force. For example, support for the United States "tak[ing] action to help stop the killing of civilians" in Syria increased only from 15% in June 2013 to 26% in an August poll fielded in the immediate aftermath of the chemical weapons attack.[44]

Some survey evidence suggests that a bare majority (50% supporting vs. 44% opposing) might have backed a more limited retaliatory response that relied exclusively on air strikes and cruise missiles.[45] However, this tenuous level of public support could erode quickly in the face of vocal congressional criticism. Many members of Congress would undoubtedly disapprove of even a limited series of air strikes on policy grounds, arguing that such retaliation was either too weak to make a real difference or risked pulling the United States into an inextricable civil conflict in Syria despite the president's best efforts to limit the scope of the response. Moreover, if Obama ignored demands to first seek congressional authorization, the administration would be exposed to critiques on constitutional grounds as well. Supermajorities of Americans agreed with congressional critics who argued that military action required the prior approval of Congress. The analyses of chapter 3 plainly demonstrated that congressional challenges to unilateral action on constitutional grounds, even in foreign affairs, can significantly erode public support for the use of force. As a result, while the long-term policy benefits of striking the Assad regime were questionable, the immediate political risks of enforcing the "red line" unilaterally were clear and considerable.

At a press conference on September 4, 2013, President Obama openly acknowledged the importance of political calculations when discussing the rationale behind his decision to forgo unilateral action. If the White House acts alone, "Congress will sit on the sidelines, snipe. If it works, the sniping will be a little less; if it doesn't, a little more."[46] To be clear, Obama did not fear that congressional critics would enact legislation overriding his decision or otherwise constraining his freedom of action. Rather, he feared the public criticism that would inevitably ensue if his policies proved costlier or less immediately successful than expected.[47] He opted against acting unilaterally and instead decided to seek congressional approval in the hopes that by compelling members of Congress to vote to authorize military action against Syria, he could tie them to the mission politically, thereby minimizing the political costs downstream.[48] Of course, Obama's reversal itself produced sharp criticism and came at some political cost. But that cost paled in comparison to what he risked should he become mired in another Middle Eastern quagmire with little support from Congress.

Ultimately, this political calculation ensured that there was no US military response to Bashar al-Assad's decision to cross the red line and use chemical weapons. Instead, the Russians stepped into the void left by the administration's shock reversal by brokering a deal for the removal and destruction of Assad's chemical stockpiles. This bold diplomatic stroke provided the opening for greater Russian involvement in the Syrian conflict, which ultimately helped turn the tide of the war back in Assad's favor. With Russia now a major player, Assad's forces, backed by Russian arms and advisers, made great gains against the rebels at a horrific human cost, including additional chemical attacks against Syrian civilians.[49]

President Obama's abrupt about-face on Syria clearly shows how antic-ipatory calculations about the likely reactions of Congress and the public can produce a dramatic shift in policy. His administration knew full well that if he had acted unilaterally to order a retaliatory strike against Assad, Congress and the courts would have been all but powerless to stop him through formal means. However, the president clearly understood Con-gress's capacity to impose political costs on the White House by criticiz-ing its policies in the public sphere should they fail to succeed quickly. Calculations concerning public opinion and the informal political costs that an erosion of support would entail were enough to tilt the balance against acting unilaterally and to produce the president's dramatic Rose Garden reversal.

Revisiting Enhanced Interrogation

Throughout the 2016 presidential campaign, Donald Trump promised a foreign policy that would be simultaneously more circumspect and more aggressive. He derided the Iraq War as "a big, fat mistake" and possibly "the worst decision" in presidential history.[50] A Trump presidency, he pledged, would avoid the "stupid" and costly wars of its predecessors. Yet at the same time, Trump promised a decidedly more muscular foreign pol-icy than that of Barack Obama. He gleefully boasted that he would "bomb the hell" out of ISIS militants and pledged to return to the "enhanced in-terrogation techniques" favored by the George W. Bush administration de-spite the Detainee Treatment Act banning torture.[51] In an interview with ABC's George Stephanopoulos, Trump minced few words: "I would abso-lutely authorize something beyond waterboarding. And believe me, it will be effective." When pressed whether such a move would lower the United States to the level of its adversaries, he remained adamant: "You have to do it that way. . . . You know, when I was a young man, I studied Medieval times. That's what they did, they chopped off heads. That's what we have [to do]." And at a Republican primary debate in Manchester, New Hamp-shire, Trump doubled down, promising to bring back not only waterboard-ing but something "a hell of a lot worse."[52]

Only five days after Trump's inauguration, the *Washington Post* re-vealed the existence of a draft executive order to follow through on the new president's campaign pledge.[53] The order would not formally re-institute waterboarding or other forms of torture per se. However, it would revoke Obama-era directives (Executive Orders 13491 and 13492) banning torture and closing the terrorist detention camp at Guantanamo Bay,

Cuba, and it would direct the CIA to consider reinstating its enhanced interrogation program. Moreover, the order would open the door for the reinstitution of "black site" prisons overseas, halt the transfer of prisoners out of the Guantanamo detention camp, and send new terrorism detainees to that facility.[54]

The leaked order triggered an immediate firestorm of criticism from both sides of the aisle on Capitol Hill. Arizona Republican John McCain curtly dismissed the suggestion that Trump could bring back torture through executive fiat, noting that it was prohibited by law and that military officers would refuse to obey illegal orders: "The President can sign whatever executive orders he likes. But the law is the law. We are not bringing back torture in the United States of America." South Dakota Republican John Thune echoed Senator McCain: "With respect to torture—that's banned." House Minority Leader Nancy Pelosi decried Trump's move as inconsistent with American values and argued that it actually endangered Americans.[55] Dianne Feinstein (D-CA), the ranking member on the Senate Foreign Relations Committee, echoed these concerns and warned that "reconstituting this appalling program would compromise our values, our morals and our standing as a world leader—this cannot happen."[56]

In the face of such criticism, key administration officials immediately sought to distance themselves and the president from the draft order despite Trump's continued public support for tougher measures and his exhortations that "we have to fight fire with fire."[57] Both incoming defense secretary James Mattis and CIA director Mike Pompeo denied that they had even seen the document before it became public. White House press secretary Sean Spicer went further, declaring that the draft order "was not a White House document" and adding "I have no idea where it came from."[58]

Like many orders in the initial days and weeks of the Trump administration, the leaked draft had all the hallmarks of having been hastily produced. It even contained basic factual errors, including stating that the 9/11 terror attacks occurred in 2011 rather than 2001.[59] Nevertheless, Spicer's assertion was dubious at best. Multiple sources from within the administration boldly contradicted his claims and provided evidence that the White House had circulated the order to the National Security Council for expedited review.[60]

Two weeks later, the administration plainly backtracked in the face of considerable political pressure. On February 8, 2017, the *New York Times* leaked a new draft executive order circulating in the White House. This revised order had dropped all references to "black site" prisons and enhanced interrogation techniques and instead only kept language directing the Department of Defense to hold ISIS terrorists at Guantanamo.[61] Ultimately, however, the administration opted against issuing even this dramatically scaled-back order.[62]

It is impossible to know the exact combination of factors that precipitated President Trump's about-face and his decision not to follow through on his campaign pledge to bring back waterboarding and something "a hell of a lot worse." Political pushback from both parties, a deluge of negative media coverage, and bureaucratic resistance from key figures within the administration all undoubtedly combined to influence his strategic calculus.[63] It is clear, however, that political calculations about institutional resistance and its potentially corrosive impact on public opinion—not the fear of a formal legislative or judicial defeat should he follow through and act unilaterally—led Trump to back down.

FAILURE TO ANTICIPATE

Sometimes presidents either fail to anticipate or miscalculate how much political resistance they will face by going it alone. When such anticipatory failures occur, presidents are left with a difficult decision. They can stay the course, avoid an embarrassing retreat, and pay the resulting political costs of acting unilaterally. Or they can reverse course in the hope of minimizing the political damage, even when Congress and the courts are unlikely to legally compel them to do so. President Trump faced this dilemma in the summer of 2018 when video documenting the horrific human cost of his "zero tolerance" policy at the border went viral and changed the tenor of the public debate.

Presidents have long struggled to combat illegal border crossings. In 2005, president George W. Bush introduced a program referring undocumented border crossers for criminal prosecution; however, the program explicitly exempted parents with children.[64] Under Obama, illegal border crossings surged in 2014, with many families seeking to enter the United States in the hope that immigration laws were more favorable to families than to individual adults. To deal with the crisis, the Obama administration considered a range of proposals, including extreme calls to separate parents and children. The White House rejected these proposals. As Obama's top domestic policy adviser Celia Munoz recalled, "I do remember looking at each other like, 'We're not going to do this, are we?' We spent five minutes thinking it through and concluded that it was a bad idea. The morality of it was clear—that's not who we are."[65] Instead, the administration significantly increased family detentions while cases were processed.[66]

Unsurprisingly, the Trump administration took a different view on the morality of family separations and had fewer qualms about using it to deter illegal immigration. On March 6, 2017, Homeland Security secretary John Kelly publicly acknowledged that the administration was considering family separations.[67] On April 1, 2018, President Trump warned in a tweet that "caravans" of migrants from Central America were coming and called on Senate Republicans to eliminate the filibuster by exercising "the nuclear option to pass tough laws NOW."[68] However, stalemate had long reigned in Congress over immigration policy, and a compromise immigration bill that would actually liberalize aspects of immigration policy had passed the Senate as recently as 2014. Tougher legislative action on immigration was simply not on the table.

Blocked legislatively, the Trump administration acted unilaterally. On May 7, Attorney General Jeff Sessions issued a memorandum announcing the administration's "zero tolerance policy": all adults apprehended on suspicion of crossing the border illegally would be criminally prosecuted. The policy made no exceptions for asylum seekers or family units.[69]

While the *Houston Chronicle* had reported on cases of family separations as early as November 2017, the new policy became a flashpoint of national political debate in the summer of 2018, when the *Washington Post* reported that a Honduran asylum seeker committed suicide in federal custody after being separated from his wife and children.[70] Five days later on June 14, CNN reported that federal authorities removed a breast-feeding infant from her mother's arms.[71] This opened the floodgates of media stories complete with video documenting the stark human cost of Trump's zero tolerance policy. Congressional Democrats roundly denounced the administration. Rep. Beto O'Rourke of the border city of El Paso, Texas, decried the policy: "This is inhumane. I'd like to say it's un-American, but it's happening right now in America."[72] Many of their criticisms were echoed by a number of prominent Republicans. Former first lady Laura Bush called family separations "immoral" and openly compared them to the horrors of Japanese internment during World War II. Senator John McCain blasted the policy as an "affront to the decency of the American people, and contrary to principles and values upon which our nation was founded." Even the conservative stalwart senator Ted Cruz of Texas firmly rejected Trump's move, declaring that "all of us who are seeing images of these children being pulled away from moms and dads in tears are horrified. This has to stop."[73]

Against this backdrop of significant elite criticism, public opinion polls also showed an overwhelming majority of Americans opposed to Trump's policy. In a June *Washington Post*-Schar School survey, 69% said they opposed the zero tolerance policy separating families at the border.[74]

In the face of this intense political pushback, President Trump executed an about-face on June 20 by signing Executive Order 13841 ending the family separations policy. It was not the fear of congressional action that led to Trump's reversal. Indeed, while opponents of the family separations policy introduced a number of bills to overturn the policy, none had any hopes of passing either chamber.[75] Rather, Trump initially failed to anticipate the extent of the political costs he would pay for the zero tolerance policy. And when he began to pay those costs following the media revelations in the summer of 2018, he abruptly changed course.

THE SCOPE AND TIMING OF UNILATERAL ACTION

The preceding case studies coupled with the more systematic analysis of major executive order issuance in chapter 5 suggest that presidents routinely forgo acting unilaterally when they anticipate significant political pushback. They do this even though their opponents would almost certainly fail to overturn a presidential order. And in rare cases, presidents may even reverse course and revoke their own unilateral actions to avoid paying a steep political price after resistance materializes. Political costs, not fears of reversal, drive most of these decisions.

Yet abandoning unilateral action altogether is not the only possible response to anticipated political costs. In some cases, presidents may ultimately embrace executive action even when they anticipate political pushback. However, they may choose to moderate the content and scope of the executive action to minimize the political risks. In other cases, presidents who anticipate costly opposition may instead choose to delay taking executive action until the political environment is more favorable. Delay may not sap opposition, but it may make the costs of that opposition less biting.

In a final pair of case studies, we examine these alternate pathways through which informal political checks affect presidential decision-making regarding unilateral action. The first examines the political calculations that drove President Obama's halting and piecemeal efforts to unilaterally strengthen gun control policy. The second details how changes in the political environment shaped his efforts to liberalize immigration enforcement through executive action. Perhaps most important, Obama delayed his boldest executive actions until after the 2014 midterm elec-

tions to minimize the political fallout for himself and his party. This delay, however, ultimately proved very costly and directly contributed to the
downfall of his efforts.

THE RESPONSE TO GUN VIOLENCE

During his 2008 campaign for the presidency, Illinois senator Barack
Obama championed the need for tighter gun control. During the Democratic primaries, New York senator Hillary Clinton attempted to paint
Obama as an extremist on the issue, accusing him of telling sympathetic
crowds that he favored a ban on handguns and that he only supported the
Second Amendment to court the votes of gun owners.[76] In the general election, the National Rifle Association denounced Obama as the most anti-
gun candidate in history. "Never in NRA's history," a fundraiser mailing
warned, "have we faced a presidential candidate . . . with such a deep-
rooted hatred of firearm freedoms."[77]

Despite Obama's support for what he called commonsense gun control
on the campaign trail, initiatives to stanch the flow of guns and gun violence were low on the priority list during his first term in office. Although
Attorney General Eric Holder told reporters that President Obama would
follow through on his campaign pledge and seek to renew the 1994 assault
weapons ban that had expired in 2004, he found little support in the rest of
the administration. White House Chief of Staff Rahm Emanuel allegedly
ordered Holder to "shut the [expletive] up," making clear that with economic recovery and health care dominating the agenda, the administration was unwilling to spend much political capital on the issue.[78]

Predictably, during Obama's first term several high-profile mass shootings occurred. In November 2009, a US Army major and psychiatrist
opened fire on his comrades at Fort Hood in Texas, killing thirteen service
members and wounding more than thirty. In January 2011, a twenty-year-
old gunman stormed a "Congress on Your Corner" constituent meeting
in a Safeway parking lot in suburban Tucson, shooting Rep. Gabrielle Gif-
fords (D-AZ) in the head at point-blank range and killing United States
District Court judge John Roll before firing randomly into the crowd. On
July 20, 2012, a gunman opened fire in an Aurora, Colorado, movie theater,
killing twelve and injuring seventy. The White House met each tragedy
with expressions of sympathy for and solidarity with the victims of gun
violence. But none of these massacres produced much in the way of concrete action, either from Congress or from the executive branch.

In the assessment of *CQ Weekly*, "Obama himself has always seemed acutely aware of public support for gun rights"; this knowledge, coupled with the need to face voters again in what promised to be a bruising re-election campaign, tempered his natural inclination to pursue stricter gun control.[79] During his first term, the president did so little to advocate gun control that the Brady Campaign to Prevent Gun Violence gave him an F rating. After campaigning on tougher gun control measures, he "ran away from the issue" once in office.[80]

On November 6, 2012, President Obama defeated senator Mitt Romney (R-UT) by almost 4% to win a second term in office. Less than six weeks later, the nation was rocked by another gun tragedy when a twenty-year-old walked into the Sandy Hook Elementary School in Newtown, Connecticut, and opened fire with a Bushmaster AR-15 semiautomatic rifle, the civilian version of the M-16. Before the shooter killed himself, twenty-six people, including twenty children between the ages of six and seven, were dead. Obama grieved with the families, visibly choking back tears as he announced that "our hearts are broken today." He recounted previous instances of mass gun violence on his watch and said that "as a country, we have been through this too many times." Inaction was no longer an option. The president warned, "We're going to have to come together and take meaningful action to prevent more tragedies like this, regardless of the politics."[81]

Five days later, Obama announced the formation of a task force chaired by Vice President Joe Biden that would explore concrete legislative remedies to the gun violence epidemic plaguing the nation. In the press conference that followed the announcement, the president was pressed to explain his prior reluctance to engage the gun control issue and to address charges that this reticence was politically and electorally motivated. Summarizing the administration's past failures, ABC News correspondent Jake Tapper bluntly asked, "Where have you been?" A defensive Obama curtly replied that other issues, particularly the economic crisis, monopolized his first term, but insisted that gun control would be a "central issue" for his second term.[82]

On January 16, 2013, the Obama administration released its proposals to reduce gun violence. At the core of the initiative were three main requests to Congress: reinstate the assault weapons ban that expired in 2004; ban high-capacity magazines and armor-piercing bullets; and close existing legal loopholes to create a system of universal background checks for those wanting to purchase a firearm. However, in addition to these and other more minor legislative proposals, President Obama simultaneously announced his intention to take twenty-three separate executive actions

to address the crisis. Some of the actions sought to promote greater information sharing between federal agencies to strengthen enforcement of
the existing laws and background check system. Other actions, such as
directing the secretaries of the Education and Health and Human Services
Departments to launch a national dialogue on gun violence and to develop
emergency preparedness plans, were more routine.[83]

While Obama's executive actions were widely interpreted in the press
as bold and even surprising given his earlier reluctance to engage the issue, he plainly did not press as far as he could have unilaterally. Critically, apart from relatively minor steps such as requiring federal agencies
to make certain data available to the federal background check system,
his unilateral actions did little to address the administration's core priorities. While the president certainly knew that his legislative initiatives
were doomed in Congress—indeed, the Manchin-Toomey compromise bill
would fail on a 54–46 vote to overcome a Republican filibuster in April
2013—on Capitol Hill there was sufficient Democratic support for stricter
gun control to defeat any legislative effort to overturn a more robust executive action. However, pushing forward risked outpacing public opinion
on the issue and provoking a political backlash.

On most metrics, the Sandy Hook school shooting had surprisingly
little impact on public opinion concerning gun control. With some regu-
larity throughout President Obama's tenure in office, a handful of polling
outfits asked Americans whether they supported or opposed stricter gun
control laws. As shown in figure 6.2, support for stricter gun laws was
remarkably stable from 2009 to 2013.[84] A flurry of polls taken in the days
and weeks immediately following the Sandy Hook shooting suggest there
was only a very modest increase, if any, in support for more gun control.
And even in the immediate aftermath of the shooting, only a bare majority backed tougher laws.

Perhaps the most plausible reason for the lack of a significant shift
in public support for more gun control is the reaction of political elites.
Liberal Democrats, of course, rallied behind the president's initiative, as
did several red state Democrats who had long resisted further restrictions
on gun ownership. For example, West Virginia senator Joe Manchin, who
earned an A rating from the NRA in 2012, became a proponent of tougher
gun laws: "Seeing the massacre of so many innocent children has changed
everything." However, most members of Congress across the political
aisle remained firmly unconverted. While North Carolina's Virginia Foxx
lamented the tragedy, she expressed a common opinion among the Republican rank and file: "There are just evil people in the world. There's

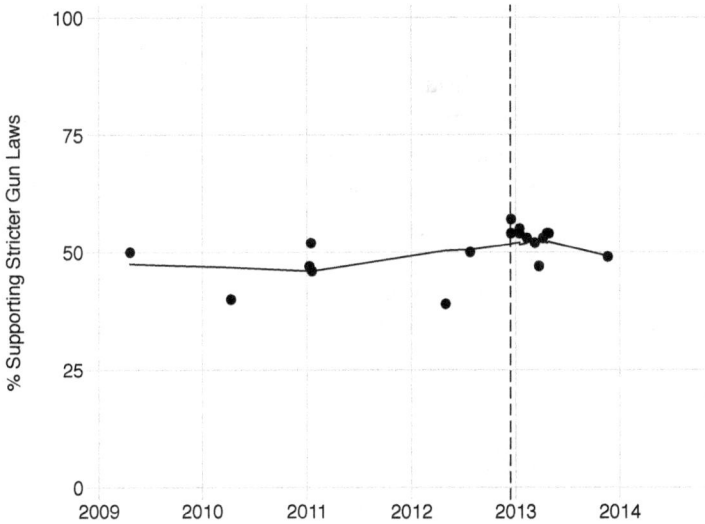

Figure 6.2. Support for stricter gun laws, 2009–13
Note: Dashed vertical line indicates the date of the Sandy Hook
school shooting. Line indicates smoothed time trend.

nothing you're going to do to prevent evil from occurring." Even Tennes-see senator Lamar Alexander, a moderate, argued that "the problem is not with the gun, but with the person pulling the trigger." More provocatively, Rep. Louie Gohmert of Texas was adamant in his belief that more guns, not fewer, was the solution to preventing such tragedies in the future.[85]

If most Republicans were unsupportive of Obama's proposed legisla-tion, they were even more vehemently opposed to the president taking any action to combat gun violence unilaterally. Immediately following the announcement of Obama's substantively modest executive actions, Republican National Committee chair Reince Priebus accused him of abusing his power and violating Americans' Second Amendment rights: "President Obama's series of gun control measures amount to an execu-tive power grab that may please his political base but will not solve the problems at hand. He paid lip service to our fundamental constitutional rights, but took actions that disregard the Second Amendment and the leg-islative process. Representative government is meant to give voice to the people; President Obama's unilateral executive action ignores this princi-ple."[86] Such scathing criticism from the Right helped quash any potential public rally behind the president's proposals. A January 2013 poll asked Americans whether the reinstatement of the ban on assault weapons—a centerpiece of Obama's legislative proposals—would have "helped avoid the Newtown, CT School Shooting tragedy." More than two-thirds replied that it would not have helped.[87] Another poll asked Americans whether they believed that "laws limiting gun ownership infringe on the public's right to bear arms under the second amendment to the U.S. Constitution." Just a month after the Newtown tragedy, 51% said yes.[88] This figure was virtually unchanged from the 49% observed in August of 2012.[89]

Against this backdrop, President Obama clearly risked incurring significant political costs if he pursued more robust executive actions to strengthen federal gun control policies. The relatively modest scope of his executive actions may thus reflect a conscious decision to not push policy as far as he could unilaterally to avoid provoking an even stronger political backlash. But could he really have done more unilaterally if he was willing to pay the ensuing political costs?

It is possible that the president pushed the bounds of his unilateral authority to strengthen gun control policy as far as he could in January of 2013 and that legally he simply could go no further. This interpretation is directly contradicted by later events. Renewing the assault weapons ban would have almost certainly required new legislation from Congress. Yet there were more aggressive alternatives at President Obama's disposal for cracking down on the availability of armor-piercing ammunition and closing loopholes in the existing background check system for gun purchasers. The Gun Control Act of 1968 and subsequent amendments banned the sale of "armor piercing ammunition," defined as a bullet that can be used in a handgun and is made of certain metals that enable it to penetrate conventional body armor. The law also allowed for an exception to exempt ammunition that is "primarily to be used for sporting purposes." The ambiguity over this clause gives government regulators significant discretion in determining which ammunition is or is not subject to the existing ban. In February 2015, the Bureau of Alcohol, Tobacco, and Firearms (ATF) announced its intention to consider new regulations that would ban .223-caliber M855 "green-tip" ammunition, which is commonly used in AR-15 rifles, the type of weapon used in the Sandy Hook shooting. Although M855 ammunition is commonly used in sporting rifles, it could also be used in a newly created handgun version of the AR-15. Given its potential use in a handgun and its ability to pierce traditional body armor worn by law enforcement, the ATF proposed a regulatory change to prohibit its sale and manufacture under existing statute.[90]

Although the impetus for the proposed rule does not seem to have come from the White House, the Obama administration publicly backed it. Shortly after the ATF announcement, White House press secretary Josh Earnest was asked whether the proposal was "a way of doing executively what Congress wouldn't do previously [after Newtown]." While Earnest emphasized that this change was going through the standard rule-making process at ATF, he concluded, "It would be fair to say, as I mentioned, that we are looking at additional ways to protect our brave men and women in law enforcement and believe that this process is valuable for that reason alone." The administration was fully behind the ATF's recommended ammunition ban: "This seems to be an area where everyone should agree that if there are armor-piercing bullets available that can fit into easily concealed weapons, that it puts our law enforcement at considerably more risk."[91]

The move prompted an outcry from gun rights advocates on Capitol Hill. Senate Judiciary Committee chair Charles Grassley lambasted it as "an affront to the Second Amendment."[92] A letter from Grassley to the ATF sharply criticizing the ban proposal was signed by fifty-one Republican senators.[93] In the face of enormous political pushback, the ATF reversed course and tabled the proposal. Celebrating the victory, NRA executive vice president Wayne LaPierre crowed, "Obama failed to pass gun control through Congress, so he tried [to] impose his political agenda through executive fiat."[94]

The ATF rule and reversal illuminate further the political calculations that President Obama had faced when he contemplated unilateral action two years earlier. First, he had potentially creative options for exploiting ambiguity and discretion within existing gun control statutes to make significant policy shifts on major administration priorities, such as limiting the availability of armor-piercing munitions. But such bold action from the administration would have undoubtedly provoked an avalanche of criticism from the gun lobby, congressional Republicans, and even some red state Democrats. Obama anticipated and understood the severity of the political costs he would incur—in terms of both his party's electoral fortunes and his other policy priorities—should he push too far unilaterally, and he moderated his unilateral response accordingly.

Finally, events in 2015–16 also show that Obama could have acted more aggressively to close loopholes in the background check system had he desired to do so after Newtown. As 2015 drew to a close, secretary of state Hillary Clinton found herself in an unexpectedly tight contest for the Democratic presidential nomination with Vermont Independent Bernie Sanders. In seeking an issue in which the self-proclaimed socialist was actually to the right of the party's liberal base, Clinton—who once attacked Obama as a threat to gun rights—proposed a series of executive actions she would take as president to unilaterally strengthen gun control policy. Whereas President Obama expressed his belief that there was nothing more he could do on his own to reduce gun violence, Secretary Clinton believed that additional executive action was possible.[95] Specifically, she supported taking regulatory action to classify any high-volume gun seller as being "in the business of selling arms" in order to close existing loopholes exempting many gun show and internet arms purchases from background checks.[96]

Clinton's vigorous campaigning for stronger executive action on gun control led more than 120 House and Senate Democrats to write President Obama, urging him to act unilaterally at once to close the internet and gun show loopholes.[97] In January 2016, Obama did just that and signed new executive actions modeled on those proposed by Clinton. Gun control advocates cheered the move, but many questioned why it took the president so long. "That's certainly the question that we've been asking," said Dan Gross, president of the Brady Campaign to Prevent Gun Violence. Gross and others failed to appreciate the difficult balancing act presidents face in pursuing a host of policy and political priorities.

That the administration did ultimately act rebuts its earlier assertions that the executive branch simply lacked the legal authority to take stronger actions than the modest moves made in 2013. Surprisingly, events during the Trump administration offer further evidence that politics, not law, was the dominant constraint on his predecessor. Following deadly mass shootings in Las Vegas and Parkland, Florida, President Trump moved to ban bump stocks, which allow semiautomatic rifles to mimic the performance of fully automatic weapons.[98] Clearly, there were a number of other ways in which President Obama could have pushed even further on gun control. Political calculations based on the anticipated reaction of most Republicans and some Democrats in Congress as well as large segments of the mass public offer a better explanation than formal institutional constraints for his initial moderation and lengthy delay in taking action.

IMMIGRATION REFORM AND THE DREAMERS

During his barrier-breaking campaign for the presidency in 2008, Barack Obama routinely promised to fix the nation's broken immigration system. In trying to find middle ground between reform advocates and those demanding tougher border controls, he pledged to pursue legislation that would both secure the nation's borders and dissuade employers from hiring unlawful immigrants while offering a pathway to citizenship for undocumented immigrants in good standing.[99]

Shortly after taking office, President Obama called for comprehensive immigration reform and tasked Homeland Security secretary Janet Napolitano with coordinating the effort to craft a legislative proposal.[100] The president again promoted the need for reform in his 2010 State of the Union address, and that March, senators Chuck Schumer (D-NY) and Lindsey Graham (R-SC) announced their intention to begin work on a bipartisan immigration overhaul blueprint.[101] These talks quickly broke down, however. In April, Senate Democrats announced their own framework for comprehensive reform. But this proposal attracted no Republican support, and even the Democrat-controlled House of Representatives' response was tepid, prompting President Obama to acknowledge that there simply may "not be an appetite" for reform.[102] Instead, reform advocates turned their focus to a more narrowly tailored piece of legislation: the Development, Relief, and Education for Alien Minors (DREAM) Act.[103] This bill would grant legal status only to undocumented immigrants who were brought to the United States as children and who met various educational or service requirements.

Although the DREAM Act did garner some bipartisan support, the momentum behind it quickly stalled. Republican gains in the 2010 midterm elections seemed to spell the death knell for any immigration reform. Desperate to try one last time before the new Congress took office in January 2011, Democrats tried once more in the lame duck session to push the DREAM Act through. The revived bill passed the House, but failed to overcome a determined Senate filibuster.

With Republicans now in control of the House, the prospects for legislative action seemed all but hopeless. In this transformed environment, immigration reform advocates began to pressure President Obama to take unilateral action to protect the Dreamers from deportation. On March 28, 2011, Obama participated in a town hall meeting sponsored by the Spanish-language network Univision. Following a question about the continued deportation of students, moderator Jorge Ramos pressed Obama to explain whether he could stop such deportations via an executive order. The president responded by reaffirming his strong support for the DREAM Act, but simultaneously asserted that he had no legal authority to address the problem through unilateral action:

> With respect to the notion that I can just suspend deportations through
> Executive order, that's just not the case, because there are laws on the

books that Congress has passed. And I know that everybody here at Bell is studying hard, so you know that we've got three branches of Government. Congress passes the law. The executive branch's job is to enforce and implement those laws. . . . There are enough laws on the books by Congress that are very clear in terms of how we have to enforce our immigration system that for me to simply through Executive order ignore those congressional mandates would not conform with my appropriate role as President.[104]

Despite such professions that he lacked the authority to act unilaterally on immigration, Obama executed an abrupt about-face as the 2012 election neared. With the stroke of a pen, he took bold executive action to protect many undocumented persons from deportation. On June 15, 2012, the administration announced the Deferred Action for Childhood Arrivals program, or DACA. DACA directed the various immigration enforcement agencies to exercise prosecutorial discretion in order to shield from deportation undocumented immigrants who were brought to the United States as children, earned a high school degree or served in the military, and have a clean criminal record.[105] While DACA did not create a path to citizenship, it did temporarily protect program applicants from deportation and grant them work permits. Approximately eight hundred thousand people have benefited from the program as of March 2017.[106]

What can explain Obama's dramatic reversal? The legal constraints on executive action in the sphere of immigration policy, to which the president had alluded in 2011, did not change. Rather, the political incentives governing the administration's actions did. For most of his first term, unilateral action on immigration had carried more political risk than reward. President Obama supported comprehensive immigration reform and plainly preferred a legislative solution, if at all possible. And once that door closed after the 2010 midterm losses, if he had acted on immigration he would have risked antagonizing Republicans on whom he now depended to move any other priority through Congress, including simply passing a budget and raising the debt ceiling to keep the government open. A bruising public fight complete with charges that he was abusing executive authority held little appeal.

But as the 2012 election neared, the political calculus changed. Latinos overwhelmingly supported the DREAM Act, and Latino leaders were among the loudest voices calling for Obama to take unilateral action.[107] Polls taken immediately after the announcement of DACA, which came less than five months before the election, suggest that it significantly bolstered support for the president among this key voting bloc. Polling in early 2012 preceding the DACA announcement showed that a majority of Latino voters reported being less enthusiastic about Obama's candidacy in 2012 than in 2008. However, subsequent polling showed that the DACA announcement helped erase this skepticism and reenergize support for the president among the Latino community.[108]

In addition, the president's action won over erstwhile critics, including one of the main sponsors of the DREAM Act, Rep. Luis Gutiérrez (D-IL), who hailed DACA as a "tremendous first step."[109] Obama's bold move to help shield many Dreamers from deportation also provided a blunt contrast to the presumptive Republican nominee, Mitt Romney, who argued during his campaign for the nomination that undocumented immigrants should commit to "self-deportation." Romney also publicly pledged that if Congress were ever to pass the DREAM Act during his presidency, he would veto it.[110]

In sum, Obama resisted the temptation to simply implement most of the DREAM Act unilaterally throughout much of his first term. This decision seems to have been a function of legal concerns, a preference for legislative action (as that would ensure a long-lasting policy change—a consideration that seems quite prescient, given President Trump's efforts to rescind many of Obama's executive actions, including this one), and, perhaps most important, broader fears about the political costs such an action could entail. After all, it would have been a clear affront to a Congress that had refused to enact the DREAM Act legislatively. A political backlash against executive action on immigration could erode public support for the president and imperil the administration's prospects of securing other major items on its legislative and programmatic agendas. Indeed, many Republicans greeted the announcement of DACA with charges of unprecedented executive overreach.[111] Ultimately, however, President Obama decided to act unilaterally in 2012—not because he suddenly deduced that Congress would be unable to overturn his action legislatively, but because he believed in the policy, of course, and the electoral benefits of executive action at that time outweighed the anticipated political costs of doing so.

By instituting DACA unilaterally, Obama achieved some of what he had long failed to accomplish through traditional legislative routes. DACA was the most important policy accomplishment in the field of immigration reform during his first term in office. However, for immigration activists and many on the Left, it failed to go far enough. In a September 2013 interview with Spanish-language network Telemundo, the president faced tough questions about why he had not protected even more undocumented immigrants from deportation. Obama declared that while he was proud of his earlier action to protect the Dreamers, existing law precluded him from going further: "If we start broadening that, then essentially I'll be ignoring the law in a way that I think would be very difficult to defend legally, so that's not an option."[112]

Yet the president's argument emphasizing the legal limits on his power failed to sway many on the Left. Two months later, during his speech on immigration in San Francisco, protesters shouted Obama down, demanding that he unilaterally block deportations. A visibly irritated Obama reiterated that his hands were tied, and he had gone as far as he could on this issue unilaterally: "If in fact I could solve all of these problems without passing something in Congress, I would do so. But we're also a nation of laws, that's part of our tradition. And so the easy way out is to yell and pretend that I can do something by violating our laws. What I'm proposing is the harder path, which is to use our democratic process to achieve the same goal that you want to achieve."[113] Despite these public statements questioning his legal authority to further liberalize immigration enforcement, by early 2014 the Obama administration signaled that further unilateral action on immigration reform was imminent. And yet in the summer of 2014, the administration executed an about-face and delayed any final decision on new action in immigration policy. This delay energized critics on the Left to intensify their demands as the midterm elections approached. At a campaign stop in Connecticut, President Obama was greeted by a swarm of protesters, including one wearing a T-shirt that read "Obama deports parents." Though Obama tried to quell the protests by shifting the blame onto Republicans for blocking comprehensive reform and by reminding the crowd that this is why they needed to work to elect more Democrats to Congress, many protesters explicitly blamed the president himself for failing to take bolder unilateral action. Maria Praeli, a member of the immigration protest group United We Dream, summed up the group's demand for action: "Our community expects President Obama to be broad in using his executive authority to provide deportation relief to millions of people from our community, including parents of Dreamers, and we're here to hold him accountable to his promise."[114] Despite the protests, Obama continued to resist the pressure for immediate executive action on immigration.

Electoral incentives are again key to understanding the Obama administration's strategic calculus. Executive action on immigration so close to the election was seen as potentially damaging to red state Democrats, on whom the party's prospects for retaining control of the Senate depended.[115] Illustrating the political risks, a September 2014 poll showed that while large majorities of black and Latino voters supported Obama taking executive action in the face of congressional inaction on immigration reform, a majority of whites opposed it.[116] An enormous surge in illegal immigration, during which about fifty-two thousand unaccompanied children were picked up by border patrols between October 2013 and September 2014, only heightened the issue's salience and stoked fears of a backlash among white voters.[117] Obama therefore postponed action until after the midterms.[118]

Ultimately, however, the delay failed to pay political dividends. Democrats suffered another wave of midterm defeats and lost control of the Senate. Many, including former president Bill Clinton, opined that Obama's decision to delay further action on immigration, rather than helping defend red state Democrats from electoral pushback, actually hurt Democrats by depressing turnout among Latino voters. Summarizing the difficult tradeoff, Clinton concluded, "It was a tough call for him because had he done so [signed another executive memorandum on immigration] a lot of others would have lost by even more."[119]

Weeks after suffering his second consecutive midterm loss, President Obama issued a new executive action to tackle one of the most pressing concerns of reform advocates—that deportations were breaking up families. The new program, Deferred Action for Parents of Americans and Lawful Permanent Residents (DAPA), would shield up to another 5 million undocumented immigrants from deportation.[120]

In authorizing DAPA, Obama rejected his own publicly expressed fears about the legal constraints on his unilateral authority in the immigration sphere. Indeed, the greatest constraints on the president's actions were political rather than legal. In the summer of 2014, many Democrats believed that unilateral action on immigration would risk provoking a backlash among white voters and endanger the party's hold on the Senate. Obama deferred a final decision accordingly—not because Congress would overturn his action, but because acting unilaterally promised to be politically costly. By December, other political risks remained. After the midterms, Washington was abuzz with speculation as to how congressional Republicans would retaliate against Obama should he act unilaterally on immigration, with many warning of another budget shutdown. A veteran of a previous shutdown, former House Speaker Newt Gingrich, warned Obama against acting unilaterally, calling the resulting war it would initiate with Congress one that the president could not win.[121]

Paradoxically, the Republican landslide in the midterm election may have reduced the political costs of acting unilaterally. With Congress hopelessly gridlocked, President Obama may rationally and rightly have calculated that the prospects for movement on his other legislative priorities were so bleak that they were unlikely to be damaged further by acting unilaterally on immigration and moving policy away from congressional preferences and toward his own. There was little to nothing to lose at this point, thereby freeing Obama to act as unilaterally as he liked. To be sure, his move did provoke a vociferous response from congressional Republicans, who endeavored to use the power of the purse to block DAPA's implementation.[122] Moreover, while several polls showed that the policy itself was fairly popular,[123] others showed that in an interbranch showdown over the propriety of instituting DAPA unilaterally, a majority sided with Congress.[124] Had Obama acted before the midterms, the political costs for his administration might have been even steeper.

Yet while the decision to delay announcing DAPA may have made sense politically, it did more than simply postpone the implementation of a policy with immense implications for millions of persons living in the United States. It may have contributed to DAPA's ultimate demise. As discussed in chapter 4, opponents of DAPA immediately challenged its constitutionality in federal court. Lower courts granted opponents an injunction temporarily blocking implementation of the program, and the Supreme Court failed to decide the matter when the vacancy caused by the death of justice Antonin Scalia prevented it from reaching a majority decision. Thus, DAPA never went into effect before Trump's election, allowing him to easily rescind it. Of course, it is possible that if Obama had issued DAPA earlier, the Supreme Court with Scalia would have struck it down. However, if he had done so and the courts had allowed it to go into effect, President Trump may have had more trouble rescinding the program, as his effort to revoke DACA protections remains blocked in federal courts.

CONCLUSION

The formal constraints on presidential unilateral power are weak. In none of the cases examined in this chapter could Congress have successfully overturned the president if he had acted swiftly and boldly to move policy toward his ideal outcome.[125] But in each instance, the president took a step back. In the cases of gays in the military and retaliating against Syrian president Bashar al-Assad for his use of chemical weapons against his own people, ultimately Bill Clinton and Barack Obama, respectively, decided not to act unilaterally at all despite having publicly promised to do so. In both cases, the president anticipated opposition from Congress and feared that this pushback would further erode support among the American public for his proposed action, not to mention the rest of their policy agendas. In the end, both Clinton and Obama judged that the benefits of acting unilaterally no longer exceeded the steep political costs they stood to pay should they do so.

Even President Trump, who campaigned as a nonpolitician with a disdain for being politically correct, showed that he can be quite sensitive to the political costs of unilateral action—at least in specific circumstances. During the campaign, Trump explicitly pledged to bring back torture and to crack down on illegal immigration. Yet he backed away from a draft executive order to loosen the legal strictures on interrogations and reversed his zero tolerance family separations policy in the face of intense political pushback.

Finally, in the gun control and immigration cases, President Obama issued multiple executive actions to move policy in a more liberal direction. However, both the scope and the timing of his actions were significantly influenced by anticipations of political pushback. Obama repeatedly opted not to move policy as far to the left as he could have for fear of provoking too much opposition from Congress and the public and what that would mean for his broader policy agenda.

CHAPTER SEVEN

Democratic Decline?

For almost half a century, warnings of an "imperial" presidency have echoed throughout the nation's political discourse. In at least two respects, the imperial presidency paradigm captures important features of contemporary politics. First, presidential power undoubtedly expanded over the course of the twentieth century as the power of the federal government itself grew. Indeed, the advent of the modern administrative state may all but require executive-centered government.[1] Second, our contemporary polity does not and may never have functioned as James Madison envisioned in *Federalist 51*. The constitutional order endeavored to pit institutions against each other as a defense against aggrandizement. But the presidency's institutional structure gives it significant advantages in interinstitutional power struggles vis-à-vis both the highly fragmented collective body that is Congress and a judiciary that lacks independent means of enforcement.[2] As a result, the institutional checks exercised by Congress and the courts on presidential unilateralism are weak.

Where the imperial paradigm errs, however, is in inferring from the weakness of these institutional checks that presidential unilateral power is all but unfettered. The unilateral president is still constrained. But the most important check on presidential unilateralism is political rather than institutional.

Perhaps the clearest evidence of this check is the relative paucity of significant unilateral action. To be sure, when presidents have used their unilateral tool kit, they have often won significant policy victories, many of which they never would have secured if legislative action in Congress had been required. Yet there are scores of other policies that presidents have opted not to unilaterally move toward their preferences. In most cases, though, presidents could do so, secure in the knowledge that neither

Congress nor the courts could stop them. The reason they often refrain from acting unilaterally is because they anticipate the political costs of executive action—particularly the risk of alienating public opinion.

This popular check on unilateralism is not automatic. Americans do not instinctively oppose all executive action taken on the grounds that it conflicts with deeply held constitutional mores about how policymaking should work in our separation of powers system. However, such concerns can be activated when other political elites challenge the unilateral president in the public sphere. Congressional allegations that an executive action is an unconstitutional power grab or just bad public policy significantly decrease support for the president and his exercise of unilateral power. Similarly, even public speculation that the courts may strike down an action as exceeding presidential prerogatives can seriously erode popular support for the president. These negative effects hold strong across a range of presidents, policies, and contexts.

Public opinion can exercise an important check on the unilateral president. But the strength of this check is largely dependent on the willingness of other political actors to challenge presidents who push too far. The parchment barriers erected by the Framers to guard against presidential aggrandizement remain important despite the conventional wisdom decrying their irrelevance in contemporary unilateral politics. However, rather than using their constitutional powers to formally check the unilateral president, other institutional actors are most influential by challenging the chief executive in the public sphere and raising the political costs of unilateral action.

By analyzing more than sixty-five years of empirical data on executive order issuance and presidential approval, we found systematic evidence that political checks have greatly constrained the president's exercise of unilateral power. Because they anticipate greater political pushback from both other elites and the mass public, presidents with low approval ratings have systematically issued fewer major executive orders than presidents who enjoy greater public support. Moreover, far from being policies opposed by majorities of Americans, most major executive actions—at least before the iconoclastic presidency of Donald Trump—were met with broad support among the public. Finally, case studies show the importance of public opinion and anticipated political costs to presidents' decision calculus when contemplating unilateral action. These calculations have led presidents routinely to forgo acting unilaterally when the political costs outweigh the anticipated policy benefits of doing so. Even when presidents do decide to take unilateral action, such calculations have also shaped both its scope and its timing, with significant consequences for politics and policymaking.

Our assessment of the health of separation of powers in the contemporary polity is more sanguine than that of many observers. While presidential power has waxed and waned over time, presidents have rarely if ever wielded "imperial" power. Presidents have effected major policy changes on their own without ever securing legislative approval. However, brazen assertions of unilateral power are relatively rare. When presidents do effect major policy changes unilaterally, their gambits generally receive ample public support. And those that do not, such as presidents Lyndon Johnson's and George W. Bush's unilateral conduct of increasingly unpopular wars, have routinely provoked significant institutional resistance and have come at a significant political cost.[3]

Nevertheless, three ongoing developments in contemporary politics hold the potential to weaken the popular check, which for so long has significantly constrained presidents' abuse of their unilateral authority. Each current—an erosion of democratic norms; increasing partisan polarization in Congress; and rising political "tribalism" among many Americans—has fostered vigorous debate over its implications for the course and conduct of American democracy. Each has undoubtedly influenced contemporary politics; and as we have explored throughout the book, in important respects President Trump has exercised unilateral power differently and perhaps more aggressively than his predecessors.[4] Nevertheless, we conclude that political checks on presidential unilateralism remain resilient thus far.

THE EROSION OF DEMOCRATIC NORMS

A common lament in the early Trump administration is that long-held democratic norms are under assault like never before.[5] Trump has brazenly fired law enforcement officials who refused to end politically damaging investigations; berated his Attorney General for failing to protect him from his accusers; and threatened to fire the special counsel appointed by his own Justice Department to investigate Russian interference in the 2016 election and possible collusion between the Russians and the Trump campaign.[6] He has demanded investigations into and possible imprisonment of his political opponents, including leveraging the full power of his office to pressure Ukraine to investigate his political opponent's son; attacked the integrity of the independent judiciary; denounced the press as an "enemy of the American people"; and alleged the existence of a "deep state" conspiring to undermine his administration.

While this erosion of democratic norms has accelerated under Trump, comparative politics scholars Steven Levitsky and Daniel Ziblatt maintain that cherished democratic norms have been crumbling for some time, placing the United States at genuine risk of democratic backsliding and of succumbing, at least in part, to a global tide of increasing authoritarianism. Perhaps most important, Levitsky and Ziblatt argue that in recent years there has been a serious erosion in what they call "norms of institutional forbearance." "Where norms of forbearance are strong," they point out, "politicians do not use their institutional prerogatives to the hilt, even if it is technically legal to do so, for such action could imperil the existing system."[7] In effect, they argue that presidents have long engaged in self-censoring, employing their unilateral powers only when there was a broad consensus that the action was democratically legitimate and avoiding executive actions that transgressed these norms.

No one would list self-restraint among President Trump's character traits. Even a quick perusal of his Twitter feed readily confirms his impetuousness and disdain for conventions. However, the erosion of the norm of forbearance did not begin with Trump; rather, Levitsky and Ziblatt contend that it has been unraveling for some time. For example, after failing to secure legislative action on a host of key priorities, president Barack Obama executed end runs around Congress to raise fuel economy standards, protect from deportation persons brought to the country illegally as children, and institute new rules that regulated greenhouse gas emissions. "The president's actions were not out of constitutional bounds," Levitsky and Ziblatt argue, "but by acting unilaterally to achieve goals that had been blocked by Congress, President Obama violated the norm of forbearance."[8] Informal rules exist only when politicians voluntarily agree to be bound by them. As such, they can be both very powerful and quick to unravel.[9] Presidents' increasingly frequent violation of democratic norms has seriously weakened the "guardrails" of democracy itself.

If self-censoring norms were the primary mechanism restraining presidents' exercise of unilateral power, then recent erosions in these norms could portend a slide toward authoritarianism and the emergence of a genuinely imperial presidency. However, our analysis identifies a very different motivation for past presidents' restraint. Presidents do not forgo unilateral action solely or even primarily because they view it as going against democratic norms and therefore illegitimate. They forgo acting alone when they anticipate a popular backlash and incurring significant political costs from doing so.

President Obama's decision to unilaterally extend protections to potentially millions of undocumented immigrants after failing to secure legislative action was not norm shattering. Rather, the political calculations that drove both the substance and the timing of his actions are remarkably similar to those that governed president John F. Kennedy's unilateral moves on civil rights more than fifty years prior. During the 1960 campaign, Kennedy pledged vigorous action to address discrimination in federal housing.[10] However, legislative action faced an inevitable filibuster by southern Democrats. Kennedy could have acted unilaterally, but he resisted calls for an executive order because he feared that doing so would strain the Democratic coalition and jeopardize the rest of his programmatic agenda. In August of 1962, the White House counsel finally prepared a draft executive order; but Kennedy worried that it would anger both southern Democrats in Congress and, ultimately, southern voters key to the party's electoral prospects in the midterm elections.[11] As a result, he kept it secret for months.[12] Presaging Obama's timing in issuing Deferred Action for Parents of Americans and Lawful Permanent Residents (DAPA) more than a half century later, Kennedy signed Executive Order 11063 prohibiting discrimination in federal housing the day after the 1962 midterms to minimize the potential political fallout.[13] Political calculations, not norms of forbearance, best explain presidents' use—and deferral—of their office's unilateral power.

Norms may play an important role in shaping the public's response to unilateral action. The results of experiments discussed in chapter 2 conclusively show that few Americans instinctively recoil from executive action as an affront to deeply held constitutional mores. However, the experiments in chapters 3 and 4 show that when other institutional actors accuse the unilateral president of transgressing constitutional limits on presidential power, the public responds. In specific experiments investigating unilateral action in foreign policy—where presidents are routinely held to possess greater inherent constitutional powers—such challenges significantly erode public support, even when presidents contest the claims and emphasize their powers as commander in chief. Constitutional challenges may be influential with the public because they activate underlying concerns that democratic norms are being broken. As such, if norms about what constitutes a legitimate versus an illegitimate exercise of unilateral presidential power are being eroded in the contemporary polity, this could undermine the ability of other elites to rally the public against the president. There are three reasons to be skeptical of such conclusions, however.

First, while democratic norms may bolster the efficacy of institutional challenges to presidential unilateralism, it is also possible that what really matters in shaping public opinion is simply the presence of institutional criticism.[14] The experiments in chapter 3 found that congressional challenges to executive action on both constitutional and strictly policy-based grounds have roughly the same effect on public opinion. Thus, prominent institutional resistance to unilateralism may still resonate with the public, even if norms concerning its exercise change.

Second, it is not clear from the data that such norms are or should be changing. While their critics frequently labeled both Bush and Obama "imperial," chapter 1 described how they issued relatively few executive actions meriting even a modest level of coverage in major media outlets. Of course, these presidents did effect significant policy changes unilaterally. Yet a holistic assessment of the intensity of their unilateral activity shows little evidence that either relied on unilateralism more heavily than their predecessors. As for President Trump, at the time of writing it is too early to determine definitively whether he is embracing unilateralism more aggressively than previous presidents. His first year in office produced an unprecedented number of executive actions that generated prominent media coverage, although his second-year tally fell considerably to more normal levels. Moreover, his outlying score in 2017 may reflect the media feeding frenzy with all things Trump as much as a genuinely unprecedented increase in the resort to unilateral power. It is also important to remember that many of his orders simply rescinded those of his predecessor. However, even if Trump does ultimately rely on unilateralism more than his predecessors, it is impossible to say whether this is evidence of a fundamental shift in unilateral politics or an anomaly resulting from a most atypical chief executive. There is certainly not a clear trend prior to Trump.

Finally, even if restrictive norms about what constitutes legitimate unilateral executive action have weakened in the twenty-first century, it is important to remember that when recent presidents have pushed too far, they faced significant political pushback. Several of Bush's most extreme executive actions in the context of the war on terror were dealt defeats in federal courts. The protracted process that ultimately produced Obama's efforts to liberalize immigration policy, Deferred Action for Childhood Arrivals (DACA) and DAPA, provoked considerable resistance in Congress, and DAPA was essentially blocked by the courts. Likewise, Trump's brazen embrace of unilateral power has sparked major resistance from Congress, including members of his own party on multiple occasions. An unprecedented number of Trump's actions have suffered stinging defeat in federal courts. And almost all his unilateral moves have encountered significant opposition from strong majorities of Americans. This recent history suggests that norms about the proper scope of executive unilateralism remain intact.

PARTISAN POLARIZATION IN CONGRESS

Institutional opposition to executive action is absolutely central to mobilizing public opinion against the administration and activating a political check on the unilateral president. Open challenges to an executive action both force the issue onto the agenda of an often inattentive public and sway popular opinion by convincing many Americans to oppose the president's action. If other elites are silent, many executive actions may go unnoticed by the public. And in the absence of elite criticism, presidents rarely incur significant political costs, provided that they avoid advancing highly controversial policies.

Members of Congress have institutional incentives to push back against presidential power grabs. For presidential copartisans, however, the incentive to stand by their party leader may overwhelm the drive for institutional self-defense. While always a concern, this tendency should be particularly true in an era of intense partisan polarization. For the last forty years, the Democratic and Republican caucuses in Congress have simultaneously grown internally more ideologically homogenous and drifted further apart from each other.[15] As this ideological polarization has increased, so, too, has what Frances Lee calls "teamsmanship"—by which sheer partisan animosity and intense competition for control of Congress, not ideological disputes over policy outcomes, drive conflict between the parties within Congress and across branches of the federal government.[16] These tandem developments suggest that congressional pushback against bold assertions of unilateral power may be increasingly limited to members of the partisan opposition. If the opposition is in the minority, the president's partisan allies may use their control of the floor and, perhaps more important, of the committees to blunt hearings, investigations, and other means of opposition against executive action.[17]

Nevertheless, recent experience suggests that enough members of Congress often remain willing to oppose presidential aggrandizement in order to erode public support for the president. President Trump's first year in office offers perhaps the clearest examples. To be sure, many congressional Republicans went to great lengths to shield him from investigations that could be politically costly. One need look no further than House Intelligence Committee chair Devin Nunes and his clumsy efforts to shift the focus of the Russia investigation from Trump to Hillary Clinton, the Democrats, and even the FBI and the Department of Justice. Yet many of Trump's executive actions—particularly those that struck out in new directions instead of merely rolling back Obama-era moves—provoked extensive criticism even from prominent Republicans. As described in chapter 5, these Republicans publicly broke with Trump over his first travel ban, transgender military service ban, and discontinuation of DACA. Similarly, his increasingly aggressive use of the national security exemptions to slap tariffs on imports, even from key US allies, produced strong denunciations from leading Republicans on Capitol Hill.

Perhaps his most controversial executive action—his 2019 declaration of a national emergency to build the wall along the US border with Mexico—also provoked from a significant number of copartisans not just criticism but even votes for legislation to rescind the emergency declaration. Of course, President Trump vetoed the joint resolution. However, its passage through both chambers of Congress may play an important role in energizing a judicial check, and the strong signal of bipartisan opposition has hindered administration efforts to build support for the president's action.[18] Equally important, our experiments in chapter 3 suggest that congressional criticism of executive action, even if limited to members of the opposition party, still erodes support for presidential unilateralism. Even opposition party criticism seems able to activate many Americans' latent unease with unilateral action.

As the parties continue to polarize to an unprecedented degree, same-party criticism of presidential unilateralism may become rarer, and opposition party critics may increasingly struggle to ensure that their challenges to executive action resonate with voters and are not dismissed as mere partisan ploys. Yet the continued influence of public congressional resistance to unilateralism in the highly polarized contemporary polity suggests that these informal checks remain resilient.

POLITICAL "TRIBALISM" AMONG THE PUBLIC

Finally, while political scientists continue to debate whether the public, like political elites, is polarizing along ideological lines, most Americans' allegiance to their partisan team is undeniably strengthening.[19] Growing partisan "tribalism" has been blamed for everything from the rise of "fake news," to extremely cold feelings toward presidential candidates, to singles increasingly prioritizing finding politically like-minded partners, to shorter Thanksgiving dinners when hosts and guests are politically divided.[20] This trend could have significant consequences for the strength of a popular check on presidential unilateralism.

First, rising tribalism suggests that presidents may have a stronger hold on their base than ever before. It is the deeper societal force underlying Donald Trump's infamous campaign observation that he could probably shoot someone on Fifth Avenue and not lose any votes among his core supporters. This suggests that public support for presidential executive actions may have a higher floor than in the past. Indeed, we saw evidence consistent with floor effects in chapter 3's experiment investigating public support for the border wall. In this experiment, congressional challenges to Trump's executive order to begin construction of the wall decreased support for that action from 40% in the control group to 35% in the treatment group. This 5% decrease in support was the smallest effect observed for a congressional challenge across the chapter's eight experiments. This does not, however, suggest that Congress is somehow unable to move public opinion on the border wall, or that Trump is insulated from the political consequences of institutional resistance. Rather, support for the wall was already so low—almost certainly because of the considerable public resistance to it from a wide spectrum of political elites—that there was little room left for additional downward movement. The roughly 30% of Americans who represent President Trump's core base may be unshakable in their support for his unilateral policies. But what is striking in an era of intense partisan tribalism is that a supermajority of Americans opposed his executive order for the border wall.

The flip side of the equation is that while partisan tribalism may give presidents a higher floor of popular support for their unilateral actions, it may simultaneously impose a lower ceiling on popular support. For example, Barack Obama's executive actions to ease the burden of student loan debt were nonideological and noncontroversial; indeed, they benefited a wide swath of young Americans from all backgrounds and political persuasions. Yet as chapter 2 showed, fewer than 45% of Republicans backed President Obama's actions. The most likely explanation for this is that partisan tribal affinities all but precluded many Republicans from supporting executive actions taken by Obama, and vice versa for Democrats in other contexts involving a Republican president. The overwhelming support for Obama's actions among Democrats and independents still ensured that he enjoyed an overall approval rating in excess of 70% for his student loan actions. But on other, more controversial issues, rising partisan tribalism could conceivably strengthen the political check on unilateralism by imposing a much lower ceiling on popular support, which in turn could invite greater pushback from other political elites.

However, it is important not to push arguments about floor and ceiling effects too far. Even in today's era of intense partisan tribalism, support for executive action is not completely frozen along partisan lines. Rather, across a range of experiments in chapters 3 and 4 we found public opinion moving significantly in response to institutional challenges to presidents' exercise of unilateral power.

Whereas classic models of campaign strategy emphasize the imperative to cater to the median voter, the Trump campaign challenged this basic tenet by focusing, almost exclusively at times, on mobilizing its base.[21] If future presidents follow suit, the popular check on unilateralism could weaken as presidents discount the opinions of many Americans, provided that they can maintain support among their base. However, while the core partisan base may be increasingly important, it still is not enough to get a candidate over the finish line. President Trump won the presidency because he also won self-declared independent voters in key midwestern states.[22] His reelection will likely depend on maintaining a slim edge in this group as well. Thus, increasing tribalism may have raised the floor of public support presidents can count on when acting unilaterally, but it has eliminated neither the political imperative to anticipate the electorate's response to an executive action nor the incentive to consider forgoing acting unilaterally when a significant public backlash is likely.

≈

Despite ongoing threats to democratic norms, unprecedented levels of polarization in Congress, and increasingly tribal partisan loyalties among the mass public, the political checks on presidential unilateral action remain resilient. Presidents anticipate the response of the public and other political elites should they act unilaterally, as well as the political costs such opposition would entail. The result is that they routinely forgo acting alone to move a range of policies closer to their preferences, even when such action would be extremely unlikely to be reversed by Congress or the courts.

While often powerful, these political checks remain informal, in contrast to the parchment barriers erected by the Framers. By using their formal powers to either pass new legislation reversing executive action or strike it down as unconstitutional, Congress and the courts can legally compel a change in policy. By contrast, presidents who are determined to ignore the *vox populi* and who are willing to pay the political costs of executive action are institutionally empowered to effect significant policy change on their own initiative. However, presidents who give in to such "imperial" tendencies risk incurring significant costs, most important among them being reduced political capital that threatens the rest of their programmatic agenda and ultimately electoral retribution at the ballot box.

NOTES

CHAPTER ONE

1. Neustadt 1990, xix.

2. McCarty, Poole, and Rosenthal 2006.

3. Binder 2015; Koger 2010.

4. Moe and Howell 1999a, 133.

5. Jonathan Karl, "Obama's Long Lost Campaign Promise," ABCNews.com, February 17, 2014, http://abcnews.go.com/blogs/politics/2014/02/obamas-long-lost-campaign -promise/.

6. Rebecca Kaplan, "Obama: I Will Use My Pen and Phone to Take On Congress," CBSNews.com, January 14, 2014, http://www.cbsnews.com/news/obama-i-will-use-my -pen-and-phone-to-take-on-congress/.

7. Gregory Korte, "Trump's Executive Actions Come Faster and in Different Forms Than Before," *USA Today*, January 30, 2017, http://www.usatoday.com/story/news/ politics/2017/01/30/trumps-executive-actions-come-faster-and-different-forms-than -before/97255592/.

8. Schlesinger 1973, ix.

9. Goldsmith 2012; Howell and Pevehouse 2007; Kriner 2010. For Congress's influence in foreign policymaking more generally, see Carter and Scott (2009); Milner and Tingley (2015).

10. For an argument that an "invisible" Congress is equally if not even more to blame than an "imperial" president, see Rudalevige (2005), 261–85.

11. Pfiffner 2008; Rudalevige 2005; Savage 2008.

12. Ackerman 2010.

13. Linda Chavez, "Like Obama, Trump Takes to Imperial Presidency," *Boston Herald*, February 7, 2017, http://www.bostonherald.com/opinion/op_ed/2017/02/chavez_like _obama_trump_takes_to_imperial_presidency. For a broader critique of Trump and his early use and possible abuse of executive power, see Crouch, Rozell, and Sollenberger (2017).

14. Levitsky and Ziblatt 2018.

15. Huq and Ginsburg 2018.

16. Cato, Letter V, *New York Journal*, November 22, 1787.

17. Howell 2003; Levinson and Pildes 2006.

18. David Eldridge, "Boehner's Memo to Members on Obama Lawsuit (Complete Text)," *Roll Call*, June 25, 2014, https://www.rollcall.com/news/boehner-lawsuit-memo -letter-members.

19. Whittington 2009.

20. Howell 2003, 152–57. President Trump's many defeats, particularly of his efforts to roll back Obama-era regulations (see, for example, the list maintained by the Institute for Policy Integrity, accessed November 1, 2019, https://policyintegrity.org/ deregulation-roundup), are a notable exception. We discuss recent trends in judicial pushback in greater detail in chapter 4.

21. Edwards 2016, 16–17.

22. Edwards 2016, 19.

23. Electoral forecast models have long shown that presidential approval is one of the strongest predictors of presidential electoral fortunes (e.g., Abramowitz 1996).

24. Jacobson 2012, 2015. On the increasing nationalization of US elections more generally, see Hopkins (2018).

25. Abramowitz 2016.

26. This is an important respect in which our argument differs from that of Posner and Vermeule (2010). Posner and Vermeule emphasize the importance of public opinion as a check on rampant unilateralism, but they pay little attention to the key role that other institutional actors, including Congress and the courts, continue to play in activating this popular check.

27. It is impossible to determine precisely how many memoranda recent presidents have issued: unlike executive orders, presidents are not bound by statute to publish all memoranda in the *Federal Register*. Nevertheless, research shows that recent presidents have issued hundreds of these; see Lowande (2014).

28. Data for 1945 to 2000 were generously provided by William Howell (2005). We updated this data set through 2018. We follow Howell's procedure of coding an executive action as significant if it was mentioned at least once in the *New York Times* within one year of its issuance.

29. Howell et al. 2000; Mayhew 1991.

30. Of course, even procedural executive orders can be impactful; however, they are far from the bold expressions of unilateral power to dramatically shift policy with the stroke of a pen that concern scholars and pundits warning of an imperial presidency.

31. For a thorough overview of the president's unilateral tool kit, see Cooper (2002).

32. Specifically, we searched for articles that contained any of the following words: "executive order," "executive action," "proclamation," "memorandum," "memoranda," or "executive agreement." These search terms were used to capture the most prevalent forms of unilateral action and included the more generic catchall term of "executive action" sometimes used in media reports.

33. Figure 1.2 plots the number of nonceremonial unilateral actions reported in the *Times*. Classifying executive actions as ceremonial can involve some subjectivity. For example, a small number of executive orders in the bottom panel of figure 1.1 deal with

waiving the mandatory retirement age for specific executive branch officials. These could be considered ceremonial, but one of them (Executive Order 11154) waived the mandatory retirement age for FBI director J. Edgar Hoover—a move with obvious policy consequences! As such, in figure 1.1 we present all executive orders mentioned in the *Times*, and we note that those we coded as ceremonial (including eleven executive orders dealing with waivers from mandatory retirement requirements) represent a small fraction—less than 5%—of the total. By contrast, almost a quarter of the non-executive-order actions mentioned in the *Times* from 2001 through 2018 are clearly ceremonial. This is particularly true of proclamations. While some, such as the third iteration of President Trump's travel ban, were clearly policy relevant, more than two-thirds were strictly ceremonial—including Trump's proclamation declaring his inauguration day a "National Day of Patriotic Devotion," and multiple proclamations honoring Martin Luther King Day, lowering flags to half-mast, etc. As a result, we exclude all ceremonial unilateral actions from figure 1.2. That said, including the thirty-nine ceremonial executive actions mentioned in the *Times* over this eighteen-year period yields time trend graphs almost indistinguishable from those presented in the text.

34. Recent research by Michelle Belco and Brandon Rottinghaus (2014, 2017) makes the important point that many executive actions involve presidents actively cooperating with Congress, rather than seeking to circumvent the legislature. Thus, the frequency with which presidents use their unilateral tool kit to make an end run around Congress is far less than raw counts of executive orders or executive memoranda suggest.

35. Howell 2003, 20–21; Schubert 1957.

36. For example, Edward Corwin's (1957) *The President, Office and Power* never used the word *unilateral*. To be sure, such powers were occasionally discussed; for example, Corwin assessed the constitutionality of executive agencies created by Franklin D. Roosevelt via executive order pursuant to his authority as commander in chief. These powers were far from a point of emphasis, however. See also Rossiter (1960).

37. Neustadt 1990.

38. Cooper 2002; Krause and Cohen 1997; Mayer 2001; Moe and Howell 1999b. On the increase in the use of major unilateral actions over time, see Howell (2003, 84–85).

39. Black 1948; Downs 1957.

40. To simplify matters, Krehbiel (1998) posits a unicameral legislature in explicating his theory.

41. Howell goes on to add additional features to the model, such as the discretion that the judiciary will allow presidents to exercise. See Howell (2003, 30–31). However, the basic features and conclusions that presidents enjoy wide latitude to act unilaterally remain.

42. Howell acknowledges that presidents must act within the discretion allowed them in each policy context. However, his model suggests that presidents routinely enjoy the discretion to move policy in either a more liberal or a more conservative direction in order to bring it into closer alignment with presidential preferences. By contrast, recent research by Fang-Yi Chiou and Lawrence Rothenberg (2014, 2017) suggests that presidential discretion may be directionally limited—that is, they explore whether presidents may only be able to move policy toward the chamber median or toward the

preferences of the median member of the majority party. Empirically, they find support for the latter possibility. Accordingly, they argue that presidents are much more constrained by Congress, particularly by opposition party leaders wielding negative agenda power, than commonly supposed in the literature.

43. For a similar emphasis on the veto override and presidential anticipation thereof, see Deering and Maltzman (1999).

44. Katyal 2006, 106. On Congress's institutional weakness vis-à-vis the executive, see also Bradley and Morrison (2013); Devins (2008).

45. Howell 2003, 101.

46. On collective action dilemmas, see Moe (1994); Moe and Wilson (1994).

47. Chiou and Rothenberg (2017) offer an important challenge to this line of argument. They do not contest that legislative reversals of unilateral action are empirically rare (though this alone cannot rule out that presidents simply avoid issuing orders that Congress would overturn), and that mustering the requisite supermajorities is quite difficult. However, they argue that past scholarship has overlooked the extrastatutory tools at Congress's disposal, including its power over the legislative calendar, budgets, and the executive branch appointment process. Even when Congress cannot overturn an executive action directly, it may be able to exercise these other formal levers of influence to impose costs on the White House. As a result, presidents may rescind executive orders that provoke pushback in Congress, and forgo others altogether that might spark a congressional response. Chiou and Rothenberg's argument and evidence represent an important new perspective on how we think about the nature of the legislative constraint that Congress exercises on presidential unilateralism. But the constraint that they describe is still a formal one; Congress can use formal institutional tools aside from enacting legislation reversing a unilateral action to affect presidential strategic calculations. Our argument here takes a different tack. We focus on the *informal* constraint placed on the unilateral executive by public opinion, and how other political actors, primarily Congress and the courts, can activate and strengthen this informal check by contesting the exercise of unilateral power in the public sphere.

48. Moe and Howell 1999a, 138. This expectation that presidents have strong incentives to act unilaterally when they are blocked legislatively is the crux of the "strategic" model of unilateral action. See Belco and Rottinghaus (2014); Cooper (2002); Deering and Maltzman (1999); Fine and Warber (2012); Nathan (1983); Peterson (1990).

49. Timothy H. Edgar, "Memorandum to Congress on President Bush's Order Establishing Military Tribunals," ACLU, November 29, 2001, https://www.aclu.org/memorandum-congress-president-bushs-order-establishing-military-tribunals#1.

50. For an overview of the extensive congressional pushback, see Howell and Kriner (2008, 118–21).

51. To mute congressional criticism, the administration did announce several "refinements" in March 2002. However, the crux of the order, including the admissibility of hearsay evidence, the absence of any civilian judicial review, and the possibility for continued detention even after an acquittal, remained (Howell and Kriner 2008, 121–22).

52. James Risen and Erich Lichtblau, "Bush Lets U.S. Spy on Callers without Courts," *New York Times*, December 16, 2005, https://www.nytimes.com/2005/12/16/politics/bush-lets-us-spy-on-callers-without-courts.html.

53. Howell 2003, 151–57.

54. For the prevalence of gun violence, see Fleegler (2019).

55. Emily Kopp, "Republicans Have Concerns about Trump's Emergency Declaration, Too," *The Hill*, February 15, 2019, https://www.rollcall.com/news/republicans-have-concerns-about-trumps-executive-action-too.

56. Chafetz 2017; Chiou and Rothenberg 2017. See also Bolton and Thrower (2016).

57. Belco and Rottinghaus 2017. For a similar argument about the complementarity of executive action and legislation, see Dickinson and Gubb (2016).

58. Kennedy 2015; Rudalevige 2009, 2012, 2015. See also Dickinson (2008); Krause and Cohen (2000); Lowande (2018).

59. Another strand of scholarship that has also not focused heavily on formal legislative constraints examines problems of bureaucratic implementation.

60. Mayer 2009. Yet, on the question of what constraint other institutional actors impose, Mayer (2009, 448) later seems to equate legislative constraint with formal legislative responses: "When do the constraints on unilateral action come into play, and what triggers them? Can we make any statements about *when* . . . Congress will respond with a legislative reaction?"

61. Moe and Howell 1999a, 138. Similarly, Matthew Dickinson (2009, 758) has argued, "If by issuing an executive order or directive presidents weaken their influence across a range of other issue areas, one would be hard-pressed using Neustadt's criteria to label the unilateral action an example of 'power.' At the very least, to validly compare unilateral action with Neustadt's bargaining model of presidential power, scholars must assess the relative gains from using administrative means to achieve an immediate objective with its cost on a president's effective influence in other areas and at other times."

62. Neustadt 1960.

63. For example, see Barrett and Eshbaugh-Soha (2007); Beckmann (2010); Canes-Wrone and de Marchi (2002); Marshall and Prins (2007); Rivers and Rose (1985).

64. Posner and Vermeule 2010, 12.

65. This view is far from universally shared, even when focusing specifically on the president's powers as commander in chief. For example, Jack Goldsmith, former head of the Office of Legal Counsel, argues that a more nuanced assessment of the war on terror shows that Congress and the courts were much more powerful than often acknowledged: "The other two branches of government, aided by the press and civil society, pushed back against the Commander in Chief like never before in our nation's history" (Goldsmith 2012, 38). For a defense of Congress's capacity to check the unilateral president even in times of foreign and domestic crisis, see Huq (2012). For the important role played by civil society, particularly citizen activist groups, in checking many of President Bush's unilateral actions through their actions both inside and outside the courtroom, see Cole (2016).

66. Posner and Vermeule 2010, 209. Similarly, Josh Chafetz (2017, 14) argues, "the American constitutional separation of powers focuses on the creation of (or the attempt to create) space for conflict between the branches of government, without an overarching adjudicator to resolve the conflict in a principled, binding, and lasting way. These conflicts play out in public and the branch that most successfully engages the public will accrete power over time."

67. Posner and Vermeule 2010, 77–78. The hypothetical constitutional battle discussed here concerns contested claims by the president and Congress over the power to end a war. For additional discussion about the importance of public opinion as a constraint on presidential war power, see Goldsmith (2012); Howell and Kriner (2007); Kriner (2010). For a game-theoretic argument that electoral pressure is insufficient to check presidential power when confronting a terrorist threat, see Dragu and Polborn (2014).

68. Bertaut 1916, 31.

69. Smith 2005, 59.

CHAPTER TWO

1. This chapter builds on research in Christenson and Kriner (2017a).

2. Delli Carpini and Keeter 1997.

3. Nick Gass, "Americans Bomb Pew Test of Basic Public Knowledge," *Politico*, April 28, 2015, https://www.politico.com/story/2015/04/pew-news-iq-test-results-117421.

4. Kuklinski and Hurley 1994; Lau and Redlawsk 1997; Lodge and Hamill 1986; Lupia 1994; Lupia and McCubbins 1998; Mondak 1993a, 1993b; Popkin 1991; Schaffner and Streb 2002; Sniderman, Brody, and Tetlock 1991; Zaller 1992.

5. Michael Rozansky, "Americans Know Surprisingly Little about Their Government, Survey Finds," Annenberg Public Policy Center, September 17, 2014, https://www.annenbergpublicpolicycenter.org/americans-know-surprisingly-little-about-their-government-survey-finds/.

6. Howell 2003, 19–21.

7. Bailey and Rottinghaus 2014.

8. Franklin D. Roosevelt, "Proclamation 2087—Forbidding the Shipment of Arms to the Combatants in the Chaco," May 28, 1934; online by Gerhard Peters and John T. Woolley, the American Presidency Project, University of California, Santa Barbara, accessed November 1, 2019, https://www.presidency.ucsb.edu/node/208841.

9. Technically, the memorandum was issued by the secretary of the Department of Homeland Security, Janet Napolitano: https://www.dhs.gov/xlibrary/assets/s1-exercising-prosecutorial-discretion-individuals-who-came-to-us-as-children.pdf, accessed November 1, 2019.

10. Pew Research Center for the People & the Press, Pew Research Center for the People & the Press Poll: February 2017, Question 63, USPSRA.030217A.R61E, Princeton Survey Research Associates International (Cornell University, Ithaca, NY: Roper Center for Public Opinion Research, 2017), accessed November 1, 2019.

11. PublicInterestPolling.com, PublicInterestPolling.com Poll # 2007-CON: Constitution and Governance Issues Survey, Question 1, USPARKER.07PIP.R01, the Parker Group (Cornell University, Ithaca, NY: Roper Center for Public Opinion Research, 2007), data set, accessed November 1, 2019.

12. Fox News, Fox News Poll: December 2014, Question 20, USASFOX.121014.R25, Anderson Robbins Research/Shaw & Co. Research (Cornell University, Ithaca, NY: Roper Center for Public Opinion Research, 2014), data set, accessed November 1, 2019.

13. Fox News, Fox News Poll: January 2016, Question 14, USASFOX.010916.R14, Shaw & Co. Research/Anderson Robbins Research (Cornell University, Ithaca, NY: Roper Center for Public Opinion Research, 2016), data set, accessed November 1, 2019.

14. For a recent overview of presidential power in foreign affairs, see Ramsay (2007).

15. CBS News/*New York Times*, CBS News/New York Times Poll # 2002-10A: 2002 Congressional Election/Politics/Foreign Policy/Iraq, Question 25, USCBSNYT.100602. R44, CBS News/*New York Times* (Cornell University, Ithaca, NY: Roper Center for Public Opinion Research, 2002), data set, accessed November 1, 2019. Almost two-thirds of Americans also believed that the first President Bush, George H. W., should seek congressional approval before using force against Iraq in 1991. Associated Press, Associated Press Poll # 1991-901G: Gulf Crisis, Question 2, USAP.91901.R2, ICR Survey Research Group (Cornell University, Ithaca, NY: Roper Center for Public Opinion Research, 1991), data set, accessed November 1, 2019.

16. In so doing, their research builds on analyses of public attitudes toward other governing institutions. For a similar analysis examining the influence of core beliefs on attitudes toward Congress and its procedures, see Park and Smith (2016); Smith and Park (2013). In the context of popular attitudes toward judicial legitimacy, see Caldeira and Gibson (1992); Gibson, Caldeira, and Spence (2005).

17. Their survey instrument also queried support for the president to choose judges as well as to decide how agencies will implement the law (Reeves and Rogowski 2016, 140).

18. Support was also quite stable at the individual level. See Reeves and Rogowski (2016, 141). In a second study employing a series of survey experiments, Reeves and Rogowski (2018) find that the public punishes hypothetical presidential candidates for announcing their intention to pursue policy goals unilaterally.

19. For complete approval data for the Obama administration, see https://www .presidency.ucsb.edu/statistics/data/presidential-job-approval, accessed November 1, 2019.

20. On the link between presidential approval and support for unilateral action, see also Reeves and Rogowski (2015).

21. Margulies 2013, 230. Interestingly, Margulies argues that times of crisis actually *heighten* the importance of Americans' creedal commitments; this in turn strengthened the public backlash to Bush's unilateral gambits (233–34).

22. E.g., Rahn (1993).

23. Gaines et al. 2007.

24. Bartels 2002; Duch, Palmer, and Anderson 2000; Gerber and Huber 2010.

25. For a review of economic voting literature, see Anderson (2007), but see also Lacy and Christenson (2017).

26. An alternative literature argues that Americans engage in partisan-motivated reasoning when processing new information and incorporating it into their political judgments (Bartels 2002; Campbell et al. 1960; Petersen et al. 2013). Following past research (Druckman, Peterson, and Slothuus 2013, 59), we acknowledge that partisanship could influence assessments of unilateral action through both pathways, and that discriminating between them is exceedingly difficult. While we believe that our

experiments show evidence consistent with both motivated reasoning and heuristics, we focus here on the simpler partisan-cues explanation, which is consistent with our results across the experiments.

27. Druckman, Peterson, and Slothuus 2013; Petersen et al. 2013.

28. All the original survey questions and survey experiments discussed in the text were fielded by YouGov. Replication materials to reproduce all the statistical analyses in the book are available at https://dataverse.harvard.edu/dataset.xhtml?persistentId= doi:10.7910/DVN/3MHYP0.

29. Indeed, while President Bush signed the order on January 24, 2007, congressional Democrats codified it into law two years later as part of the 2009 Omnibus Appropriations Act.

30. Converse 1964; Zaller 1992.

31. Green, Palmquist, and Schickler 2002; Lenz 2012.

32. Levendusky 2009.

33. Cohen 2003; Rahn 1993.

34. Arceneaux 2008; Boudreau and Mackenzie 2014; Bullock 2011.

35. There is a massive literature debating the relative importance of self-interest in opinion formation. For recent evidence that self-interest matters in the context of two policies examined in subsequent chapters, immigration and the use of force, see Gerber et al. (2017); Kriner and Shen (2010).

36. See, e.g., Achen and Bartels (2017).

37. Lee 2016.

38. All surveys were conducted by YouGov, which uses a two-stage sample matching methodology to produce nationally representative results from a large opt-in panel. For more information on YouGov's sampling strategy, as well as the results of a recent Pew Study showing YouGov outperforming other online competitors, see https://today .yougov.com/news/2016/05/13/pew-research-yougov/, accessed November 1, 2019.

39. ABC News/*Washington Post*, ABC News/Washington Post Poll: 2014 Congressional Election/Congress/Affordable Care Act, Question 23, USABCWP.012614.R12, Langer Research Associates/Capital Insight/Abt SRBI, Inc. (Cornell University, Ithaca, NY: Roper Center for Public Opinion Research, 2014), data set, accessed November 1, 2019. The dependent variable in this and each subsequent experiment (except for the Partisan Source Experiment) was measured on a four-point Likert scale. We collapsed the strongly support and somewhat support response categories to construct a measure of the percentage of Americans supporting the president's unilateral action, which is the most politically relevant quantity emphasized in media reports.

40. Republicans controlled the House in the 113th Congress and gained control of the Senate in the 2014 elections.

41. Lebo and Cassino 2007; Zaller 1992.

42. Full results of the logistic regression models are presented in appendix table 2.1.

43. We also examined an alternate hypothesis, that the justification treatment effect is moderated by a subject's level of political knowledge. However, we find that partisanship, not political knowledge, is the key moderating variable.

44. In all the figures for this chapter, we examine the effect of each factor on the

probability of supporting unilateral action while holding all other variables constant at their median values.

45. E.g., Lenz (2012).

46. E.g., Canes-Wrone, Howell, and Lewis (2008).

47. Wildavsky 1966, 9–10.

48. Italics added here for emphasis.

49. The prompt and question wording were adapted from a 2014 *Washington Post* poll: ABC News/*Washington Post*, ABC News/Washington Post Poll: 2014 Congressional Election/Congress/Affordable Care Act, Question 23, USABCWP.012614.R12, Langer Research Associates/Capital Insight/Abt SRBI, Inc. (Cornell University, Ithaca, NY: Roper Center for Public Opinion Research, 2014), data set, accessed November 1, 2019.

50. For full results, see appendix table 2.2.

51. See appendix table 2.3.

52. For a comparative assessment of the frequency with which recent presidents have reversed their predecessors' orders, see Potter et al. (2019, 3).

53. Half our sample of one thousand Americans was assigned to the first experiment, while the other half was assigned to the second.

54. Italics added here for emphasis.

55. However, because the experiment was administered to only five hundred subjects, the 95% confidence interval around this estimate includes the null hypothesis of no opinion change. See appendix table 2.4 for full results. Throughout the book, we report the results concerning the change in predicted probabilities of supporting executive action as percent change. For example, if a factor increased the predicted probability of supporting executive action from .40 to .60, we refer to this as a 20% increase in the probability of supporting executive action.

56. The pipeline was later blocked by the federal district court in Montana. But in March 2019, President Trump signed a new permit to sidestep the court order, though challenges in state court still cloud the pipeline's future.

57. In this and several other experiments, we use the term *executive order* to describe the president's unilateral action, even if it was accomplished using a different unilateral tool, such as a presidential memorandum. We did this because *executive order* is more familiar to most Americans, as the media commonly use this as a catchall term to label any unilateral action taken by the administration.

58. For full results, see appendix table 2.5.

59. Glennon 2015.

60. The only modification to the Gallup question was the addition of "to combat terrorism." *USA Today*, Gallup News Service Poll: Presidential Election/Bush Administration, Question 37, USGALLUP.200621.Q11, Gallup Organization (Cornell University, Ithaca, NY: Roper Center for Public Opinion Research, 2006), data set, accessed November 1, 2019.

61. Simple past tense was also used instead of the present perfect.

62. For full results, see appendix table 2.6.

63. In the June 2006 Gallup survey, 74% of Democrats said Bush had gone too far.

64. This experiment was embedded in the preelection wave of the 2014 Cooperative Congressional Election Study.

65. Of course, executive orders are not the only option in the president's unilateral tool kit (Lowande 2014; Rottinghaus and Maier 2007). However, given the null results for the executive order treatment in both experiments, we think it highly unlikely that the public would respond differently to unilateral action through other instruments.

66. For example, recent research by Grimmer, Westwood, and Messing (2014) shows that voters give members of Congress as much credit for proposing legislation to bring dollars to their districts as they do for actually securing legislation with the funds.

67. Reeves and Rogowski 2015.

68. The standard approval variable was a component of the Common Content of the Cooperative Congressional Election Study: https://dataverse.harvard.edu/dataset.xhtml ?persistentId=doi%3A10.7910/DVN/XFXJVY, accessed November 5, 2019. Because of space limitations, we were unable to include the approval question on our other You-Gov surveys. However, in three separate experiments (one each in chapters 2, 3, and 4) we find that approval is consistently a strong predictor of support for executive action.

69. Additional analyses in appendix table 2.7 examine whether the relationship between the executive order treatment and support for Obama's student loan efforts was moderated by partisanship or policy preferences. Model 2 includes the interactions of the executive order treatment with the Democratic and Republican indicator variables. None of the coefficients are statistically significant. Across partisan groups, whether Obama pursued limits on student loan debt repayments by legislation or unilateral action has no significant influence on the probability of a subject backing the president. Model 3 includes the interaction of the executive order treatment and the student loan debt indicator variable. The resulting coefficients for both the main effect and the interaction are also statistically insignificant. Whether Obama pursued student loan debt relief legislatively or unilaterally had no effect on either those with student debt or those without it.

70. Italics added here for emphasis.

71. Reestimating this model with the interaction of the Latino and Republican dummy variables confirms that Latinos of all partisan stripes—including the approximately 20% who identified as Republican—were more supportive of Obama's immigration efforts, all else being equal. Additional analyses in appendix table 2.8 show that the effect of the executive order treatment was not conditional on any partisan or racial subgroup. Model 2 includes the partisan interactions; neither coefficient is statistically significant. Democrats backed Obama's efforts and Republicans vehemently opposed them, regardless of whether the president chose a legislative or a unilateral policy course. Similarly, model 3 shows that neither Latinos nor non-Latinos were affected by the executive order treatment. As in the Student Loans Experiment, partisan cues and policy preferences alone shaped assessments of Obama's immigration actions.

72. The order did not contain any funding to actually construct the wall. However, our language here echoes that of the order itself: "In accordance with existing law, including the Secure Fence Act and IIRIRA [Illegal Immigration Reform and Responsibility Act], take all appropriate steps to immediately plan, design, and construct a physical wall along the southern border." Executive Order: Border Security and Immigration

Enforcement Improvements, January 25, 2017, https://www.whitehouse.gov/presidential
-actions/executive-order-border-security-immigration-enforcement-improvements/.

73. Additional analyses presented in appendix table 2.9 again show that the executive order treatment did not have any effect among any partisan or racial group.

74. Reeves and Rogowski 2016, 2018.

75. What might explain the divergent results? Perhaps most important, our analysis employs a different methodological approach to studying popular assessments of
unilateral action. As much as possible, our questions and experiments (in this chapter and those that follow) asked subjects to evaluate unilateral actions, both real and
anticipated, taken by contemporary presidents. By contrast, Reeves and Rogowski's
survey instruments employ more general questions and examine popular reactions to
hypothetical unilateral actions. For example, in their first study, Reeves and Rogowski
endeavor to measure public support for unilateral action as exercised by "the office of
the presidency and not any particular president." Focusing on popular perceptions of
the office and its proper exercise of power, they find that large majorities of Americans
oppose unilateral executive action in the abstract, and that core democratic values, primarily support for the rule of law, are among the main drivers of this opposition. Similarly, in a follow-up study they employ a series of survey experiments to examine how a
presidential candidate's decision to pursue policy goals either legislatively or unilaterally affects support for that hypothetical candidate. Using more abstract questions and
hypothetical scenarios does afford some important advantages. For example, examining
support for actual unilateral actions can lead to strategic selection bias, as presidents
should only act unilaterally either when they anticipate little public resistance to a
unilateral action or when the anticipated benefits outweigh the costs (we develop this
argument further in chapter 5; see also [Reeves and Rogowski 2018, 427–28]). Similarly,
as Reeves and Rogowski note, it is all but impossible to identify two identical real-world
policy outcomes that were achieved through different means (one unilaterally and the
other legislatively). As we acknowledge above, there is necessarily some asymmetry in
our ends versus means experiments. Yet, particularly on relatively low-salience issues,
we are confident that the manipulations are plausible. However, because such questions
asked subjects to evaluate unilateral action in an apolitical context—perhaps most
important, in a setting devoid of partisan cues—it is difficult to generalize from these
findings to how Americans view unilateralism in today's intensely polarized political environment. As a result, we believe that our experiments provide a more realistic
window on preference formation in contemporary politics.

76. The sharp differences in public responses to abstract versus specific questions
parallel those observed in other policy areas, such as federal spending (Jacoby 2000) and
health care (Christenson and Glick 2015b).

CHAPTER THREE

1. This chapter builds on research in Christenson and Kriner (2017b).

2. Jacobs et al. 1998; Mayhew 2000.

3. On the presidential strategy of "going public" and its limits, see Canes-Wrone
(2005); Cohen (2008, 2010); Edwards (2006); Kernell (1997); Rottinghaus (2010).

4. Jacobs 2010; Jacobs and Shapiro 2000; Mayhew 2000.

5. On Congress's capacity to shape wartime public opinion, see Berinsky (2009); Howell and Pevehouse (2007); Kriner (2017); Kriner and Shen (2014). On the president's advantages in foreign policy, see Wildavsky (1966).

6. Zaller 1992.

7. Reeves and Rogowski 2015, 2016, 2018.

8. Berinsky 2007.

9. Althaus et al. 1996; Bennett 1990; Entman 2004.

10. Cappella and Jamieson 1997; Groeling 2010; Patterson 1996.

11. Chong and Druckman 2007.

12. Canes-Wrone, Howell, and Lewis 2008; Wildavsky 1966.

13. For contrasting evidence, see Reeves and Rogowski (2016).

14. Bennett 1990.

15. Mermin 1999.

16. Kriner and Schickler 2014.

17. Berinsky 2009; Brody 1991; Zaller 1992.

18. Baum and Groeling 2009; Calvert 1985.

19. For example, a trio of polls in October–December of 1992 showed a fairly evenly divided public on the question of whether gays should be allowed to serve openly in the military. By May 1993, a CNN poll showed only 36% backing Clinton's plan versus 55% opposing it. Similarly, almost immediately after Obama signed Executive Order 13492 to begin the process of closing Guantanamo, polls showed roughly an evenly split public. However, by the summer of 2009 opposition to Obama's order clearly outpaced support, and by the beginning of 2010 the president's executive action was roughly 20% underwater with the American public.

20. In an important respect, the Clean Power Plan was not a unilateral presidential action akin to an executive order. Rather, it was a regulatory action undertaken by the EPA. As such, it was subject to the Administrative Procedures Act, involved periods of public comment, and ultimately was a rule issued by the EPA (RIN 2060-AR33), not the White House. However, the EPA began the process to develop the Clean Power Plan at the direction of President Obama, and the eventual plan was broadly consistent with the policy preferences of the president and administration. Indeed, it was repeatedly hailed in the press as President Obama's "signature climate change policy." To exclude such cases from an assessment of presidential unilateral power would overlook the significant influence that presidents can have on policy outcomes through the regulatory process.

21. Entman 2004.

22. Throughout the chapter, we label these treatments "constitutional" challenges. To clarify, not all "constitutional challenges" take direct aim at the scope of the president's Article II powers. For example, the legal challenges to President Obama's Clean Power Plan primarily involved questions of discretion. The Supreme Court in *Massachusetts vs. EPA* ruled that the EPA could regulate carbon dioxide as a greenhouse gas under the Clean Air Act. The question is whether President Obama's plan pushed too far and seized power beyond that delegated to the executive branch by existing statute. Nevertheless, critics of the executive action in the media routinely used constitutional language when challenging the legality of Obama's action. Perhaps most prominently, Harvard law professor Lawrence Tribe penned an op-ed in the December 22, 2014, edi-

tion of the *Wall Street Journal* provocatively titled "The Clean Power Plan Is Unconstitutional." Tribe argued that "the agency is asserting executive power far beyond its lawful authority," and hence that the plan is unconstitutional. Following Tribe and many other political and media elites (for example, a LexisNexis search of "clean power plan AND unconstitutional" returned over 1,400 news hits from 2014 through 2018), we describe such challenges as "constitutional," even if the legal debate focuses primarily on statutory interpretation.

23. In the first three experiments of this chapter, the congressional opposition is described as bipartisan, because many of Obama's major unilateral actions attracted at least some criticism from members of his own party. Even if most of the opposition is from the opposition party, isolated criticism from presidential copartisans is frequent enough for media outlets to label the pushback bipartisan. Later in this chapter, we will examine the effects of purely partisan opposition. In chapter 5, we further modify our experimental treatment to examine the influence of alternate language in which *"some members of Congress from both parties"* challenge the president's unilateral actions. In all cases, we continue to find statistically significant negative effects of congressional criticism on support for unilateral action (or, in chapter 5, for the president himself).

24. In each experiment, support for the president's action was measured on a four-point Likert scale. We collapsed the strongly support and somewhat support categories to calculate the percentage supporting the president. Ordered logit models yielded substantively similar results.

25. Although subjects were randomly assigned to the three experimental groups, randomization checks indicated an uneven partisan balance across the three samples. A multivariate logit model allowed us to account for this uneven distribution of Democratic and Republican partisans across the three groups.

26. Full results are presented in appendix table 3.1.

27. The small difference in estimated effect sizes across the two treatments is not statistically significant.

28. As shown in model 3 of appendix table 3.1, the coefficient for the constitutional objections interaction is almost zero. The coefficient for the policy criticism interaction is positive and substantively larger; however, it also fails to reach conventional levels of statistical significance.

29. NBC News/*Wall Street Journal*, NBC News/Wall Street Journal Poll: November 2014, Question 47, USNBCWSJ.120214.R21A, Hart Research Associates/Public Opinion Strategies (Cornell University, Ithaca, NY: Roper Center for Public Opinion Research, 2014), data set, accessed November 1, 2019.

30. President Obama's decision to launch air strikes against ISIS targets in September 2014 received considerable support in Congress, but also provoked strong criticism from some members, including senator Tim Kaine (D-VA), on constitutional grounds. While Kaine's call for Congress to take up a new authorization to use military force gained little traction in Congress, his and others' criticism of Obama's unilateral action received substantial media coverage.

31. President Obama first instituted (https://www.whitehouse.gov/the-press-office/ 2012/06/07/presidential-memorandum-improving-repayment-options-federal-student -loan) and then expanded (https://www.whitehouse.gov/the-press-office/2014/06/09/

presidential-memorandum-federal-student-loan-repayments) this program through a pair of memoranda. The treatment wording follows media coverage, which frequently uses the more familiar term *executive order* to describe a range of executive actions.

32. Full results are presented in appendix table 3.2.

33. In words echoing our experimental treatment, Manchin argued, "If these regulations go into effect, American jobs will be lost, electricity prices will soar and economic uncertainty will grow." Dan Cappiello, "Obama Moves to Limit Power-Plant Carbon Pollution," *Atlanta Journal-Constitution*, September 20, 2013, https:// www.myajc.com/news/national/obama-moves-limit-power-plant-carbon-pollution/ dS4BwFjd3Ipr7kMQTKuq2M/.

34. Deirdre Walsh, "Most Positive Reaction to Syria Airstrikes Comes from Obama's Critics," CNN, September 23, 2014, http://www.cnn.com/2014/09/23/politics/ syria-airstrikes-congress-reaction/.

35. Groeling 2010.

36. To ensure adequate subgroup sample sizes for our partisan interactions, our treatments in this experiment combined constitutional objections and policy criticisms, which were equally influential in the first EPA experiment. This choice also reflects much congressional criticism of unilateral actions.

37. Full results are presented in appendix table 3.3.

38. Full results are presented in appendix table 3.4.

39. However, Wald tests on the regression coefficients reported in appendix table 3.5 cannot confirm that the differences in magnitude between either of the congressional treatments and the two noncongressional source treatments are statistically significant, given the small sample sizes involved.

40. Full results are presented in appendix table 3.5.

41. Jacobson 2015.

42. Trump's Executive Order 13767 directed "the immediate construction of a physical wall on the southern border." However, absent congressional appropriation of the requisite funds, his efforts were thwarted, leading him to declare a national emergency in February 2019 in order to reprogram funds to build the wall.

43. Full results are presented in appendix table 3.6.

44. Full results are presented in appendix table 3.7.

45. Whether the policy criticism treatment effect meets conventional thresholds of statistical significance depends on which controls are included in the model.

46. "Here's Donald Trump's Announcement Speech," *Time*, June 16, 2015, http:// time.com/3923128/donald-trump-announcement-speech/.

47. Ashley Parker, Nick Corasaniti, and Erica Berenstein, "Voices from Donald Trump Rallies, Uncensored." *New York Times*, August 3, 2016, https://www.nytimes .com/2016/08/04/us/politics/donald-trump-supporters.html.

48. Fowler 2015; Kriner and Schickler 2016; Mayhew 2000.

CHAPTER FOUR

1. This chapter builds on research in Christenson and Kriner (2017c).

2. Howell 2003, 19–21.

3. For example, as Curtis Bradley and Trevor Morrison (2013, 1109) note, "If courts routinely reviewed contested issues of presidential power, they could decide whether and when to credit historical practice in this area. They could also decide whether novel presidential assertions of authority were justified, before such assertions became established practice. But judicial review in this area is anything but routine."

4. Howell 2003, 152–57.

5. Bellia 2002; Silverstein 1994, 1997.

6. Posner and Vermeule 2010, 4. For a contrasting view that sees potential for a legal constraint through practice-based law, see Bradley and Morrison (2013).

7. Ellis 1974.

8. For example, courts have used the political questions doctrine, as well as other maneuvers, to sidestep ruling on the constitutionality of president-initiated wars, both large and small (Fisher 2005).

9. Recent research by Epstein and Posner (2017) finds that presidential "win rates" in the Supreme Court have declined precipitously in recent years, with President Obama winning just over 50% of the cases involving the administration. While Epstein and Posner's data include all cases in which the United States or an executive actor was a party, not just cases involving challenges to assertions of unilateral executive power, the trend they observe is consistent with the greater pushback to executive action described qualitatively here.

10. Jody Freeman, "How Obama Plans to Beat His Climate Critics," *Politico*, August 3, 2015, https://www.politico.com/agenda/story/2015/08/how-obama-plans-to-beat-his-climate-critics-000186.

11. Under President Obama and continuing under President Trump, opponents of administration actions have increasingly engaged in venue shopping in the hopes of having their case heard by judges or in circuits with a track record of ruling against the administration (Botoman 2017). See also Russell Wheeler, "Trump Wants to 'Break Up the Ninth Circuit': How Would That Help Him?," Brookings *Fixgov* (blog), May 16, 2017, https://www.brookings.edu/blog/fixgov/2017/05/16/trump-wants-to-break-up-the-ninth-circuit-how-would-that-help-him/.

12. As an even further example of court activism, in *NLRB v. Canning* the Supreme Court struck down President Obama's aggressive use of recess appointments as unconstitutional. This decision has had major implications for the Obama administration's efforts to shape policy implementation. See Ostrander (2015).

13. The Department of Justice formally announced in October 2017 that it would not appeal the district court ruling, effectively killing Obama's overtime rules.

14. Howell 2003, 160–64.

15. Mayhew 2000.

16. Mitch McConnell, "States Should Reject Obama Mandate for Clean-Power Regulations," *Lexington (KY) Herald-Leader*, March 3, 2015, http://www.kentucky.com/opinion/op-ed/article44558769.html.

17. Cappella and Jamieson 1997; Groeling 2010; Patterson 1996.

18. Josh Gerstein, "Appeals Court Chilly to Feds' Argument for NSA Surveillance Program," *Politico*, September 2, 2014, https://www.politico.com/blogs/under-the-radar/2014/09/appeals-court-chilly-to-feds-arguments-for-nsa-surveillance-program-194760.

19. George Will, "Will the Supreme Court Strike Back at Obama's Overreach?" *Washington Post*, January 22, 2016, https://www.washingtonpost.com/opinions/will-the -supreme-court-strike-back-at-obamas-overreach/2016/01/22/1af0b1b0-c077-11e5-83d4 -42e3bceea902_story.html?utm_term=.137b41c2a471. See also David Savage, "Supreme Court to Render a Verdict on Obama's Use of Executive Authority," *Los Angeles Times*, February 7, 2016, http://www.latimes.com/nation/la-na-court-presidential-power-78020160208-story.html.

20. For example, see David Rivkin and Elizabeth Price Foley, "Federal Courts Need to Stop Obama from Flouting the Constitution," *Washington Post*, July 25, 2014, https:// www.washingtonpost.com/opinions/federal-courts-need-to-stop-obama-from-flouting -the-constitution/2014/07/25/138f5bfc-12bc-11e4-98ee-daea85133bc9_story.html; Ben Adler, "Can Polluters Block Obama's Clean Power Plan in Court?" *Grist*, November 5, 2015, http://grist.org/climate-energy/can-polluters-block-obamas-clean-power-plan-in -court/.

21. Andrew Napolitano, "Why Obama's Executive Action on Guns Is Unconstitutional," Fox News, January 5, 2016, http://www.foxnews.com/opinion/2016/01/05/judge -napolitano-why-obamas-executive-action-on-guns-is-unconstitutional.html.

22. Mica Rosenberg, Dan Levine, and Andy Sullivan, "Sanctuary Cities See Legal Holes in Trump's Immigration Orders," Reuters, January 26, 2017, http://www.reuters .com/article/us-usa-immigration-legal-idUSKBN15B03H.

23. Andrew Napolitano, "Trump's Brazen, Unconstitutional Overreach," Fox News, February 21, 2019, https://www.foxnews.com/opinion/judge-andrew-napolitano -trumps-brazen-unconstitutional-overreach. Napolitano places Trump's declaration firmly within Justice Jackson's framework in *Youngstown* and argues that in this case, presidential power is at its nadir: "But when the president acts in an area that the Constitution gives exclusively to Congress—such as spending money—and when he acts in defiance of Congress, his acts are unconstitutional and are to be enjoined."

24. Caldeira and Gibson 1992; Gibson 2007; Gibson, Caldeira, and Baird 1998.

25. Gibson, Caldeira, and Spence 2003.

26. Robert Barnes, "Ginsburg Expresses 'Regret' for Remarks Criticizing Trump," *Washington Post*, July 14, 2016, https://www.washingtonpost.com/politics/ginsburg -expresses-regret-over-remarks- criticizing-trump/2016/07/14/f53687bc-49cc-11e6-bdb9-701687974517_story.html.

27. Howell 2003. More generally, see Ducat and Dudley (1989); Yates and Whitford (1998).

28. Dunlap and McCright 2008. A June 2012 poll mentioning Obama's EPA plan found that a majority of Republicans supported Congress taking action to stop the EPA from regulating greenhouse gas emissions, 52 to 39%. By contrast, Democrats opposed legislative efforts to block the plan by more than two to one, 28 to 65%. Survey by United Technologies, National Journal; methodology: conducted by Princeton Survey Research Associates International, June 14–17, 2012, and based on 1,002 telephone interviews. Sample: National adult; 601 respondents were interviewed on a landline telephone, and 401 were interviewed on a cell phone, including 187 who had no landline telephone [USPSRA.061812CC.R04, accessed November 1, 2019].

29. Finally, these and related comments questioning the constitutionality of the

Clean Power Plan may have already decreased support for the executive action, thus further stacking the deck against finding evidence of treatment effects.

30. Notably, the magnitude of the effects in this final experiment with the "softer" treatment is substantively similar to those observed with the "stronger" treatment in experiments 1 and 2.

31. Emphasis added. Mitch McConnell, "States Should Reject Obama Mandate for Clean-Power Regulations," *Lexington (KY) Herald-Leader*, March 3, 2015, http://www.kentucky.com/opinion/op-ed/article44558769.html; Laurence Tribe, "The Clean Power Plan Is Unconstitutional," *Wall Street Journal*, December 23, 2014, https://www.wsj.com/articles/laurence-tribe-the-epas-clean-power-plan-is-unconstitutional-1419293203.

32. Emphasis added. Tucker Higgins, "Trump's Attack on Birthright Citizenship Will Likely Hit a Constitutional Dead End," CNBC, October 30, 2018, https://www.cnbc.com/2018/10/30/trump-attack-on-birthright-citizenship-unlikely-to-fly-with-supreme-court.html.

33. In the experiment, support for the president's action was measured on a four-point Likert scale. To guard against satisficing, we omitted a neutral midpoint category (e.g., Krosnick 1991, 1999). In the analyses, we collapsed the strongly support and support categories to create a dummy variable of general support for the unilateral action.

34. Full results are presented in appendix table 4.1.

35. A common critique of experimental research is that the observed treatment effects may overstate what would be observed in the real world. Experiments expose all the subjects in the treatment group to the treatment; in more realistic settings, many low-information Americans may not receive such elite cues. To examine whether our results are driven exclusively by low-information subjects, we used education as a proxy for political sophistication. We then reestimated the logit model from table 4.1 with the interaction of the SCOTUS treatment and education. The resulting coefficient was actually negative, and not statistically significant. As a result, there is no evidence that our treatment effect was concentrated solely among less politically sophisticated subjects.

36. Bartels and Johnston 2013; Christenson and Glick 2015a.

37. Crawford and Sobel 1982; Druckman 2001; Lupia and McCubbins 1994.

38. Zaller 1992.

39. Bradley Jones, "Americans' Views of Immigrants Marked by Widening Partisan, Generational Divides," Pew Research Center, April 15, 2016, http://www.pewresearch.org/fact-tank/2016/04/15/americans-views-of-immigrants-marked-by-widening-partisan-generational-divides/.

40. Hoekstra 1995.

41. Bartels and Johnston 2013; Christenson and Glick 2015a; Gibson, Caldeira, and Spence 2003.

42. We used the respondents' levels of agreement with six related statements: disagreeing with a lot of Supreme Court rulings means "it might be better to do away with the Supreme Court altogether"; judges "who consistently make decisions at odds with what a majority of the people want should be removed from their position as judge"; the court "ought to be made less independent so that it listens a lot more to what the people

want"; the court "favors some groups"; the court "can usually be trusted to make decisions that are right for the country" and in "the best interests of the American people."
Each of these was measured on a six-point scale on which respondents indicated their
agreement with the statements. The six responses were summed, resulting in values
ranging from 6 (minimum agreement or lowest legitimacy) to 36 (greatest agreement
or highest legitimacy). To test our hypothesis that those who believe that the Supreme
Court is legitimate will be more responsive to the judicial check cue than those who
do not believe that the court is legitimate, we dichotomized our measure. Subjects who
scored an 18 or lower on our scale gave answers that, on average, were inconsistent with
court legitimacy. These subjects, 30% of our sample, were coded 0 on our legitimacy
indicator variable. The remaining 70%, who gave the court higher legitimacy ratings,
were coded 1.

43. Full results are presented in appendix table 4.2. As in the Clean Power Plan
Experiment, we also looked for evidence that the effect varied by level of political
sophistication. In the Immigration Experiment, we used six factual political knowledge questions on the Common Content of the CCES to construct a seven-point scale.
We then reestimated the model in column 2 of appendix table 4.2 with two additional
variables: this index of political knowledge and its interaction with the SCOTUS treatment. The coefficient on the interaction is positive, consistent with the hypothesis that
the treatment effect is smaller for more politically sophisticated subjects. But there is
considerable uncertainty about this estimate, and the standard error is larger than the
coefficient estimate itself. As a result, we again found little evidence that our effect is
concentrated solely among low-information subjects who might not receive such cues
in the real world.

44. The error bars representing the 95% confidence interval around our effect size
estimate span the origin. The treatment coefficient in the regression is statistically
significant, $p < .10$, two-tailed test.

45. By contrast, 69% of subjects supported Obama's actions to reduce carbon dioxide emissions in the control group.

46. By contrast, 35% of Republicans supported Obama's Clean Power Plan in the
control group of the first experiment.

47. See model 3 of appendix table 4.2. The coefficient for the main effect is statistically significant $(p = .055)$.

48. Kriner and Howell 2012; Nyhan and Reifler 2010.

49. Kunda 1990; Taber and Lodge 2006.

50. Donald J. Trump, "Remarks on Signing an Executive Order on Promoting
Energy Independence and Economic Growth," March 28, 2017; online by Gerhard Peters
and John T. Woolley, the American Presidency Project, University of California, Santa
Barbara, accessed November 1, 2019, https://www.presidency.ucsb.edu/node/326500.

51. Full results are presented in appendix table 4.3.

52. Our sample was almost evenly divided on the question of the border wall. Over
47% of all subjects supported Trump's unilateral action to begin constructing the wall,
as did 49% of independents. Because subjects who opposed the wall were almost certain
to oppose Trump's EPA actions, figure 4.4 presents the estimated effect of both treat-

ments on the median independent respondent who supported Trump taking unilateral action to begin building the border wall.

53. Bartels and Mutz 2009; Christenson and Glick 2015b; Johnson and Martin 1998; Wlezien and Goggin 1993.

CHAPTER FIVE

1. Beckmann 2010; Canes-Wrone and de Marchi 2002.

2. Many electoral forecasts find that a measure of presidential approval is among the strongest predictors of presidential electoral fortunes as well as those of their would-be partisan successors. For example, see Abramowitz (2016).

3. Hopkins 2018; Jacobson 2015.

4. Edwards 1989.

5. As noted previously, empirical tests of one of the main hypotheses of the strategic model, that executive action will increase in periods of divided government, have met with mixed results. As Belco and Rottinghaus (2017) note, executive action can sometimes be used to implement or complement legislation, which might make it more frequent in periods of unified government.

6. See also Reeves and Rogowski (2015).

7. This effect is illustrated in figure 2.8.

8. These predicted probabilities are derived from simulations of model 3 in appendix table 3.1.

9. These predicted probabilities are derived from simulations of model 2 in appendix table 4.2.

10. Delli Carpini and Keeter 1997.

11. This survey was fielded by YouGov between January 11 and January 14, 2019.

12. Full results are presented in appendix table 5.1.

13. Indeed, research by Thrower (2017) shows that approval ratings even influence the willingness of future presidents to reverse or amend the executive actions taken by their predecessors.

14. For example, congressional investigations can systematically erode popular support for the president. However, the relationship between investigative activity and public opinion cuts both ways, as Congress is also less likely to investigate aggressively a president who is riding high in the polls. See Kriner and Schickler (2016, 83–89).

15. Ducat and Dudley 1989; Howell 2003; Yates and Whitford 1998.

16. Reeves and Rogowski 2018.

17. In the *Los Angeles Times* poll fielded January 25–26, 1995, 79% of Americans opposed US loan guarantees for Mexico (64% strongly) versus only 18% who supported doing so. Another poll taken shortly after Clinton's announcement (February 9–12, 1995) similarly showed 55% of Americans disapproving Clinton's action versus only 30% approving it. *Los Angeles Times*, Los Angeles Times Poll: National Politics, State of the Union, Question 36, USLAT.95JA25.R33, Los Angeles Times (Cornell University, Ithaca, NY: Roper Center for Public Opinion Research, 1995), data set, accessed November 1, 2019; *Times Mirror*, Times Mirror Poll: February 1995, Question 59, USPSRA.021795.

R31A, Princeton Survey Research Associates (Cornell University, Ithaca, NY: Roper Center for Public Opinion Research, 1995), accessed November 1, 2019.

18. Clinton 2004, 644.

19. By contrast, while presidential memoranda are increasingly important and often used interchangeably with executive orders in the contemporary polity (Lowande 2014), their use has evolved significantly over the past sixty years (Cooper 2002). This evolution complicates over-time comparisons.

20. Mayer 2001, 35.

21. Pfiffner 2018.

22. In recent work (Christenson and Kriner 2019), we replicate the analyses and results in this section with another measure of executive order importance offered by Fang-Yi Chiou and Lawrence Rothenberg. Their measure is based on a Bayesian hierarchical item response theory (IRT) model that assigns a significance score to each executive order based on eighteen "raters," which include various news and government source publications. For more detail, see Chiou and Rothenberg (2014, 2017). Although the two measures are distinct, a visual comparison of the two time series (Christenson and Kriner 2019) shows that they are strongly correlated. Moreover, the results are strongly complementary; that is, by using either measure we arrive at the same substantive findings.

23. Gallup asked the approval question before 1953; however, there are significant gaps in this earlier coverage. To fill in the few, small remaining gaps in the approval series (primarily in the 1950s), we used Kalman filtering (Green, Gerber, and de Boef 1999).

24. Since the late 1990s, a number of scholars have explored the factors driving temporal variation in executive order issuance. Many of these studies examined the relationship between executive action and presidential approval. Some studies conclude that presidents issue more unilateral actions when their approval rating is low (Deering and Maltzman 1999; Mayer 1999, 2001; Mayer and Price 2002). Others find at least some evidence that unilateral action increases as approval ratings increase (Fine and Warber 2012; Marshall and Pacelle 2005). Still others find little evidence of any systematic relationship between the two (Gleiber and Shull 1992; Krause and Cohen 1997). However, all these studies simply include approval on the right-hand side of a regression equation; none account for the potential endogeneity in the relationship.

25. Further methodological details and robustness checks are provided in the Supporting Information to Christenson and Kriner (2019).

26. For example, Deering and Maltzman (1999) find evidence for this strategic model, while Mayer (1999) and Howell (2003) actually find that presidents issue more executive orders in unified government.

27. We coded Korea, Vietnam, the Persian Gulf War, and the wars in Afghanistan and Iraq as wars.

28. E.g., Belco and Rottinghaus (2017).

29. More generally, this approach also allowed us to examine whether the causal arrow runs in both directions or whether there is no causal relationship between the two factors.

30. Reeves and Rogowski 2018.

31. For example, prior research on presidential budgetary proposals has found that

presidents are more responsive to public opinion as the next election approaches (Canes-Wrone and Shotts 2004).

32. Kriner and Schickler 2016.

33. Having established that the direction of causality runs only from approval to orders with the vector autoregressive models, we here employed negative binomial event count models to simplify the testing of the interactions and their interpretation. The election year dummy variable is coded 1 for the first ten months of the presidential election year. The divided government dummy variable is coded 1 if either chamber of Congress is controlled by the opposition party. Presidential approval is lagged one month. In each model, we included the relevant dummy variable and its interaction with lagged approval. Appendix table 5.4 presents the full regression results.

34. Edwards 2016.

35. As a general illustration, a search for any poll containing the phrase "executive order" yielded only six hits for 1953–2000, with four of those six polls measuring opinion on Clinton's Mexican bailout and 1998 antidiscrimination order. By contrast, as unilateral action has become more publicly salient the same search returned seventy-four hits between 2001 and 2017.

36. NBC News/*Wall Street Journal*, NBC News/Wall Street Journal Poll: Clinton/Starr/HMOs, Question 77, USNBCWSJ.98JL25.R30C, Hart-Teeter Research Companies (Cornell University, Ithaca, NY: Roper Center for Public Opinion Research, 1998), data set, accessed November 1, 2019.

37. Most of the polls were fielded within weeks or several months of the president taking action. The lone exception was Obama's executive order closing the terrorist detention facility at Guantanamo Bay, Cuba. To highlight the initial popularity of the action (rather than how it evolved over time), for this order we focused on the four polls fielded within one hundred days of Obama's order.

38. The strong popular support for the Clean Power Plan may be superficially surprising given the resistance it produced from many in Congress. However, many pro-environmental policies, such as support for wind and solar energy, enjoy robust public support, and even in our experiments more than 60% of subjects routinely backed the Clean Power Plan in our treatment conditions. In this case, congressional criticism lowered support for unilateral action from a very high baseline level.

39. E.g., Potter et al. (2019).

40. Paul Waldman, "Republicans Are Now Big Fans of Presidential Tyranny," *Washington Post*, April 26, 2017, https://www.washingtonpost.com/blogs/plum-line/wp/2017/04/26/republicans-are-now-big-fans-of-presidential-tyranny/?noredirect=on&utm_term=.24f4f0e12c40.

41. Nick Gass, "Donald Trump's Polling Obsession," *Politico*, December 10, 2015, https://www.politico.com/story/2015/12/trump-polls-216640.

42. Michael D'Antonio, "The Three Things Donald Trump Really Cares About," CNN, December 15, 2016, http://www.cnn.com/2016/11/25/opinions/what-does-trump-care-about-dantonio/index.html

43. We included Trump's national emergency declaration to build the Mexican border wall. It was issued in February 2019, just over two years into his presidency.

44. Gallup Organization, Gallup Organization Poll: March 2017, 2017 [data set],

Roper #31114289, Version 2. Gallup Organization [producer]. Cornell University, Ithaca, NY: Roper Center for Public Opinion Research [distributor], accessed November 1, 2019.

45. Jenna Johnson, "Trump Calls for 'Total and Complete Shutdown of Muslims Entering the United States,'" *Washington Post*, December 7, 2015, https://www.washingtonpost.com/news/post-politics/wp/2015/12/07/donald-trump-calls-for-total-and-complete-shutdown-of-muslims-entering-the-united-states/?utm_term=.f1bf6d5ad161.

46. The order also called for the indefinite suspension of the Syrian refugee program begun by President Obama.

47. An NPR analysis identified 237 Democrats as being on the record for opposing Trump's first travel ban versus none in favor, 1 with no statement, and 2 whose public statements on the issue were unclear as to their position. Laurel Wamsley, "Where Does Your Member of Congress Stand on Trump's Immigration Order?," NPR, February 1, 2017, https://www.npr.org/2017/02/01/512860167/congress-tracker-trumps-refugee-and-immigration-executive-order.

48. Julie Hirschfeld Davis, "Obama, Out of Office 10 Days, Speaks Out against Immigration Ban," *New York Times*, January 30, 2017, https://www.nytimes.com/2017/01/30/us/politics/obama-trump-immigration-ban.html.

49. Nicholas Fandos, "Lawmakers Criticize Trump's Refugee Policy," *New York Times*, January 29, 2017, https://www.nytimes.com/2017/01/29/us/politics/republicans-congress-trump-refugees.html.

50. Lamar Alexander, "Alexander Statement on Refugee Executive Order," January 29, 2017, https://www.alexander.senate.gov/public/index.cfm/pressreleases?ID=C007E222-C999-4341-AB41-7E5A2A752F50.

51. Ariane de Vogue and Eli Watkins, "Judges Temporarily Block Part of Trump's Immigration Order, WH Stands by It," CNN, January 29, 2017, http://www.cnn.com/2017/01/28/politics/2-iraqis-file-lawsuit-after-being-detained-in-ny-due-to-travel-ban/index.html.

52. Jonathan Adler, "Acting Attorney General Orders Justice Department Attorneys Not to Defend Immigration Executive Order," *Washington Post*, January 30, 2017, https://www.washingtonpost.com/news/volokh-conspiracy/wp/2017/01/30/acting-attorney-general-orders-justice-department-attorneys-not-to-defend-immigration-executive-order/?utm_term=.bbcdb9bc2c53.

53. Kim Soffen and David Cameron, "How Trump's Travel Ban Broke from the Normal Executive Order Process," *Washington Post*, February 9, 2017, https://www.washingtonpost.com/graphics/politics/trump-travel-ban-process/.

54. Cory Booker, "Booker Statement on Second Trump Muslim Ban," March 6, 2017, https://www.booker.senate.gov/?p=press_release&id=550.

55. In June 2017, the new secretary of defense, James Mattis, delayed this mandate for six months to give the Department of Defense more time to study the issue.

56. Julie Hirschfeld Davis and Helene Cooper, "Trump Says Transgender People Will Not Be Allowed in the Military," *New York Times*, July 26, 2017, https://www.nytimes.com/2017/07/26/us/politics/trump-transgender-military.html.

57. Noa Yadidi and Grace Hauck, "McCain Criticizes 'Unclear' Trump Policy on

Transgender Military Ban." CNN, July 26, 2017, https://www.cnn.com/2017/07/26/politics/congress-reaction-transgender-military-policy/index.html.

58. Aaron Blake, "Trump's Transgender Military Ban Is Another Case of Political Malpractice," *Washington Post*, July 26, 2017, https://www.washingtonpost.com/news/the-fix/wp/2017/07/26/trumps-transgender-military-ban-looks-like-another-political-blunder/.

59. Yadidi and Hauck, "McCain Criticizes 'Unclear' Trump Policy on Transgender Military Ban."

60. Quinnipiac University Polling Institute, Quinnipiac University Polling Institute Poll: July 2017, Question 65, USQUINN.080317.R52, Quinnipiac University Polling Institute (Cornell University, Ithaca, NY: Roper Center for Public Opinion Research, 2017), data set, accessed November 1, 2019.

61. Ann Marimow, "Federal Judge Says Trump Administration Can't Stop Funding Sex-Reassignment Surgeries for Military Members," *Washington Post*, November 21, 2017, https://www.washingtonpost.com/local/public-safety/a-second-judge-blocks-trump-administrations-proposed-transgender-military-ban/2017/11/21/d91f65e4-cee1-11e7-81bc-c55a220c8cbe_story.html.

62. James N. Mattis, Memorandum for the President, "Military Service for Transgender Individuals," Office of the Secretary of Defense, March 23, 2018, https://media.defense.gov/2018/Mar/23/2001894037/-1/-1/0/MILITARY-SERVICE-BY-TRANSGENDER-INDIVIDUALS.PDF.

63. The gunshot ricocheted off the concrete pavement for seventy-eight feet before striking Steinle. A jury acquitted Zarate of murder and involuntary manslaughter in December 2017.

64. Theodore Schleifer, "Trump: San Francisco Killing Shows Perils of Illegal Immigration," CNN, July 3, 2015, https://www.cnn.com/2015/07/03/politics/trump-san-francisco-killing/index.html.

65. Liz Robbins, "'Sanctuary City' Mayors Vow to Defy Trump's Immigration Order," *New York Times*, January 25, 2017, https://www.nytimes.com/2017/01/25/nyregion/outraged-mayors-vow-to-defy-trumps-immigration-order.html/.

66. Russel Spivak, "Case Summary: Federal District Court Issues Nationwide Injunction against Trump's Sanctuary City Executive Order," *Lawfare* (blog), April 26, 2017, https://www.lawfareblog.com/case-summary-federal-district-court-issues-nationwide-injunction-against-trumps-sanctuary-city.

67. Jeff Sessions, "Memorandum for All Department Grant-Making Components," Office of the Attorney General, May 22, 2017, https://www.justice.gov/opa/press-release/file/968146/download.

68. Cristiano Lima, "Judge Declines to Remove Block on Trump Sanctuary Cities Order," *Politico*, July 20, 2017, https://www.politico.com/story/2017/07/20/judge-declines-to-remove-trump-block-sanctuary-cities-240780.

69. Matt Zaposky, "Judge Rules Justice Department Can't Keep Grant Money from Uncooperative Sanctuary Cities," *Washington Post*, September 15, 2017, https://www.washingtonpost.com/world/national-security/judge-rules-justice-dept-cant-keep-grant-money-from-uncooperative-sanctuary-cities/2017/09/15/40f0ec66-9a52-11e7-82e4-f1076f6d6152_story.html.

70. Nick Visser, "Judge Permanently Blocks Trump's Executive Order on Sanctuary Cities," *Huffington Post*, November 20, 2017, https://www.huffingtonpost.com/entry/sanctuary-cities-executive-order-blocked_us_5a139666e4b0aa32975d6b3f.

71. Jonathan Stempel, "Philadelphia Beats U.S. Appeal in Sanctuary City Case," Reuters, February 15, 2019, https://www.reuters.com/article/us-usa-immigration-philadelphia/philadelphia-beats-us-appeal-in-sanctuary-city-case-idUSKCN1Q42BS.

72. Trump did not distinguish between DACA and DAPA in this speech, but given that the latter's implementation had already been blocked by federal court injunction in February 2015, it is likely that DACA was foremost on his mind. "Here's Donald Trump's Presidential Announcement Speech," *Time*, June 16, 2015, http://time.com/3923128/donald-trump-announcement-speech/. Moreover, at an August 2016 campaign rally he explicitly promised to terminate Obama's "two illegal executive amnesties"—a clear reference to both DACA and DAPA.

73. In the same speech, he went on to denounce Hillary Clinton's campaign promise to act even further unilaterally on the immigration issue. Katie Reilly, "Here's What President Trump Has Said about DACA in the Past," *Time*, September 5, 2017, http://time.com/4927100/donald-trump-daca-past-statements/.

74. "Full Text: Donald Trump Immigration Speech in Arizona." *Politico*, August 31, 2016, https://www.politico.com/story/2016/08/donald-trump-immigration-address-transcript-227614.

75. Michael Scherer, "2016 Person of the Year, Donald Trump." *Time*, December 19, 2016, http://time.com/time-person-of-the-year-2016-donald-trump/.

76. "Transcript: ABC News Anchor David Muir Interviews President Trump," ABC News, January 25, 2017, http://abcnews.go.com/Politics/transcript-abc-news-anchor-david-muir-interviews-president/story?id=45047602.

77. Brian Bennett and Michael Memoli, "The White House Has Found Ways to End Protection for 'Dreamers' while Shielding Trump from Blowback," *Los Angeles Times*, February 16, 2017, http://www.latimes.com/politics/la-na-pol-trump-daca-20170216-story.html.

78. Donald J. Trump, "The President's News Conference," February 16, 2017; online by Gerhard Peters and John T. Woolley, the American Presidency Project, University of California, Santa Barbara, accessed November 1, 2019, https://www.presidency.ucsb.edu/node/323569.

79. The court was evenly divided because of the vacancy left by the death of justice Antonin Scalia.

80. Richard Wolf, "Deadlocked Supreme Court Blocks Obama on Immigration," *USA Today*, June 23, 2016, https://www.usatoday.com/story/news/politics/2016/06/23/supreme-court-obama-immigration-undocumented-texas-deportation/83515218/.

81. Ken Paxton, "Donald Trump Should Keep His Promise to Dump DACA: Texas Attorney General," *USA Today*, July 26, 2017, https://www.usatoday.com/story/opinion/2017/07/26/trump-not-king-we-must-phase-out-daca-and-return-rule-law-column/488732001/.

82. Miriam Jordan, "'Dreamer' Plan That Aided 800,000 Immigrants Is Threatened," *New York Times*, August 27, 2017, https://www.nytimes.com/2017/08/27/us/politics/dreamers-trump-lawsuit.html.

83. Donald J. Trump, "Statement on the Deferred Action for Childhood Arrivals Policy," September 5, 2017; online by Gerhard Peters and John T. Woolley, the American Presidency Project, University of California, Santa Barbara, accessed November 1, 2019, https://www.presidency.ucsb.edu/node/331039.

84. Kathryn Watson, "Congress Reacts to Trump Ending DACA," CBS News, September 5, 2017, https://www.cbsnews.com/news/congress-reacts-to-trump-administration-rescinding-daca/.

85. Donald J. Trump on Twitter, September 5, 2017, https://twitter.com/realdonaldtrump/status/905228667336499200.

86. Dara Lind, "DREAMers Are at Risk Because of Donald Trump. Period," *Vox*, February 16, 2018, https://www.vox.com/policy-and-politics/2018/2/16/17017908/immigration-congress-fault-daca. President Trump has stated that he believed that the Supreme Court would ultimately strike down DACA, giving him greater leverage in negotiations with Democrats. However, his plan was thwarted when the court failed to act on DACA in January 2019, all but ensuring that it would slip to the next session. Adam Liptak, "Supreme Court Doesn't Act on Trump's Appeal in 'Dreamer's' Case," *New York Times*, January 22, 2019, https://www.nytimes.com/2019/01/22/us/politics/supreme-court-daca-dreamers.html.

87. Catherine Shoichet and Tal Kopan, "Court Hands DACA Recipients Another Victory," CNN, February 27, 2018, https://www.cnn.com/2018/02/27/politics/daca-revocation-ruling/index.html; Priscilla Alvarez and Ariane de Vogue, "Supreme Court Again Takes No Action on DACA, Leaving Policy in Effect for Now," CNN, January 22, 2019, https://www.cnn.com/2019/01/22/politics/daca-supreme-court/index.html.

88. For example, see FiveThirtyEight.com's continuously updated measure of Trump's approval that incorporates data from a wide range of public polling outlets: https://projects.fivethirtyeight.com/trump-approval-ratings/?ex_cid=rrpromo, accessed November 8, 2019.

89. Jacobson 2019.

90. Freeman, Williams, and Lin 1989.

91. E.g., Freeman (1983); Granger (1969).

92. Because of the inherent difficulty in identifying "significant" executive orders, in other work (Christenson and Kriner 2019) we estimate identical analyses using a different measure of significant executive activity derived from Chiou and Rothenberg (2017). The results with this alternate measure are substantively the same as those presented here.

CHAPTER SIX

1. Clinton later confided that he responded to the student's question without understanding fully the ramifications of his answer and without having consulted any of his advisers on the topic. Ann Devroy, "President Opens Military to Gays," *Washington Post*, July 20, 1993, https://www.washingtonpost.com/archive/politics/1993/07/20/president-opens-military-to-gays/06c8e220-83b0-4748-a1e8-7cd292d2b546/.

2. Eric Schmitt, "Challenging the Military: In Promising to End Ban on Homosexuals, Clinton Is Confronting a Wall of Tradition," *New York Times*, November 12, 1992,

https://www.nytimes.com/1992/11/12/us/transition-analysis-challenging-military
-promising-end-ban-homosexuals-clinton.html.

3. Schmitt, "Challenging the Military."

4. Drew 1994, 45–46.

5. Clinton 2004, 484.

6. Drew 1994, 44.

7. R. W. Apple Jr., "Clinton, Savoring Victory, Starts Sizing Up the Job Ahead,"
New York Times, November 5, 1992, https://www.nytimes.com/1992/11/05/us/1992
-elections-president-elect-overview-clinton-savoring-victory-starts-sizing.html.

8. Gallup Organization, Post Election Survey, Question 6, USGALLUP.112192.R1E,
Gallup Organization (Cornell University, Ithaca, NY: Roper Center for Public Opinion
Research, 1992), data set, accessed November 1, 2019. Scott James, "A Theory of Presidential Commitment and Opportunism: Swing States, Pivotal Groups, and Civil Rights
under Truman and Clinton," paper presented in Chicago in 1995 at the Annual Meeting
of the American Political Science Association.

9. *Newsweek*, Gallup/Newsweek Poll # 1992-305061: Clinton Transition, Question
12, USGALNEW.305061.Q09, Gallup Organization (Cornell University, Ithaca, NY:
Roper Center for Public Opinion Research, 1992), data set, accessed November 1, 2019.
By January of 1993, public support for lifting the ban had fallen even further, particularly among the swing Perot voters. In a late January Gallup Poll, only 43% of Americans supported ending the ban on gays serving in the military. Among Perot voters,
only 37% favored lifting the ban, while 55% opposed it. Cable News Network (CNN)/
USA Today, Gallup/CNN/USA Today Poll # 1993-322044: Hillary Clinton/Gays in the
Military, Question 19, USGALLUP.020493.R1, Gallup Organization (Cornell University, Ithaca, NY: Roper Center for Public Opinion Research, 1993), data set, accessed
November 1, 2019.

10. White House daily briefing, January 21, 1993, https://www.c-span.org/video/
?37841-1/white-house-daily-briefing.

11. Thomas L. Friedman, "Compromise Near on Military's Ban on Homosexuals," *New York Times*, January 29, 1993, https://www.nytimes.com/1993/01/29/us/
compromise-near-on-military-s-ban-on-homosexuals.html.

12. Drew 1994, 48.

13. Clinton 2004, 485.

14. Senate Armed Services Committee, *Policy concerning Homosexuality in the
Armed Forces*, HRG-1993-SAS-0020; Senate Hearings 103-845, 103rd Cong., 2nd Sess.
(1994), 629.

15. *Time*/Cable News Network (CNN), Yankelovich/Time Magazine/CNN Poll:
Bill Clinton, Ross Perot, Bosnia, and Health Care, Question 48, USYANKP.051493.R26,
Yankelovich Partners, Inc. (Cornell University, Ithaca, NY: Roper Center for Public
Opinion Research, 1993), data set, accessed November 1, 2019.

In an identically worded question fielded by the same survey firm January 22–25,
1993, 43% favored Clinton's plan, while 48% opposed it. *Time*/Cable News Network
(CNN), Yankelovich/Time/CNN Poll: Politics, Religion, and Morality, Question 13,
USYANKP.012893.R22, Yankelovich Partners, Inc. (Cornell University, Ithaca, NY:
Roper Center for Public Opinion Research, 1993), data set, accessed November 1, 2019.

16. Pat Towell, "Frank Suggests Compromise: 'Don't Investigate' Gays," *CQ Weekly*, May 22, 1993, p. 1302.

17. William J. Clinton, "Remarks in the 'CBS This Morning' Town Meeting," May 27, 1993; online by Gerhard Peters and John T. Woolley, the American Presidency Project, University of California, Santa Barbara, accessed November 1, 2019, https://www.presidency.ucsb.edu/node/219942.

18. For further analysis of these political calculations, see James (1995).

19. "Clinton: Policy on Gays in Military Is 'Sensible Balance,'" *Washington Post*, July 20, 1993, https://www.washingtonpost.com/archive/politics/1993/07/20/clinton-policy-on-gays-in-military-is-sensible-balance/30aa4aa0-e692-41c0-b87f-30df94372e31/?utm_term=.a4965633dbc1.

20. For an overview, see Anderson (2011).

21. David Kirkpatrick, "Egypt Erupts in Jubilation as Mubarak Steps Down," *New York Times*, February 12, 2011, https://www.nytimes.com/2011/02/12/world/middleeast/12egypt.html.

22. Ian Black, "Gaddafi Threatens Retaliation in Mediterranean as UN Passes Resolution," *Guardian* (US edition), March 17, 2011, http://www.theguardian.com/world/2011/mar/17/gaddafi-retaliation-mediterranean-libya-no-fly-zone.

23. "August Produces Worst Toll in Syria Conflict, Says UN," Reuters, September 17, 2012, http://www.reuters.com/article/2012/09/17/syria-crisis-un-idUSL1E8KH8ZN20120917.

24. Michael Gordon and Mark Landler, "Backstage Glimpses of Clinton as Dogged Diplomat, Win or Lose," *New York Times*, February 2, 2013, https://www.nytimes.com/2013/02/03/us/politics/in-behind-scene-blows-and-triumphs-sense-of-clinton-future.html; Michael Gordon and Mark Landler, "Senate Hearing Draws Out a Rift in U.S. Policy on Syria," *New York Times*, February 7, 2013, https://www.nytimes.com/2013/02/08/us/politics/panetta-speaks-to-senate-panel-on-benghazi-attack.html.

25. Neil MacFarquhar and Eric Schmitt, "Syria Threatens Chemical Attack on Foreign Force," *New York Times*, July 24, 2012, https://www.nytimes.com/2012/07/24/world/middleeast/chemical-weapons-wont-be-used-in-rebellion-syria-says.html.

26. Barack Obama, "Remarks at the Veterans of Foreign Wars National Convention in Reno, Nevada," July 23, 2012; online by Gerhard Peters and John T. Woolley, the American Presidency Project, University of California, Santa Barbara, accessed November 1, 2019, https://www.presidency.ucsb.edu/node/301910.

27. Barack Obama, "Remarks and an Exchange with Reporters following a Press Briefing by White House Press Secretary James F. 'Jay' Carney," August 20, 2012; online by Gerhard Peters and John T. Woolley, the American Presidency Project, University of California, Santa Barbara, accessed November 1, 2019, https://www.presidency.ucsb.edu/node/302263.

28. For a chronology, see Arms Control Association, "Timeline of Syrian Chemical Weapons Activity, 2012–2014," accessed November 1, 2019, http://www.armscontrol.org/factsheets/Timeline-of-Syrian-Chemical-Weapons-Activity.

29. Letter reprinted in "White House Letter on Syria Chemical Weapons to Senators," Associated Press, April 25, 2013, http://www.huffingtonpost.com/2013/04/25/white-house-letter-syria-senators_n_3156099.html.

30. United Nations, Office of the High Commissioner for Human Rights, "Updated UN Study Indicates at Least 93,000 People Killed in Syria Conflict," June 13, 2013, http://www.ohchr.org/EN/NewsEvents/Pages/DisplayNews.aspx?NewsID=13447& LangID=E#3.

31. For news coverage, including video footage of the attacks, see Loveday Morris and Karen DeYoung, "Syrian Activists Accuse Government of Deadly Chemical Attack near Damascus," *Washington Post*, August 22, 2013, http://www.washingtonpost.com/ world/syrian-activists-accuse-government-of-deadly-chemical-attack-near-damascus/ 2013/08/21/aea157e6-0a50-11e3-89fe-abb4a5067014_story.html.

32. See, for example, Adam Entous and Carol Lee, "At the Last Minute, Obama Alone Made Call to Seek Congressional Approval: Change in President's Thinking Confounded White House Insiders," *Wall Street Journal*, September 1, 2013, http:// online.wsj.com/articles/SB10001424127887324009304579047542466837078.

33. Office of the Press Secretary, the White House, "Government Assessment of the Syrian Government's Use of Chemical Weapons on August 21, 2013," August 30, 2013, http://www.whitehouse.gov/the-press-office/2013/08/30/government-assessment-syrian -government-s-use-chemical-weapons-august-21.

34. Barack Obama, "Statement by the President on Syria," September 1, 2013, Office of the Press Secretary, the White House, http://www.whitehouse.gov/the-press-office/ 2013/08/31/statement-president-syria.

35. For example, in a *Lawfare* blog post, Jack Goldsmith wrote, "I have been hard on the President—on this blog last week, and today in the *NYT*—for what just about everyone (except Philip Bobbitt) thought was going to be his strike in Syria without congressional authorization. I was thus surprised, but very happily surprised, when the President announced this afternoon that he would seek congressional authorization for the strike." Jack Goldsmith, "Congratulations President Obama," August 31, 2013, *Lawfare* (blog), http://www.lawfareblog.com/2013/08/congratulations-president-obama/.

36. Mark Memmot, "Kerry Says Assad, 'A Thug and a Murderer,' Was behind Attack," NPR, August 29, 2013, http://www.npr.org/blogs/thetwo-way/2013/08/30/ 217211589/coming-up-kerry-statement-about-the-crisis-in-syria.

37. Adam Entous and Carol Lee, "At the Last Minute, Obama Alone Made Call to Seek Congressional Approval: Change in President's Thinking Confounded White House Insiders," *Wall Street Journal*, September 1, 2013, http://online.wsj.com/articles/ SB10001424127887324009304579047542466837078.

38. Caroline D. Krass, "Authority to Use Military Force in Libya," April 1, 2011, http://www.justice.gov/sites/default/files/olc/opinions/2011/04/31/authority-military -use-in-libya_0.pdf.

39. Charlie Savage, "Obama Tests Limits of Power in Syrian Conflict," *New York Times*, September 9, 2013, http://www.nytimes.com/2013/09/09/world/middleeast/ obama-tests-limits-of-power-in-syrian-conflict.html?pagewanted=all#.

40. Barack Obama, "Statement by the President on Syria," September 1, 2013, Office of the Press Secretary, the White House, http://www.whitehouse.gov/the-press-office/ 2013/08/31/statement-president-syria.

41. Many journalistic accounts have emphasized the Obama administration's concerns about the legitimacy of a unilateral response, particularly after British prime

minister David Cameron was forced to abandon planned British participation in air strikes following a shock defeat in the House of Commons. Legitimacy concerns likely did factor into the administration's calculus; however, concerns about legitimacy alone are unlikely to have been decisive. For a more detailed critique of such arguments, see Christenson and Kriner (2015). For a fuller explication of this argument and empirical evidence of the tangible political benefits that congressional authorizations give presidents, see Kriner (2014).

42. Rebecca Shabad, "140 House Members Say Obama Needs Approval from Congress on Syria," *The Hill*, August 29, 2013, http://thehill.com/blogs/blog-briefing-room/news/319127-55-house-members-say-obama-needs-approval-from-congress-in-syria-strikes.

43. NBC News, NBC News Poll: August 2013, Question 11, USNBC.083013.R12, Hart and McInturff Research Companies (Cornell University, Ithaca, NY: Roper Center for Public Opinion Research, 2013), data set, accessed November 1, 2019. It is also important to note that this strong public preference for legislative authorization is not unique to the Syrian case. For example, in 2002, despite president George W. Bush's 68% approval rating, three-quarters of Americans said that Bush should first secure congressional authorization for any use of force against Iraq. For the public's belief that Bush should seek congressional authorization, see ABC News/*Washington Post*, ABC News/Washington Post Poll: August 2002, Question 8, USABCWP.081202.R07, ABC News/*Washington Post* (Cornell University, Ithaca, NY: Roper Center for Public Opinion Research, 2002), data set, accessed November 1, 2019. For Bush's 68% approval rating, see Gallup Organization, Gallup Organization Poll: August 2002, Question 18, USGALLUP.02AG05.R01, Gallup Organization (Cornell University, Ithaca, NY: Roper Center for Public Opinion Research, 2002), data set, accessed November 1, 2019.

44. NBC News/*Wall Street Journal*, NBC News/Wall Street Journal Poll: May 2013, Question 56, USNBCWSJ.13MAY.R32, Hart and McInturff Research Companies (Cornell University, Ithaca, NY: Roper Center for Public Opinion Research, 2013), data set, accessed November 1, 2019; NBC News, NBC News Poll: August 2013, Question 4, USNBC.083013.R06, Hart and McInturff Research Companies (Cornell University, Ithaca, NY: Roper Center for Public Opinion Research, 2013), data set, accessed November 1, 2019.

45. NBC News, NBC News Poll: August 2013, Question 7, USNBC.083013.R08X, Hart and McInturff Research Companies (Cornell University, Ithaca, NY: Roper Center for Public Opinion Research, 2013), data set, accessed November 1, 2019.

46. Barack Obama, "The President's News Conference with Prime Minister John Fredrik Reinfeldt of Sweden in Stockholm, Sweden," September 4, 2013; online by Gerhard Peters and John T. Woolley, the American Presidency Project, University of California, Santa Barbara, accessed November 1, 2019, https://www.presidency.ucsb.edu/node/304691.

47. See also William Howell, "All Syria Policy Is Local: The Political Expediency of Obama's Congressional Push on Syria." *Foreign Policy*, September 3, 2013, https://foreignpolicy.com/2013/09/03/all-syria-policy-is-local/.

48. At the time of his decision, President Obama also seemed confident that he could secure the necessary votes in Congress. Chuck Todd, "The White House Walk-

and-Talk That Changed Obama's Mind on Syria," NBC News, August 31, 2013, http://firstread.nbcnews.com/_news/2013/08/31/20273128-the-white-house-walk-and-talk-that-changed-obamas-mind-on-syria.

49. Julie Hirschfeld Davis and Helene Cooper, "White House Accuses Russia of Cover-Up in Syria Chemical Attack," *New York Times*, April 11, 2017, https://www.nytimes.com/2017/04/11/world/middleeast/russia-syria-chemical-weapons-white-house.html.

50. Richard Cohen, "On Iraq, Trump Was Right, and It Could Hurt Him," *Washington Post*, February 15, 2016, https://www.washingtonpost.com/opinions/on-iraq-trump-was-right-and-it-could-hurt-him/2016/02/15/637a0920-d41a-11e5-be55-2cc3c1e4b76b_story.html?utm_term=.50b4279c9bc7; Shane Goldmacher, "Donald Trump Calls Iraq 'Worst Decision' but Won't Repeat That Bush 'Lied,'" *Politico*, February 19, 2016, https://www.politico.com/blogs/south-carolina-primary-2016-live-updates-and-results/2016/02/2016-south-carolina-trump-george-w-bushs-iraq-219475.

51. Michael Crowly and Bryan Bender, "Trump's Syria Identity Crisis," *Politico*, April 14, 2018, https://www.politico.com/story/2018/04/14/trump-syria-identity-crisis-523103.

52. Chris Cillizza, "Donald Trump's Answer on Torture Is Really Out There—Even for Trump," *Washington Post*, February 8, 2016, https://www.washingtonpost.com/news/the-fix/wp/2016/02/08/donald-trumps-answer-on-torture-is-really-out-there-even-for-trump/?noredirect=on&utm_term=.8b0799d9d029; Nicki Rossol, "Donald Trump Wants to Authorize 'Something beyond Waterboarding,'" ABC News, February 7, 2016, https://abcnews.go.com/Politics/donald-trump-authorize-waterboarding/story?id=36760677.

53. The draft order, "Executive Order—Detention and Interrogation of Enemy Combatants," is available at http://apps.washingtonpost.com/g/documents/national/read-the-draft-of-the-executive-order-on-cia-black-sites/2288/.

54. As Jack Goldsmith notes, the order does not so much mandate a "return to the bad old days" as open the door for it by undoing the hurdles to such a return erected by Barack Obama. In Goldsmith's view, considerable legal and cultural hurdles to a wholesale return to the policies in place immediately after 9/11 would remain. Jack Goldsmith, "Trump's Self-Defeating Order on Interrogation." *Lawfare* (blog), January 25, 2017, https://www.lawfareblog.com/trumps-self-defeating-executive-order-interrogation.

55. Eli Yokley, "McCain to Trump: 'We Are Not Bringing Back Torture,'" *Morning Consult*, January 25, 2017, https://morningconsult.com/2017/01/25/mccain-trump-not-bringing-back-torture/; Abigail Tracy, "Trump's Fevered Executive Orders Leave Capitol Hill in Chaos," *Vanity Fair*, January 26, 2017, https://www.vanityfair.com/news/2017/01/donald-trump-executive-orders.

56. Dan Merica, "Trump on Waterboarding: 'We Have to Fight Fire with Fire,'" CNN, January 26, 2017, https://www.cnn.com/2017/01/25/politics/donald-trump-waterboarding-torture/index.html.

57. Merica, "Trump on Waterboarding."

58. Paul Shinkman, "Spicer: 'Black Site' Order 'Not a White House Document,'"

US News & World Report, January 25, 2017, https://www.usnews.com/news/politics/articles/2017-01-25/sean-spicer-draft-cia-black-site-order-not-a-white-house-document.

59. The draft order itself correctly identified the year as 2001, but the explanatory statement preceding it erroneously placed the attacks in 2011.

60. Mark Mazzetti and Charlie Savage, "Leaked Draft of Executive Order Could Revive C.I.A. Prisons," *New York Times*, January 25, 2017, https://www.nytimes.com/2017/01/25/us/politics/executive-order-leaked-draft-national-security-trump-administration.html.

61. Charlie Savage, "Draft Trump Order on ISIS Detainees and Guantanamo," *New York Times*, February 8, 2017, https://www.nytimes.com/interactive/2017/02/08/us/document-Revised-draft-Trump-EO-on-detainees-and-Gitmo.html. Notably, this order would revoke Obama's Executive Order 13492, but not 13491 banning enhanced interrogation techniques.

62. As late as February 2019, the Trump administration still insisted that holding ISIS detainees at Guantanamo Bay, Cuba, was an option (although no new detainee had arrived since 2008), but it had still not issued an executive order directing the policy change. Carol Rosenberg, "U.S.: Guantanamo Still an Option for ISIS Captives in Syria Who Can't Go Home," *McClatchy*, February 6, 2019, https://www.mcclatchydc.com/news/nation-world/national/national-security/guantanamo/article225544185.html.

63. On the importance of bureaucratic resistance in this case, see Phillip Carter, "Thank the 'Deep State' for Quashing Trump's Torture Plans," *Slate*, February 10, 2017, https://slate.com/news-and-politics/2017/02/meet-the-people-who-helped-quash-trumps-plans-to-reinstitute-torture.html.

64. Linda Chiu, "Fact-Checking Trump's Family Separation Claim about Obama's Policy," *New York Times*, April 9, 2019, https://www.nytimes.com/2019/04/09/us/politics/fact-check-family-separation-obama.html.

65. Julie Hirschfeld Davis and Michael Shear, "How Trump Came to Enforce a Practice of Separating Migrant Families," *New York Times*, June 16, 2018, https://www.nytimes.com/2018/06/16/us/politics/family-separation-trump.html.

66. Dara Lind, "What Obama Did with Migrant Families vs. What Trump Is Doing," *Vox*, June 21, 2018, https://www.vox.com/2018/6/21/17488458/obama-immigration-policy-family-separation-border.

67. Daniella Diaz, "Kelly: DHS Is Considering Separating Undocumented Children from Their Parents at the Border." CNN, March 7, 2017, https://www.cnn.com/2017/03/06/politics/john-kelly-separating-children-from-parents-immigration-border/index.html.

68. Joseph Tafani and Cindy Carcamo, "Children Are Likely to Be Separated from Parents Illegally Crossing the Border under New Trump Administration Policy," *Los Angeles Times*, May 7, 2018, https://www.latimes.com/politics/la-na-pol-border-crossers-20180507-story.html.

69. "The Trump Administration's 'Zero Tolerance' Immigration Enforcement Policy," Congressional Research Service, February 26, 2019, https://fas.org/sgp/crs/homesec/R45266.pdf.

70. Lomi Kriel, "Trump Moves to End 'Catch and Release,' Prosecuting Parents and

Removing Children Who Cross Border," *Houston Chronicle*, November 25, 2017, https://
www.houstonchronicle.com/news/houston-texas/houston/article/Trump-moves-to-end
-catch-and-release-12383666.php; Nick Miroff, "A Family Was Separated at the Border,
and This Distraught Father Took His Own Life," *Washington Post*, June 9, 2018.

71. Ed Lavandera, "She Says Federal Officials Took Her Daughter while She Breast-
fed the Child in a Detention Center," CNN, June 14, 2018, https://www.cnn.com/2018/
06/12/us/immigration-separated-children-southern-border/index.html.

72. Karoun Demirjian, "GOP, Democrats Are Outraged but at Odds over Ending Family Separation at the Border," *Washington Post*, June 17, 2018, https://www
.washingtonpost.com/powerpost/gop-democrats-are-outraged-but-at-odds-over-ending
-family-separation-at-border/2018/06/17/6667f3a4-7247-11e8-b4b7-308400242c2e_story
.html.

73. Eli Watkins, "These Republicans Have Criticized Trump's 'Zero Tolerance'
Immigration Policy," CNN, June 18, 2019, https://www.cnn.com/2018/06/18/politics/
republican-party-family-separation/index.html.

74. Dan Balz and Scott Clement, "Most Americans Oppose Key Parts of Trump
Immigration Plans, including Wall, Limits on Citizens Bringing Family to U.S., Poll
Says," *Washington Post*, July 6, 2018, https://www.washingtonpost.com/politics/most
-americans-oppose-key-elements-of-trump-immigration-policy/2018/07/05/36124360
-7e3d-11e8-b0ef-fffcabeff946_story.html?noredirect=on. The poll was fielded from June
27 through July 2, 2018.

75. "The Trump Administration's 'Zero Tolerance' Immigration Enforcement
Policy," Congressional Research Service, February 26, 2019, p. 20, https://fas.org/sgp/
crs/homesec/R45266.pdf.

76. Ben Smith, "Clinton Mailing Attacks Obama on Guns," *Politico*, May 4, 2008,
http://www.politico.com/blogs/ben-smith/2008/05/clinton-mailing-attacks-obama-on
-guns-008390.

77. Ben Smith, "NRA: Obama Most Anti-gun Candidate Ever, Will Ban Guns,"
Politico, August 6, 2008, http://www.politico.com/blogs/ben-smith/2008/08/nra-obama
-most-anti-gun-candidate-ever-will-ban-guns-010821.

78. Phillip Rucker and Sari Horwitz, "On Gun Control, Obama's Record Shows
an Apparent Lack of Political Will—Until Now," *Washington Post*, December 23,
2012, https://www.washingtonpost.com/politics/on-gun-control-obamas-record-shows
-an-apparent-lack-of-political-will--until-now/2012/12/23/913a3626-4937-11e2-ad54
-580638ede391_story.html.

79. John Gramlich, "Even after Newtown, Little Change," *CQ Weekly*, February 11,
2013, 290–92.

80. Michael O'Brien, "Gun Control Group Gives Obama an 'F,'" *The Hill*, January 19, 2010, http://thehill.com/homenews/administration/76717-gun-control-group
-gives-obama-an-f.

81. Barack Obama, "Remarks on the Shootings in Newtown, Connecticut," December 14, 2012; online by Gerhard Peters and John T. Woolley, the American Presidency
Project, University of California, Santa Barbara, accessed November 1, 2019, https://
www.presidency.ucsb.edu/node/303118.

82. Barack Obama, "The President's News Conference," December 19, 2012; online

by Gerhard Peters and John T. Woolley, the American Presidency Project, University of California, Santa Barbara, accessed November 1, 2019, https://www.presidency.ucsb.edu/node/303118.

83. For a complete list of the executive actions, see "Obama's Response to School Shooting," *CQ Weekly*, December 31, 2012, 173, http://library.cqpress.com/cqweekly/weeklyreport113-000004207506.

84. Figure 6.2 pools data from polls using the following question wordings: In general, do you think gun control laws should be made more strict, less strict, or kept as they are now?; Do you favor or oppose stricter gun control laws?; Do you favor or oppose stricter gun control laws in this country? (If Favor/Oppose, ask:) Is that strongly or somewhat favor/oppose?

85. Zachary Roth, "After Newtown, GOP Unmoved," NBC News, December 18, 2012, http://www.msnbc.com/msnbc/after-newtown-gop-unmoved.

86. Rachel Maddow, "Defining 'Power Grabs' Down," *The MaddowBlog*, MSNBC, January 16, 2013, http://www.msnbc.com/rachel-maddow-show/defining-power-grabs-down.

87. Arthur N. Rupe Foundation/Reason Foundation, Reason-Rupe Poll: January 2013, Question 39, USREASON.13JAN.R34, Princeton Survey Research Associates International (Cornell University, Ithaca, NY: Roper Center for Public Opinion Research, 2013), data set, accessed November 1, 2019.

88. Associated Press, Associated Press Poll: January 2013, Question 3, USAP.011613G.R03, Gfk Roper Public Affairs & Corporate Communications (Cornell University, Ithaca, NY: Roper Center for Public Opinion Research, 2013), data set, accessed November 1, 2019.

89. Associated Press, Associated Press Poll: August 2012, Question 71, USAP.091512G.R12, Gfk Roper Public Affairs & Corporate Communications (Cornell University, Ithaca, NY: Roper Center for Public Opinion Research, 2012), data set, accessed November 1, 2019.

90. Bureau of Alcohol, Tobacco, Firearms, and Explosives, "ATF Framework for Determining Whether Certain Projectiles Are 'Primarily Intended for Sporting Purposes' within the Meaning of 18 U.S.C. 921(a)(17)(C)," https://www.atf.gov/resource-center/docs-0/download; Frank Minter, "Why Is the ATF Moving to Ban Common Rifle Ammo?," *Forbes*, February 24, 2015, https://www.forbes.com/sites/frankminiter/2015/02/24/why-is-the-atf-moving-to-ban-common-rifle-ammo/.

91. "Press Briefing by Press Secretary Josh Earnest," March 2, 2015, https://obamawhitehouse.archives.gov/the-press-office/2015/03/02/press-briefing-press-secretary-josh-earnest-3215.

92. David Boyer, "Obama Loses Another Second Amendment Battle as ATF Drops Proposed Ammo Ban," *Washington Times*, March 10, 2015, http://www.washingtontimes.com/news/2015/mar/10/atf-drops-proposed-ammo-ban/.

93. Adam Lerner, "Obama Administration Drops Proposed Ammo Ban after Conservative Outcry." *Politico*, March 10, 2015, http://www.politico.com/story/2015/03/obama-administration-drops-proposed-ammo-ban-after-conservative-outcry-115965.

94. Boyer, "Obama Loses Another Second Amendment Battle."

95. For Obama's declaration that there was nothing else he could do alone, see

Barack Obama, "The President's News Conference," October 2, 2015; online by Gerhard Peters and John T. Woolley, the American Presidency Project, University of California, Santa Barbara, accessed November 1, 2019, https://www.presidency.ucsb.edu/node/311290. The Obama administration began looking for ways in which it could legally go further on gun control unilaterally at some point during October 2015. Whether this was before or after Clinton's public announcement is unknown. However, in the assessments of many, Clinton's public statements ratcheted up the political pressure on Obama to act. Juliet Eilperin, "Obama Weighs Expanding Background Checks through Executive Authority," *Washington Post*, October 8, 2015, https://www.washingtonpost.com/politics/obama-weighs-expanding-background-checks-through-executive-authority/2015/10/08/6bd45e56-6b63-11e5-9bfe-e59f5e244f92_story.html.

96. Sam Stein, "Hillary Clinton Goes Big on Gun Policy, Creates Contrast with Bernie Sanders," *Huffington Post*, October 5, 2015, http://www.huffingtonpost.com/entry/hillary-clinton-gun-control_us_5611d70ae4b0dd85030c6b3b?9lpojemi=.

97. Jennifer Bendery, "Democrats Urge Obama to Act on Hillary Clinton's Gun Control Proposal," *Huffington Post*, November 23, 2015, http://www.huffingtonpost.com/entry/obama-gun-control-executive-action_us_5652501ce4b0879a5b0b6ca0.

98. The ban was challenged in court but upheld by a federal judge in February 2019 and went into effect that March.

99. Josh Hicks, "Obama's Failed Promise of a First-Year Immigration Overhaul," *Washington Post*, September 25, 2012, https://www.washingtonpost.com/blogs/fact-checker/post/obamas-failed-promise-of-a-first-year-immigration-overhaul/2012/09/25/06997958-0721-11e2-a10c-fa5a255a9258_blog.html.

100. Barack Obama, "Remarks following a Meeting with Members of Congress," June 25, 2009; online by Gerhard Peters and John T. Woolley, the American Presidency Project, University of California, Santa Barbara, accessed November 1, 2019, https://www.presidency.ucsb.edu/node/287115.

101. Charles Schumer and Lindsey Graham, "The Right Way to Mend Immigration," *Washington Post*, March 19, 2010, http://www.washingtonpost.com/wp-dyn/content/article/2010/03/17/AR2010031703115.html.

102. Perry Bacon Jr., "Democrats Unveil Immigration-Reform Proposal," *Washington Post*, April 29, 2010, http://www.washingtonpost.com/wp-dyn/content/article/2010/04/29/AR2010042904512.html.

103. This legislation underwent several incarnations in various bills since its initial appearance in Rep. Luis Gutiérrez's (D-IL) Immigrant Children's Educational Advancement and Dropout Prevention Act of 2001 (H.R. 1582).

104. Barack Obama, "Remarks at Univision's 'Es el Momento' Town Hall Meeting and a Question-and-Answer Session," March 28, 2011; online by Gerhard Peters and John T. Woolley, the American Presidency Project, University of California, Santa Barbara, accessed November 1, 2019, https://www.presidency.ucsb.edu/node/289823.

105. Janet Napolitano, "Exercising Prosecutorial Discretion with Respect to Individuals Who Came to the United States as Children," Department of Homeland Security, June 15, 2012, https://www.dhs.gov/xlibrary/assets/s1-exercising-prosecutorial-discretion-individuals-who-came-to-us-as-children.pdf.

106. Department of Homeland Security, U.S. Citizenship and Immigration Services, "Number of Form I-821D, Consideration of Deferred Action for Childhood Arrivals, by Fiscal Year, Quarter, Intake, Biometrics and Case Status Fiscal Year 2012–2017," March 31, 2017, https://www.uscis.gov/sites/default/files/USCIS/Resources/Reports%20and%20Studies/Immigration%20Forms%20Data/All%20Form%20Types/DACA/daca_performancedata_fy2017_qtr2.pdf.

107. Matt Barreto, "New LD Poll Finds Latinos Favor Obama over Romney, Oppose Rubio DREAM," *Latino Decisions*, June 8, 2012, http://www.latinodecisions.com/blog/2012/06/08/new-ld-poll-finds-latinos-favor-obama-over-romney-oppose-rubio-dream/.

108. Matt Barreto, "New Poll: Latino Voters in Battle Ground States Enthusiastic about Obama DREAM Announcement, Oppose Romney 'Self-Deport' Alternative," *Latino Decisions*, June 17, 2012, http://www.latinodecisions.com/blog/2012/06/17/new-poll-latino-voters-enthusiastic-about-obama-dream-announcement-oppose-romney-policy-of-self-deport/.

109. Elise Foley, "Obama Administration to Stop Deporting Younger Undocumented Immigrants and Grant Work Permits," *Huffington Post*, June 15, 2012, http://www.huffingtonpost.com/2012/06/15/obama-immigration-order-deportation-dream-act_n_1599658.html.

110. "'Self Deportation': Exploring Mitt Romney's Odd New Phrase," *Huffington Post*, January 24, 2012, http://www.huffingtonpost.com/2012/01/24/self-deportation-romney_n_1228296.html; Elise Foley, "Mitt Romney Says Immigration 'Dream Act' Would Get Veto from Him," *Huffington Post*, December 31, 2011, http://www.huffingtonpost.com/2011/12/31/mitt-romney-immigration-dream-act-veto_n_1178060.html.

111. Foley, "Obama Administration to Stop Deporting Younger Undocumented Immigrants."

112. Michael Shear, "For Obama, Executive Order on Immigration Would Be a Turnabout," *New York Times*, November 18, 2014, https://www.nytimes.com/2014/11/18/us/by-using-executive-order-on-immigration-obama-would-reverse-long-held-stance.html. Many legal experts, however, do not share Obama's concerns about the legality of such an action. For example: Peter Shane, "How Obama's Immigration 'Executive Action' Respects the Rule of Law," *Washington Monthly*, December 1, 2014, https://washingtonmonthly.com/2014/12/01/how-obamas-immigration-executive-action-respects-the-rule-of-law/.

113. Philip Bump, "Obama's Immigration Speech Was Interrupted by a Heckler on Stage with Him," *Atlantic*, November 25, 2013, https://www.theatlantic.com/politics/archive/2013/11/obamas-immigration-speech-was-interrupted-one-people-stage-him/355504/.

114. Dave Boyer, "Immigration Hecklers Interrupt Obama at Connecticut Campaign Rally: President Stumps for Governors in Friendly States," *Washington Times*, November 2, 2014, http://www.washingtontimes.com/news/2014/nov/2/immigration-hecklers-interrupt-obama-connecticut-c/.

115. David Nakamura and Ed O'Keefe, "Obama Delays Executive Immigration Action until after Midterm Elections in November," *Washington Post*, September 6,

2014, http://www.washingtonpost.com/politics/obama-delays-executive-immigration
-action-until-after-midterm-elections-in-november/2014/09/06/e3ecf346-35cf-11e4-9e92
-0899b306bbea_story.html.

116. *Washington Post*/ABC News, ABC News/Washington Post Poll: Obama/Congress/Iraq, Question 59, USABCWP.090914.R36, Abt SRBI, Inc./Capital Insight/Langer Research Associates (Cornell University, Ithaca, NY: Roper Center for Public Opinion Research, 2014), data set, accessed November 1, 2019.

117. "Why Are So Many Children Trying to Cross the US Border?," BBC, September 30, 2014, http://www.bbc.com/news/world-us-canada-28203923.

118. Thomas Sparrow, "Can Obama Pass US Immigration Reform?," BBC, November 5, 2014, http://www.bbc.com/news/world-us-canada-29890300.

119. Maggie Haberman, "Clinton: No Obama Immigration Action May Have Hurt in Midterms," *Politico*, November 15, 2014, http://www.politico.com/story/2014/11/clinton-no-obama-immigration-action-may-have-hurt-in-midterms-112924.html #ixzz3JGuhwrjD.

120. Jeh Jonson, "Exercising Prosecutorial Discretion with Respect to Individuals Who Came to the United States as Children and with Respect to Certain Individuals Who Are the Parents of U.S. Citizens or Permanent Residents," Department of Homeland Security, November 20, 2014, https://www.dhs.gov/sites/default/files/publications/14_1120_memo_deferred_action_2.pdf; Michael Shear and Robert Pear, "Obama's Immigration Plan Could Shield Five Million," *New York Times*, November 20, 2014, https://www.nytimes.com/2014/11/20/us/politics/obamacare-unlikely-for -undocumented-immigrants.html. Barack Obama, "Address to the Nation on Immigration Reform," November 20, 2014; online by Gerhard Peters and John T. Woolley, the American Presidency Project, University of California, Santa Barbara, accessed November 1, 2019, https://www.presidency.ucsb.edu/node/308498.

121. Newt Gingrich, "Gingrich: You Won't Win a War with Congress," CNN, November 13, 2014, http://www.cnn.com/2014/11/12/opinion/gingrich-obama-congress -confrontation/index.html.

122. Rebecca Shabad and Cristina Marcos, "House Passes Bill to Defund Obama's Immigration Orders," *The Hill*, January 14, 2015, http://thehill.com/blogs/floor-action/house/229469-house-votes-to-defund-obamas-immigration-orders.

123. For example, a December 2014 poll asked, "[Barack] Obama has taken an executive action under which as many as four million of the country's undocumented immigrants will not face deportation over the next three years if they pass a background check and meet other requirements. Most will need to show that they have been in the United States for at least five years and have children who were born here. Do you support or oppose this immigration program?" In this survey, 52% backed the president's action versus 44% who opposed it. *Washington Post*/ABC News, ABC News/Washington Post Poll: CIA/Afghanistan, Question 18, USABCWP.121714A.R16, Abt SRBI, Inc./Capital Insight/Langer Research Associates (Cornell University, Ithaca, NY: Roper Center for Public Opinion Research, 2014), data set, accessed November 1, 2019.

124. For example, a December 2014 poll asked, "Do you think Barack Obama acted within his authority under the Constitution or exceeded his authority under the Constitution when he issued executive orders on immigration without Congressional

approval?" A majority, 54%, answered that Obama exceeded his authority, while only 34% said that he had not done so. Fox News, Fox News Poll: December 2014, Question 19, USASFOX.121014.R24, Anderson Robbins Research/Shaw & Co. Research (Cornell University, Ithaca, NY: Roper Center for Public Opinion Research, 2014), data set, accessed November 1, 2019.

125. The only questionable case is Bill Clinton and whether gays can serve in the military. If Clinton had unilaterally lifted the ban in toto, it is possible that enough members of Congress would have joined efforts to override a veto of any legislation to write into law the old policy banning homosexuals from military service. However, Clinton almost certainly could have acted unilaterally to dramatically expand protections for gays serving in the military—for example, something more along the line of Rep. Barney Frank's compromise, in which gay service members would remain closeted while on their military base—while leaving enough face-saving elements of the old policy intact in order to peel off enough votes to defeat a veto override attempt. In short, Clinton almost certainly could have moved policy closer to his personal preference unilaterally than he ultimately did through the don't ask, don't tell compromise.

CHAPTER SEVEN

1. Posner and Vermeule 2010.

2. Moe and Howell 1999a.

3. To be fair, Congress clearly authorized the Iraq War in October 2002. However, President Bush repeatedly made recourse to his commander in chief powers to conduct the war as he alone saw fit, even when it contrasted with the express will of Congress. This is perhaps most clear in his decision to continue with the troop surge in Iraq in 2007, even as he vetoed legislation that would place a timetable on winding down the US military commitment in Iraq.

4. Perhaps most important, as shown in chapter 5, Trump is an outlier in terms of both the frequency with which he has resorted to executive action given his low approval rating and the broad popular opposition to most of the unilateral actions he has taken (in stark contrast to recent experience under Presidents Bush and Obama).

5. For example, see Brendan Nyhan, "Norms Matter: Turns Out a Lot of Politics Isn't Governed by Written Rules. Which Was a Good Thing, Until Now," *Politico*, September/October 2017, https://www.politico.com/magazine/story/2017/09/05/why-norms-matter-politics-trump-215535.

6. Indeed, the Mueller Report revealed that Trump explicitly ordered White House counsel Don McGahn to fire the special counsel. McGahn refused. Glenn Kessler, "Trump Says He Did Not Try to Fire Mueller. Here's What Mueller's Report Says," *Washington Post*, April 26, 2019, https://www.washingtonpost.com/politics/2019/04/26/trump-says-he-did-not-try-fire-mueller-heres-what-muellers-report-says/?utm_term=.659648f1a9e5.

7. Levitsky and Ziblatt 2018, 105.

8. Levitsky and Ziblatt 2018, 163.

9. On the importance of democratic norms more generally, see Azari and Smith (2012).

10. John F. Kennedy, "Remarks of Senator John F. Kennedy, NAACP Rally, Sunday July 10, 1960, Los Angeles, CA," John F. Kennedy Presidential Library, https://www .jfklibrary.org/Asset-Viewer/Archives/JFKSEN-0910-013.aspx.

11. Importantly, this shows that presidents contemplating executive action are sometimes more responsive to the anticipated reactions of particular segments of the public than to aggregate public opinion. Further exploration of this dynamic is fertile ground for future research.

12. Dallek 2003, 492–93.

13. Reeves 1993, 432.

14. This logic is consistent with top-of-the-head models of opinion formation, e.g. Zaller (1992).

15. McCarty, Poole, and Rosenthal 2006.

16. Lee 2009, 2016.

17. Kriner and Schickler 2016.

18. On the potential legal ramifications of the congressional vote, see Li Zhoi, "If Congress Votes to Block Trump's Emergency, It Could Be Used against Him in Court," *Vox*, March 13, 2019, https://www.vox.com/2019/3/13/18256607/congress -trump-emergency. On Trump's failure to rally public support for the wall in the face of congressional opposition, see Emily Guskin, "A Clear Majority of Americans Oppose Trump's Emergency Declaration," *Washington Post*, March 15, 2019, https://www .washingtonpost.com/politics/2019/03/15/clear-majority-americans-oppose-trumps -emergency-declaration/?noredirect=on&utm_term=.ac7ed47e1b3c.

19. Iyengar and Westwood 2015; Mason 2013; Rogowski and Sutherland 2016.

20. Chen and Rohla 2018; Christenson and Weisberg 2018; Klofstad, McDermott, and Hatemi 2013; Lazer et al. 2018.

21. Downs 1957.

22. According to the 2016 exit polls, Trump narrowly carried independents 46 to 42%. The exit polls are available from CNN at https://www.cnn.com/election/2016/ results/exit-polls/, accessed November 1, 2019.

REFERENCES

Abramowitz, Alan I. 1996. "Bill and Al's Excellent Adventure." *American Politics Quarterly* 24 (4): 434–42.

Abramowitz, Alan I. 2016. "Will Time for Change Mean Time for Trump?" *PS: Political Science and Politics* 49 (4): 659–60.

Achen, Christopher H., and Larry M. Bartels. 2017. *Democracy for Realists: Why Elections Do Not Produce Responsive Government*. Princeton, NJ: Princeton University Press.

Ackerman, Bruce. 2010. *The Decline and Fall of the American Republic*. Cambridge, MA: Harvard University Press.

Althaus, Scott L., Jill A. Edy, Robert M. Entman, and Patricia Phalen. 1996. "Revising the Indexing Hypothesis: Officials, Media, and the Libya Crisis." *Political Communication* 13 (4): 407–21.

Anderson, Christopher J. 2007. "The End of Economic Voting? Contingency Dilemmas and the Limits of Democratic Accountability." *Annual Review of Political Science* 10 (1): 271–96.

Anderson, Lisa. 2011. "Demystifying the Arab Spring: Parsing the Differences between Egypt, Tunisia, and Libya." *Foreign Affairs* 90 (3): 2–7.

Arceneaux, Kevin. 2008. "Can Partisan Cues Diminish Democratic Accountability?" *Political Behavior* 30 (2): 139–60.

Azari, Julia R., and Jennifer K. Smith. 2012. "Unwritten Rules: Informal Institutions in Established Democracies." *Perspectives on Politics* 10 (1): 37–55.

Bailey, Jeremy D., and Brandon Rottinghaus. 2014. "Reexamining the Use of Unilateral Orders." *American Politics Research* 42 (3): 472–502.

Barrett, Andrew W., and Matthew Eshbaugh-Soha. 2007. "Presidential Success on the Substance of Legislation." *Political Research Quarterly* 60 (1): 100–112.

Bartels, Brandon L., and Christopher D. Johnston. 2013. "On the Ideological Foundations of Supreme Court Legitimacy in the American Public." *American Journal of Political Science* 57 (1): 184–99.

Bartels, Larry M. 2002. "Beyond the Running Tally: Partisan Bias in Political Perceptions." *Political Behavior* 24 (2): 117–50.

Baum, Matthew A., and Tim J. Groeling. 2009. *War Stories: The Causes and Consequences of Public Views of War*. Princeton, NJ: Princeton University Press.

Beckmann, Matthew N. 2010. *Pushing the Agenda: Presidential Leadership in U.S. Lawmaking, 1953–2004*. New York: Cambridge University Press.

Belco, Michelle, and Brandon Rottinghaus. 2014. "In Lieu of Legislation." *Political Research Quarterly* 67 (2): 413–25.

Belco, Michelle, and Brandon Rottinghaus. 2017. *The Dual Executive: Unilateral Orders in a Separated and Shared Power System*. Stanford, CA: Stanford University Press.

Bellia, Patricia L. 2002. "Executive Power in Youngstown's Shadows." *Constitutional Commentary* 19: 87–90.

Bennett, W. Lance. 1990. "Toward a Theory of Press-State Relations in the United States." *Journal of Communication* 40 (2): 103–27.

Berinsky, Adam J. 2007. "Assuming the Cost of War: Events, Elites, and American Public Opinion for Military Conflict." *Journal of Politics* 69 (4): 975–97.

Berinsky, Adam J. 2009. *In Time of War: Understanding American Public Opinion from World War II to Iraq*. Chicago: University of Chicago Press.

Bertaut, Jules. 1916. *Napoleon in His Own Words*. Chicago: A. C. McClurg.

Binder, Sarah. 2015. "The Dysfunctional Congress." *Annual Review of Political Science* 18 (1): 85–101.

Black, Duncan. 1948. "On the Rationale of Group Decision-Making." *Journal of Political Economy* 56 (1): 23–34.

Bolton, Alexander, and Sharece Thrower. 2016. "Legislative Capacity and Executive Unilateralism." *American Journal of Political Science* 60 (3): 649–63.

Botoman, Alex. 2017. "Divisional Judge-Shopping." *Columbia Human Rights Law Review* 49:297–344.

Boudreau, Cheryl, and Scott A. Mackenzie. 2014. "Informing the Electorate? How Party Cues and Policy Information Affect Public Opinion about Initiatives." *American Journal of Political Science* 58 (1): 48–62.

Bradley, Curtis A., and Trevor W. Morrison. 2013. "Presidential Power, Historical Practice, and Legal Constraint." *Columbia Law Review* 113 (4): 1097–1161.

Brody, Richard. 1991. *Assessing the President: The Media, Elite Opinion, and Public Support*. Stanford, CA: Stanford University Press.

Bullock, John G. 2011. "Elite Influence on Public Opinion in an Informed Electorate." *American Political Science Review* 105 (3): 496–515.

Caldeira, Gregory A., and James L. Gibson. 1992. "The Etiology of Public Support for the Supreme Court." *American Journal of Political Science* 36 (3): 635–44.

Calvert, Randall L. 1985. "The Value of Biased Information: A Rational Choice Model of Political Advice." *Journal of Politics* 47 (2): 530–55.

Campbell, Angus, Philip Converse, Warren Miller, and Donald Stokes. 1960. *The American Voter*. New York: Wiley.

Canes-Wrone, Brandice. 2005. *Who Leads Whom? Presidents, Policy, and the Public*. Chicago: University of Chicago Press.

Canes-Wrone, Brandice, William G. Howell, and David E. Lewis. 2008. "Toward a Broader Understanding of Presidential Power: A Reevaluation of the Two Presidencies Thesis." *Journal of Politics* 70 (1): 1–16.

Canes-Wrone, Brandice, and Scott de Marchi. 2002. "Presidential Approval and Legislative Success." *Journal of Politics* 64 (2): 491–509.

Canes-Wrone, Brandice, and Kenneth W. Shotts. 2004. "Conditional Nature of Presidential Responsiveness to Public Opinion." *American Journal of Political Science* 48 (4): 690–706.

Cappella, Joseph N., and Kathleen H. Jamieson. 1997. *Spiral of Cynicism: The Press and the Public Good*. New York: Oxford University Press.

Carter, Ralph G., and James M. Scott. 2009. *Choosing to Lead: Understanding Congressional Foreign Policy Entrepreneurs*. Durham, NC: Duke University Press.

Chafetz, Josh. 2017. *Congress' Constitution: Legislative Authority and the Separation of Powers*. New Haven, CT: Yale University Press.

Chen, M. Keith, and Ryne Rohla. 2018. "The Effect of Partisanship and Political Advertising on Close Family Ties." *Science* 360 (6392): 1020–24.

Chiou, Fang-Yi, and Lawrence S. Rothenberg. 2014. "The Elusive Search for Presidential Power." *American Journal of Political Science* 58 (3): 653–68.

Chiou, Fang-Yi, and Lawrence S. Rothenberg. 2017. *The Enigma of Presidential Power: Parties, Policies, and Strategic Uses of Unilateral Action*. New York: Cambridge University Press.

Chong, Dennis, and James N. Druckman. 2007. "Framing Theory." *Annual Review of Political Science* 10 (1): 103–26.

Christenson, Dino P., and David M. Glick. 2015a. "Chief Justice Roberts' Health Care Decision Disrobed : The Microfoundations of the Supreme Court's Legitimacy." *American Journal of Political Science* 59 (2): 403–18.

Christenson, Dino P., and David M. Glick. 2015b. "Issue-Specific Opinion Change: The Supreme Court and Health Reform." *Public Opinion Quarterly* 79 (4): 881–905.

Christenson, Dino P., and Douglas L. Kriner. 2015. "Political Constraints on Unilateral Executive Action." *Case Western Reserve Law Review* 65 (4): 897–931.

Christenson, Dino P., and Douglas L. Kriner. 2017a. "Constitutional Qualms or Politics as Usual? The Factors Shaping Public Support for Unilateral Action." *American Journal of Political Science* 61 (2): 335–49.

Christenson, Dino P., and Douglas L. Kriner. 2017b. "Mobilizing the Public against the President: Congress and the Political Costs of Unilateral Action." *American Journal of Political Science* 61 (4): 769–85.

Christenson, Dino P., and Douglas L. Kriner. 2017c. "The Specter of Supreme Court Criticism: Public Opinion and Unilateral Action." *Presidential Studies Quarterly* 47 (3): 471–94.

Christenson, Dino P., and Douglas L. Kriner. 2019. "Does Public Opinion Constrain Presidential Unilateralism?" *American Political Science Review* 113 (4): 1071–77.

Christenson, Dino P., and Herbert F. Weisberg. 2019. "Bad Characters or Just More Polarization? Extremely Negative Feeling for Presidential Candidates." *Electoral Studies*, https://doi.org/10.1016/j.electstud.2019.03.008.

Clinton, William J. 2004. *My Life*. New York: Alfred Knopf.

Cohen, Geoffrey L. 2003. "Party over Policy: The Dominating Impact of Group Influence on Political Beliefs." *Journal of Personality and Social Psychology* 85 (5): 808–22.

Cohen, Jeffrey E. 2008. *The Presidency in an Era of 24 Hour News*. New York: Cambridge University Press.

Cohen, Jeffrey E. 2010. *Going Local: Presidential Leadership in the Post-Broadcast Age*. New York: Cambridge University Press.

Cole, David. 2016. *Engines of Liberty: The Power of Citizen Activists to Make Constitutional Law*. New York: Basic Books.

Converse, Philip E. 1964. "The Nature of Belief Systems in Mass Publics." In *Ideology and Discontent*, edited by David E. Apter, 206–61. New York: Free Press.

Cooper, Phillip J. 2002. *By Order of the President: The Use and Abuse of Executive Direct Action*. Lawrence: University of Kansas Press.

Corwin, Edward. 1957. *The President, Office and Powers, 1787–1957: History and Analysis of Practice and Opinion*. New York: New York University Press.

Crawford, Vincent P., and Joel Sobel. 1982. "Strategic Information Transmission." *Econometrica* 50 (6): 1431–51.

Crouch, Jeffrey, Mark J. Rozell, and Mitchel A. Sollenberger. 2017. "The Law : The Unitary Executive Theory and President Donald J. Trump." *Presidential Studies Quarterly* 47 (3): 561–73.

Dallek, Robert. 2003. *An Unfinished Life: John F. Kennedy, 1917–1968*. Boston: Little, Brown.

Deering, Christopher J., and Forrest Maltzman. 1999. "The Politics of Executive Orders: Legislative Constraints on Presidential Power." *Political Research Quarterly* 52 (4): 767–83.

Delli Carpini, Michael X., and Scott Keeter. 1997. *What Americans Know about Politics and Why It Matters*. New Haven, CT: Yale University Press.

Devins, Neal. 2008. "Presidential Unilateralism and Political Polarization: Why Today's Congress Lacks the Will and the Way to Stop Presidential Initiatives." *Willamette Law Review* 45: 395–415.

Dickinson, Matthew J. 2008. "The Politics of Persuasion: A Bargaining Model of Presidential Power." In *Presidential Leadership: The Vortex of Power*, edited by Bert A. Rockman and Richard W. Waterman, 277–10. New York: Oxford University Press.

Dickinson, Matthew J. 2009. "We All Want a Revolution: Neustadt, New Institutionalism, and the Future of Presidency Research." *Presidential Studies Quarterly* 39 (4): 736–70.

Dickinson, Matthew J., and Jesse Gubb. 2016. "The Limits to Power without Persuasion." *Presidential Studies Quarterly* 46 (1): 48–72.

Downs, Anthony. 1957. *An Economic Theory of Democracy*. New York: Harper.

Dragu, Tiberiu, and Mattias Polborn. 2014. "The Rule of Law in the Fight against Terrorism." *American Journal of Political Science* 58 (2): 511–25.

Drew, Elizabeth. 1994. *On the Edge: The Clinton Presidency*. New York: Touchstone.

Druckman, James N. 2001. "On the Limits of Framing Effects: Who Can Frame?" *Journal of Politics* 63 (4): 1041–66.

Druckman, James N., Erik Peterson, and Rune Slothuus. 2013. "How Elite Partisan Polarization Affects Public Opinion Formation." *American Political Science Review* 107 (1): 57–79.

Ducat, Craig R., and Robert L. Dudley. 1989. "Federal District Judges and Presidential Power during the Postwar Era." *Journal of Politics* 51 (1): 98–118.

Duch, Raymond M., Harvey D. Palmer, and Christopher J. Anderson. 2000. "Heterogeneity in Perceptions of National Economic Conditions." *American Journal of Political Science* 44 (4): 635–52.

Dunlap, Riley E., and Araon M. McCright. 2008. "A Widening Gap: Republican and Democratic Views on Climate Change." *Environment: Science and Policy for Sustainable Development* 50 (5): 26–35.

Edwards, George C., III. 1989. *At the Margins: Presidential Leadership of Congress.* New Haven, CT: Yale University Press.

Edwards, George C., III. 2006. *On Deaf Ears: The Limits of the Bully Pulpit.* New Haven, CT: Yale University Press.

Edwards, George C., III. 2016. *Predicting the Presidency: The Potential for Persuasive Leadership.* Princeton, NJ: Princeton University Press.

Ellis, Richard E. 1974. *The Jeffersonian Crisis: Courts and Politics in the Young Republic.* New York: Norton.

Entman, Robert M. 2004. *Projections of Power: Framing News, Public Opinion, and U.S. Foreign Policy.* Chicago: University of Chicago Press.

Epstein, Lee, and Eric A. Posner. 2018. "The Decline of Supreme Court Deference to the President." *University of Pennsylvania Law Review* 166 (4) 829–60.

Fine, Jeffrey A., and Adam L. Warber. 2012. "Circumventing Adversity: Executive Orders and Divided Government." *Presidential Studies Quarterly* 42 (2): 256–74.

Fisher, Louis. 2005. "Judicial Review of the War Power." *Presidential Studies Quarterly* 35 (3): 466–95.

Fleegler, Eric. 2019. "Mass Shootings and the Numbing of America." *JAMA Internal Medicine* 179, no. 5 (April 1): 610–11.

Fowler, Linda. 2015. *Watchdogs on the Hill: The Decline of Congressional Oversight of U.S. Foreign Relations.* Princeton, NJ: Princeton University Press.

Freeman, John R. 1983. "Causality and the Times Series Granger of Political Relationships Analysis." *American Journal of Political Science* 27 (2): 327–58.

Freeman, John R., John T. Williams, and Tse-min Lin. 1989. "Vector Autoregression and the Study of Politics." *American Journal of Political Science* 33 (4): 842–77.

Gaines, Brian J., James H. Kuklinski, Paul J. Quirk, Buddy Peyton, and Jay Verkuilen. 2007. "Same Facts, Different Interpretations: Partisan Motivation and Opinion on Iraq." *Journal of Politics* 69 (4): 957–74.

Gerber, Alan S., and Gregory A. Huber. 2010. "Partisanship, Political Control, and Economic Assessments: Results from a Natural Experiment." *American Journal of Political Science* 54 (1): 153–73.

Gerber, Alan S., Gregory A. Huber, Daniel R. Biggers, and David J. Hendry. 2017. "Self-Interest, Beliefs, and Policy Opinions: Understanding How Economic Beliefs Affect Immigration Policy Preferences." *Political Research Quarterly* 70 (1): 155–71.

Gibson, James L. 2007. "The Legitimacy of the U.S. Supreme Court in a Polarized Polity." *Journal of Empirical Legal Studies* 4 (3): 507–38.

Gibson, James L., Gregory A. Caldeira, and Vanessa A. Baird. 1998. "On the Legitimacy of National High Courts." *American Political Science Review* 92 (2): 343–58.

Gibson, James L., Gregory A. Caldeira, and Lester Kenyatta Spence. 2003. "Measuring Attitudes toward the United States Supreme Court." *American Journal of Political Science* 47 (2): 354–67.

Gibson, James L., Gregory A. Caldeira, and Lester Kenyatta Spence. 2005. "Why Do People Accept Public Policies They Oppose? Testing Legitimacy Theory with a Survey-Based Experiment." *Political Research Quarterly* 58 (2): 187–201.

Gleiber, Dennis W., and Steven A. Shull. 1992. "Presidential Influence in the Policy-making Process." *Western Political Quarterly* 45 (June): 441–67.

Glennon, Michael J. 2015. *National Security and Double Government.* New York: Oxford University Press.

Goldsmith, Jack. 2012. *Power and Constraint: The Accountable Presidency after 9/11.* New York: W. W. Norton.

Granger, C. W. J. 1969. "Investigating Causal Relations by Econometric Models and Cross-Spectral Methods." *Econometrica* 37 (3): 424–38.

Green, Donald P., Alan S. Gerber, and Suzanna L. de Boef. 1999. "Tracking Opinion over Time: A Method for Reducing Sampling Error." *Public Opinion Quarterly* 63 (2): 178–92.

Green, Donald P., Bradley Palmquist, and Eric Schickler. 2002. *Partisan Hearts and Minds: Political Parties and the Social Identities of Voters.* New Haven, CT: Yale University Press.

Grimmer, Justin, Sean J. Westwood, and Solomon Messing. 2014. *The Impression of Influence: Legislator Communication, Representation, and Democratic Account-ability.* Princeton, NJ: Princeton University Press.

Groeling, Tim. 2010. *When Politicians Attack: Party Cohesion in the Media.* New York: Cambridge University Press.

Hoekstra, Valerie J. 1995. "The Supreme Court and Opinion Change: An Experimental Study of the Court's Ability to Change Opinion." *American Politics Research* 23 (1): 109–29.

Hopkins, Daniel J. 2018. *The Increasingly United States: How and Why American Political Behavior Nationalized.* Chicago: University of Chicago Press.

Howell, William G. 2003. *Power without Persuasion: The Politics of Direct Presidential Action.* Princeton, NJ: Princeton University Press.

Howell, William G. 2005. "Unilateral Powers: A Brief Overview." *Presidential Studies Quarterly* 35 (3): 417–39.

Howell, William G., Scott Adler, Charles Cameron, and Charles Riemann. 2000. "Divided Government and the Legislative Productivity of Congress, 1945–94." *Legislative Studies Quarterly* 25 (2): 285–312.

Howell, William G., and Douglas L. Kriner. 2007. "Bending So As Not to Break: What the Bush Presidency Reveals about the Politics of Unilateral Action." In *The Polarized Presidency of George W. Bush*, edited by George C. Edwards and Desmond King, 96–141. New York: Oxford University Press.

Howell, William G., and Douglas L. Kriner. 2008. "Power without Persuasion: Identifying Executive Influence." In *Presidential Leadership: The Vortex of Power*, edited by Bert A. Rockman and Richard W. Waterman, 105–44. New York: Oxford University Press.

Howell, William G., and Jon Pevehouse. 2007. *While Dangers Gather: Congressional Checks on Presidential War Powers*. Princeton, NJ: Princeton University Press.

Huq, Aziz. 2012. "Binding the Executive (by Law or by Politics)." *University of Chicago Law Review* 79 (2): 777–836.

Huq, Aziz, and Tom Ginsburg. 2018. "How to Lose a Constitutional Democracy." *UCLA Law Review* 65: 78–169.

Iyengar, Shanto, and Sean J. Westwood. 2015. "Fear and Loathing across Party Lines: New Evidence on Group Polarization." *American Journal of Political Science* 59 (3): 690–707.

Jacobs, Lawrence R. 2010. "The Presidency and the Press: The Paradox of the White House Communications War." In *The Presidency and the Political System*, ed. Michael Nelson. Washington, DC: CQ Press, 236–63.

Jacobs, Lawrence R., Eric D. Lawrence, Robert Y. Shapiro, and Steven S. Smith. 1998. "Congressional Leadership of Public Opinion." *Political Science Quarterly* 113 (1): 21–41.

Jacobs, Lawrence R., and Robert Shapiro. 2000. *Politicians Don't Pander: Political Manipulation and the Loss of Democratic Responsiveness*. Chicago: University of Chicago Press.

Jacobson, Gary C. 2012. "The President's Effect on Partisan Attitudes." *Presidential Studies Quarterly* 42 (4): 683–718.

Jacobson, Gary C. 2015. "Obama and Nationalized Electoral Politics in the 2014 Midterm." *Political Science Quarterly* 130 (1): 1–25.

Jacobson, Gary C. 2019. *Presidents and Parties in the Public Mind*. Chicago: University of Chicago Press.

Jacoby, William G. 2000. "Issue Framing and Public Opinion on Government Spending." *American Journal of Political Science* 44 (4): 750–67.

James, Scott C. 1995. "A Theory of Presidential Commitment and Opportunism : Swing States, Pivotal Groups and Civil Rights under Truman and Clinton." Presented at the annual meeting of the American Political Science Association, Chicago. http://www.sscnet.ucla.edu/polisci/faculty/james/papers/pres_tc.pdf.

Katyal, Neal. 2006. "Internal Separation of Powers : Checking Today's Most Dangerous Branch from Within." *Yale Law Journal* 115 (9): 2314–49.

Kennedy, Joshua B. 2015. ""Do This! Do That!" and Nothing Will Happen': Executive Orders and Bureaucratic Responsiveness." *American Politics Research* 43 (1): 59–82.

Kernell, Samuel. 1997. *Going Public: New Strategies of Presidential Leadership*. Washington, DC: CQ Press.

Klofstad, Casey A., Rose McDermott, and Peter K. Hatemi. 2013. "The Dating Preferences of Liberals and Conservatives." *Political Behavior* 35 (3): 519–38.

Koger, Gregory. 2010. *Filibustering: A Political History of Obstruction in the House and Senate*. Chicago: University of Chicago Press.

Krause, George A., and David B. Cohen. 1997. "Presidential Use of Executive Orders, 1953–1994." *American Politics Quarterly* 25 (4): 458–81.

Krause, George A., and Jeffrey E. Cohen. 2000. "Opportunity, Constraints, and the Development of the Institutional Presidency: The Issuance of Executive Orders, 1939–96." *Journal of Politics* 62 (1): 88–114.

Krehbiel, Keith. 1998. *Pivotal Politics: A Theory of U.S. Lawmaking*. Chicago: University of Chicago Press.

Kriner, Douglas L. 2010. *After the Rubicon: Congress, Presidents, and the Politics of Waging War*. Chicago: University of Chicago Press.

Kriner, Douglas L. 2014. "The Contemporary Presidency: Obama's Authorization Paradox; Syria and Congress's Continued Relevance in Military Affairs." *Presidential Studies Quarterly* 44 (2): 309–27.

Kriner, Douglas L. 2017. "Congress, Public Opinion, and the Political Costs of Waging War." In *Congress Reconsidered*, edited by Lawrence C. Dodd and Bruce I. Oppenheimer, 421–50. Washington, DC: CQ Press.

Kriner, Douglas L., and William G. Howell. 2012. "Congressional Leadership of War Opinion? Backlash Effects and the Polarization of Public Support for War." In *Congress Reconsidered*, edited by Lawrence C. Dodd and Bruce I. Oppenheimer, 377–400. Washington, DC: CQ Press.

Kriner, Douglas L., and Eric Schickler. 2014. "Investigating the President: Committee Probes and Presidential Approval, 1953–2006." *Journal of Politics* 76 (2): 521–34.

Kriner, Douglas L., and Eric Schickler. 2016. *Investigating the President: Congressional Checks on Presidential Power*. Princeton, NJ: Princeton University Press.

Kriner, Douglas L., and Francis X. Shen. 2010. *The Casualty Gap: The Causes and Consequences of American Wartime Inequalities*. New York: Oxford University Press.

Kriner, Douglas L., and Francis X. Shen. 2014. "Responding to War on Capitol Hill: Battlefield Casualties, Congressional Response, and Public Support for the War in Iraq." *American Journal of Political Science* 58 (1): 157–74.

Krosnick, Jon A. 1991. "Response Strategies for Coping with the Cognitive Demands of Attitude Measures in Surveys." *Applied Cognitive Psychology* 5(3): 213–36.

Krosnick, Jon A. 1999. "Survey Research." *Annual Review of Psychology* 50 (1): 537–67.

Kuklinski, James H., and Norman L. Hurley. 1994. "On Hearing and Interpreting Political Messages: A Cautionary Tale of Citizen Cue-Taking." *Journal of Politics* 56 (3): 729–51.

Kunda, Ziva. 1990. "The Case for Motivated Reasoning, 108 PSYCHOL." *Psychological Bulletin* 108 (3): 480–98.

Lacy, Dean, and Dino P. Christenson. 2017. "Who Votes for the Future? Information, Expectations, and Endogeneity in Economic Voting." *Political Behavior* 39 (2): 347–75.

Lau, Richard R., and David P. Redlawsk. 1997. "Voting Correctly." *American Political Science Review* 91 (3): 585–98.

Lazer, David M. J., Matthew A. Baum, Yochai Benkler, Adam J. Berinsky, Kelly M. Greenhill, Filippo Menczer, Miriam J. Metzger, et al. 2018. "The Science of Fake News: Addressing Fake News Requires a Multidisciplinary Effort." *Science* 359 (6380): 1094–96.

Lebo, Matthew J., and Daniel Cassino. 2007. "The Aggregated Consequences of Motivated Reasoning and the Dynamics of Partisan Presidential Approval." *Political Psychology* 28 (6): 719–46.

Lee, Frances. 2009. *Beyond Ideology: Politics, Principles, and Partisanship in the U.S. Senate*. Chicago: University of Chicago Press.

Lee, Frances. 2016. *Insecure Majorities: Partisanship and the Perpetual Campaign*. Chicago: University of Chicago Press.

Lenz, Gabriel S. 2012. *Follow the Leader: How Voters Respond to Politicians' Policies and Performance*. Chicago: University of Chicago Press.

Levendusky, Matthew. 2009. *The Partisan Sort: How Liberals Became Democrats and Conservatives Became Republicans*. Chicago: University of Chicago Press.

Levinson, Daryl J., and Richard H. Pildes. 2006. "Separation of Parties, Not Powers." *Harvard Law Review* 119 (8): 2311–86.

Levitsky, Steven, and Daniel Ziblatt. 2018. *How Democracies Die*. New York: Crown.

Lodge, Milton, and Ruth Hamill. 1986. "A Partisan Schema for Political Information Processing." *American Political Science Review* 80 (2): 505–19.

Lowande, Kenneth S. 2014. "After the Orders : Presidential Memoranda and Unilateral Action." *Presidential Studies Quarterly* 4 (4): 724–41.

Lowande, Kenneth S. 2018. "Delegation or Unilateral Action." *Journal of Law, Economics, and Organization* 34 (1): 54–78.

Lupia, Arthur. 1994. "Shortcuts versus Encyclopedias: Information and Voting Behavior in California Insurance Reform Elections." *American Political Science Review* 88 (1): 63–76.

Lupia, Arthur, and Matthew D. McCubbins. 1994. "Who Controls? Information and the Structure of Legislative Decision Making." *Legislative Studies Quarterly* 19 (3): 361–84.

Lupia, Arthur, and Mathew D. McCubbins. 1998. *The Democratic Dilemma: Can Citizens Learn What They Need to Know?* New York: Cambridge University Press.

Margulies, Joseph. 2013. *What Changed When Everything Changed: 9/11 and the Making of National Identity*. New Haven, CT: Yale University Press.

Marshall, Bryan W., and Richard L. Pacelle. 2005. "Revisiting the Two Presidencies." *American Politics Research* 33 (1): 81–105.

Marshall, Bryan W., and Brandon C. Prins. 2007. "Strategic Position Taking and Presidential Influence in Congress." *Legislative Studies Quarterly* 32 (2): 257–84.

Mason, Lilliana. 2013. "The Rise of Uncivil Agreement: Issue versus Behavioral Polarization in the American Electorate." *American Behavioral Scientist* 57 (1): 140–59.

Mayer, Kenneth R. 1999. "Executive Orders and Presidential Power." *Journal of Politics* 61 (2): 445–66.

Mayer, Kenneth R. 2001. *With the Stroke of a Pen : Executive Orders and Presidential Power*. Princeton, NJ: Princeton University Press.

Mayer, Kenneth R. 2009. "Going Alone: The Presidential Power of Unilateral Action." In *The Oxford Handbook of the American Presidency*, edited by George C. Edwards III and William G. Howell, 427–54. New York: Oxford University Press.

Mayer, Kenneth R., and Kevin Price. 2002. "Unilateral Presidential Powers: Significant Executive Orders, 1949–99." *Presidential Studies Quarterly* 32 (2): 367–86.

Mayhew, David R. 1991. *Divided We Govern*. New Haven, CT: Yale University Press.

Mayhew, David R. 2000. *America's Congress: Actions in the Public Sphere*. New Haven, CT: Yale University Press.

McCarty, Nolan, Keith T. Poole, and Howard Rosenthal. 2006. *Polarized America: The Dance of Ideology and Unequal Riches*. Cambridge, MA: MIT Press.

Mermin, Jonathan. 1999. *Debating War and Peace: Media Coverage of U.S. Intervention in the Post-Vietnam Era*. Princeton, NJ: Princeton University Press.

Milner, Helen V., and Dustin Tingley. 2015. *Sailing the Water's Edge: The Domestic Politics of American Foreign Policy*. Princeton, NJ: Princeton University Press.

Moe, Terry M. 1994. "The Presidency and the Bureaucracy: The Presidential Advantage." In *The Presidency and the Political System*, edited by Michael Nelson, 425–57. Washington, DC: Congressional Quarterly Press.

Moe, Terry M., and William G. Howell. 1999a. "The Presidential Power of Unilateral Action." *Journal of Law, Economics, and Organization* 15 (1): 132–79.

Moe, Terry M., and William G. Howell. 1999b. "Unilateral Action and Presidential Power: A Theory." *Presidential Studies Quarterly* 29 (4): 850–72.

Moe, Terry M., and Scott A. Wilson. 1994. "Presidents and the Politics of Structure." *Law and Contemporary Problems* 57 (2): 1–44.

Mondak, Jeffery J. 1993a. "Public Opinion and Heuristc Processing of Source Cues." *Political Behavior* 15 (2): 167–92.

Mondak, Jeffery J. 1993b. "Source Cues and Policy Approval: The Cognitive Dynamics of Public Support for the Reagan Agenda." *American Journal of Political Science* 37 (1): 186–212.

Nathan, Richard. 1983. *The Administrative Presidency*. New York: John Wiley.

Neustadt, Richard E. 1960. *Presidential Power, the Politics of Leadership*. New York: Wiley.

Neustadt, Richard E. 1990. *Presidential Power and the Modern Presidents*. New York: Free Press.

Nyhan, Brendan, and Jason Reifler. 2010. "When Corrections Fail: The Persistence of Political Misperceptions." *Political Behavior* 32 (2): 303–30.

Ostrander, Ian. 2015. "Powering Down the Presidency; The Rise and Fall of Recess Appointments." *Presidential Studies Quarterly* 45 (3): 558–72.

Park, Hong Min, and Steven S. Smith. 2016. "Partisanship, Sophistication, and Public Attitudes about Majority Rule and Minority Rights in Congress." *Legislative Studies Quarterly* 41 (4): 841–71.

Patterson, Thomas E. 1996. "Bad News, Bad Governance." *Annals of the American Academy of Political and Social Science* 546 (1): 97–108.

Petersen, Michael Bang, Martin Skov, Søren Serritzlew, and Thomas Ramsøy. 2013. "Motivated Reasoning and Political Parties: Evidence for Increased Processing in the Face of Party Cues." *Political Behavior* 35 (4): 831–54.

Peterson, Mark. 1990. *Legislating Together: The White House and Capitol Hill from Eisenhower to Reagan*. Cambridge, MA: Harvard University Press.

Pfiffner, James P. 2008. *Power Play: The Bush Presidency and the Constitution*. Washington, DC: Brookings Institution.

Pfiffner, James P. 2018. "Unilateral Presidential Authority: Uses and Abuses." In *Rivals for Power: Presidential-Congressional Relations*, edited by James A. Thurber and Jordan Tama, 75–97. Lanham, MD: Rowman and Littlefield.

Popkin, Samuel L. 1991. *The Reasoning Voter: Communication and Persuasion in Presidential Campaigns*. Chicago: University of Chicago Press.

Posner, Eric A., and Adrian Vermeule. 2010. *The Executive Unbound: After the Madisonian Republic*. New York: Oxford University Press.

Potter, Rachel Augustine, Andrew Rudalevige, Sharece Thrower, and Adam L. Warber. 2019. "Continuity Trumps Change: The First Year of Trump's Administrative Presidency." *PS—Political Science and Politics* 52 (4): 613–19.

Rahn, Wendy M. 1993. "The Role of Partisan Stereotypes in Information Processing about Political Candidates." *American Journal of Political Science* 37 (2): 472–96.

Ramsay, Michael. 2007. *The Constitution's Text in Foreign Affairs.* Cambridge, MA: Harvard University Press.

Reeves, Andrew, and Jon C. Rogowski. 2015. "Public Opinion toward Presidential Power." *Presidential Studies Quarterly* 4 (4): 1–28.

Reeves, Andrew, and Jon C. Rogowski. 2016. "Unilateral Powers, Public Opinion, and the Presidency." *Journal of Politics* 78 (1): 137–51.

Reeves, Andrew, and Jon C. Rogowski. 2018. "The Public Cost of Unilateral Action." *American Journal of Political Science* 62 (2): 424–40.

Reeves, Richard. 1993. *President Kennedy: Profile of Power.* New York: Simon and Schuster.

Rivers, Douglas, and Nancy L. Rose. 1985. "Passing the President's Program: Public Opinion and Presidential Influence in Congress." *American Journal of Political Science* 29 (2): 183–96.

Rogowski, Jon C., and Joseph L. Sutherland. 2016. "How Ideology Fuels Affective Polarization." *Political Behavior* 38 (2): 485–508.

Rossiter, Clinton. 1960. *The American Presidency.* New York: Harcourt, Brace.

Rottinghaus, Brandon. 2010. *The Provisional Pulpit: Modern Presidential Leadership of Public Opinion.* College Station: Texas A&M University Press.

Rottinghaus, Brandon, and Jason Maier. 2007. "The Power of Decree: Presidential Use of Executive Proclamations, 1977–2005." *Political Research Quarterly* 60 (June): 338–43.

Rudalevige, Andrew. 2005. *The New Imperial Presidency: Renewing Presidential Power after Watergate.* Ann Arbor: University of Michigan Press.

Rudalevige, Andrew. 2009. "The Administrative Presidency and Bureaucratic Control: Implementing a Research Agenda." *Presidential Studies Quarterly* 39 (1): 10–24.

Rudalevige, Andrew. 2012. "The Contemporary Presidency: Executive Orders and Presidential Unilateralism." *Presidential Studies Quarterly* 42 (1): 138–160.

Rudalevige, Andrew. 2015. "Executive Branch Management and Presidential Unilateralism: Centralization and the Issuance of Executive Orders." *Congress and the Presidency* 42 (1): 342–65.

Savage, Charlie. 2008. *Takeover: The Return of the Imperial Presidency.* Boston: Little, Brown.

Schaffner, Brian F., and Matthew J. Streb. 2002. "The Partisan Heuristic in Low-Information Elections." *Public Opinion Quarterly* 66 (4): 559–81.

Schlesinger, Arthur, Jr. 1973. *The Imperial Presidency.* Boston: Houghton Mifflin.

Schubert, Glendon. 1957. *The Presidency in the Courts.* Minneapolis: University of Minnesota Press.

Silverstein, Gordon. 1994. "Judicial Enhancement of Executive Power." In *The President, the Congress, and the Making of Foreign Policy*, ed. Paul Peterson. Norman: University of Oklahoma Press, 23–45.

Silverstein, Gordon. 1997. *Imbalance of Powers: Constitutional Interpretation and the Making of American Foreign Policy.* Princeton, NJ: Princeton University Press.

Smith, Steven S., and Hong Min Park. 2013. "Americans' Attitudes about the Senate Filibuster." *American Politics Research* 41 (5): 735–60.

Smith, William H. C. 2005. *The Bonapartes: The History of a Dynasty.* New York: Palgrave Macmillan.

Sniderman, Paul M., Richard A. Brody, and Philip E. Tetlock. 1991. *Reasoning and Choice: Explorations in Political Psychology.* New York: Cambridge University Press.

Taber, Charles S., and Milton Lodge. 2006. "Motivated Skepticism in the Evaluation of Political Beliefs." *American Journal of Political Science* 50 (3): 755–69.

Thrower, Sharece. 2017. "To Revoke or Not Revoke? The Political Determinants of Executive Order Longevity." *American Journal of Political Science* 61 (3): 642–56.

Whittington, Keith. 2009. "Judicial Checks on the President." In *The Oxford Handbook of the American Presidency,* edited by George C. Edwards III and William G. Howell, 646–64. New York: Oxford University Press.

Wildavsky, Aaron. 1966. "The Two Presidencies." *Trans-action* 4 (2): 7–14.

Yates, Jeff, and Andrew Whitford. 1998. "Presidential Power and the United States Supreme." *Political Research Quarterly* 51 (2): 539–50.

Zaller, John. 1992. *The Nature and Origins of Mass Opinion.* New York: Cambridge University Press.

INDEX

Page numbers in italics indicate figures.

www.ingramcontent.com/pod-product-compliance
Lightning Source LLC
Chambersburg PA
CBHW060029030426
42334CB00019B/2244